84

The correctness problem
in computer science

International Lecture Series in Computer Science

These volumes are based on the lectures given during a series of specially funded chairs. The International Chair in Computer Science was created by IBM Belgium in co-operation with the Belgium National Foundation for Scientific Research. The holders of each chair cover a subject area considered to be of particular relevance to current developments in computer science.

The Correctness Problem in Computer Science (1981)
R. S. BOYER and J STROTHER MOORE

Forthcoming titles

Computer-Aided Modelling and Simulation
J. A. SPRIET and G. C. VANSTEENKISTE

The correctness problem in computer science

Edited by

R. S. Boyer and J Strother Moore

Computer Science Laboratory
SRI International
Menlo Park, CA 94025, U.S.A.

1981

ACADEMIC PRESS

A Subsidiary of Harcourt Brace Jovanovich, Publishers

London·New York·Toronto·Sydney·San Francisco

ACADEMIC PRESS INC. (LONDON) LTD.
24—28 Oval Road
London NW1 7DX

U.S. Edition published by
ACADEMIC PRESS INC
111 Fifth Avenue
New York, New York 10003

British Library Cataloguing in Publication Data

The correctness problem in computer science.
1. Computer programs—Testing
I. Boyer, Robert S.   II. Moore, J Strother
001.64′2   QA76.6

ISBN 0-12-122920-3

LCCCN 81-67887

Typeset by Bath Typesetting Ltd., Bath
and printed in Great Britain by
T. J. Press (Padstow) Ltd., Padstow, Cornwall.

Contributors

R. S. Boyer: *Computer Science Laboratory, SRI International, 333 Ravenswood Avenue, Menlo Park, California 94025, U.S.A.*

R. M. Burstall: *Department of Computer Science, The King's Building, University of Edinburgh, Mayfield Road, Edinburgh EH9 3JZ.*

E. W. Dijkstra: *Plataanstraat 5, 5671 AL NUENEN, The Netherlands.*

J. A. Goguen: *Computer Science Laboratory, SRI International, 333 Ravenswood Avenue, Menlo Park, California 94025, U.S.A.*

Z. Manna: *Computer Science Laboratory, Stanford University, Stanford, California, U.S.A. and Applied Mathematics Department, The Weizmann Institute, Rehovot, Israel.*

J Strother Moore: *Computer Science Laboratory, SRI International, 333 Ravenswood Avenue, Menlo Park, California 94025, U.S.A.*

A. Pnueli: *Applied Mathematics Department, The Weizmann Institute, Rehovot, Israel.*

Preface

The cost of "bugs" in critical software is great; consequently the problem of program correctness is being investigated intensively worldwide. Although there are many approaches to the problem, the contributions to this book are united by the view that programming is a mathematical activity. That is, a programmer ought to be able to prove, in the mathematical sense, that his programs are correct. Programming requires of the programmer the same kinds of precise thinking, creative leaps, and attention to detail normally required of the mathematician and in support of which the mathematician employs a set of powerful formal and informal tools. This view underlies most of the current research on formal programming methodologies, programming language semantics, specification languages and program proof methods.

The view of programming as a mathematical activity can be contrasted with the image of the programmer as tinker, one who produces machines that "work", without knowing precisely what they do, by changing his programs until they no longer fail under certain tests. Research into programming environments and testing methodologies is often based on this view of the programmer as tinker. Such research is not represented in this volume.

Although the contributors to this book take the view that programming is a mathematical activity, they take different approaches within that view. Among the questions to which one finds different answers in the papers collected here are:

(1) Should one strive for the formality of logicians in his proofs, or will the informality of most mathematicians suffice as a model for programmers?

(2) Should proofs of program correctness be mechanically checked?

(3) Are new programming languages required, or are the oldest languages in use—LISP and FORTRAN—adequate for producing correct programs?

(4) Is the logic used by mathematicians both theoretically and practically adequate for correctness proofs, or should new logics, designed for programming, be used?

In 1979 the Fonds National de la Recherche Scientifique (FNRS) of Belgium, with the financial support of IBM Belgium, established an annual Professorship in Computer Science, named the *"chaire internationale d'informatique"*. In addition to inviting guest lecturers to speak on a selected topic in computer science, the FNRS invited the recipients of the Professorship to contribute papers to be collected and published in book form. This book is the first volume in that series and contains previously unpublished reports of research by the contributors.

The FNRS selected the University of Liège to be the host institution for the 1979–1980 academic year and the University chose to devote the Professorship that year to "The Correctness Problem in Computer Science".

To speak on the program correctness problem Professors A. Danthine and D. Ribbens of the Institut d'Electricité Montéfiore of the University of Liège invited five guest lecturers to spend one month each in Liège. The five speakers were: Prof. E. W. Dijkstra, Dr R. S. Boyer, Dr J Strother Moore, Prof. R. M. Burstall and Prof. Z. Manna. Each lecturer delivered approximately 30 hours of lectures over the course of the month.

The topics discussed and their relation to the material published in this book were as follows:

Dijkstra spoke during November and December 1979. His inaugural address for the *chaire internationale d'informatique*, entitled "Why Correctness Must be a Mathematical Concern", is included here and argues well the point that programming is a mathematical activity. A theme of Dijkstra's lectures was that a program and its correctness proof should be developed hand in hand. Dijkstra's lectures introduced the notions of mathematical proof, predicate transformers, and program language semantics for a simple language, and considered the proof of correctness and optimization of programs in that language. Related material may be found in Dijkstra's book, "A Discipline of Programming" (Prentice-Hall, 1976).*

Boyer spoke during January 1980. The theme of his lectures was the role of recursive functions in program verification and the handling of the semantics of FORTRAN. The lectures introduced the first-order predicate calculus, recursive functions and induction, the functional and inductive assertion methods of program verification, and an accurate formalization of the semantics of ANSI FORTRAN 66 and 77. The primary text for the first two weeks of the month was the book "A Computational Logic" (Academic Press, 1979) by Boyer and Moore. The first Boyer–Moore contribution to this book, "A Verification Condition Generator for FORTRAN", served as the class notes for the final two weeks of Boyer's lectures.

---

* Extensive notes of Dijkstra's lectures were taken and have been circulated by Pierre de Marneffe of the Faculté Polytechnique de Mons, 7000 Mons, Belgium.

Moore spoke during February on the topic of mechanical theorem-proving in support of program verification. The lectures included an introduction to resolution theorem-proving, equality and term rewriting systems, heuristic use of the principle of mathematical induction, and the use of a mechanical theorem-prover to prove metatheorems establishing the correctness of extensions to the theorem-prover. Examples were taken from several program correctness problems. Unpublished notes were used during the first week; the second and third weeks were taken primarily from the Boyer–Moore book cited above, and the second Boyer–Moore paper in this collection, "Metafunctions: Proving Them Correct and Using Them Efficiently as New Proof Procedures", was used as the class notes during the final week.

Burstall spoke during March. The theme of the lectures was applicative programming languages and abstract data types. Burstall discussed the programming language HOPE developed at Edinburgh by MacQueen, Sannella and Burstall; the Darlington–Burstall unfold/fold method of program transformation; the use of abstract data types in HOPE and CLU; and correctness proofs by R. Topor's method and the temporal logic work by S. Owicki of Stanford. The Burstall–Goguen paper in this collection summarizes more recent work on the specification language CLEAR and was not part of Burstall's Liège lectures.

Manna spoke during April on the role of modal logic in program correctness. The lectures dealt with the basic concepts of modal logic and their application to deterministic, nondeterministic and parallel programs. Two axiomatic systems were studied, temporal logic and (more briefly) dynamic logic. The Manna–Pnueli paper published here was not available during the Liège lectures, but covers much of the same material.

In closing, we would like to express our belief that in establishing an international chair in computer science and the associated series of books the FNRS and IBM have contributed significantly both to the teaching of computer science and the advancement of research in the field. In addition, we believe that the decision to devote the first year to the program correctness problem was particularly inspired.

We thank the FNRS and IBM Belgium for founding the program. We thank Professors Danthine and Ribbens for honoring us with the invitations to occupy the chair during its first year. In addition, we thank them and their colleagues at the University of Liège for their excellent planning and organization and for the hospitality shown us and our families during our stay in Liège. Finally, we thank Liz Moore for helping to proofread Chapters 2 and 3 of this book.

Robert S. Boyer
J Strother Moore

August, 1981

Contents

1. Introduction: Why correctness must be a mathematical concern

E. W. DIJKSTRA

The topic to which this new international chair at Liège has been devoted has many names. On the continent of Europe the recently coined name "Informatics" has become generally accepted; in the Anglo-Saxon world the much older term "Computer Science" is most commonly used, though occasionally replaced by the now more appropriate term "Computing Science". The latter term is more appropriate because it expresses quite clearly that an activity, not a piece of equipment, constitutes the core of its subject matter. By its very nature, this subject matter is highly technical; an inaugural address, however, is specifically the occasion at which technicalities should be avoided, and it is my purpose to explain the significance of the topic without explaining the topic itself in any detail.

An explanation of what mathematics is all about cannot be expected in a few words: in order to grasp that, one has to *do* mathematics for many years oneself. But I would like to show one simple argument in order to convey some of the flavour of mathematics.

Consider the following silly game to be played by a single person with an urn and as many white balls and black balls as he needs. To begin with, an arbitrary positive number of balls is put into the urn, and as long as the urn contains two or more balls, the player repeats the following move: he shakes the urn and, without looking, he takes two balls from the urn; if those two balls are the same colour he throws one black ball back into the urn, otherwise he puts one white ball back into the urn. Because each move decreases the total number of balls in the urn by one, the game is guaranteed to terminate after a finite number of moves, and it is not difficult to see that the game ends with exactly one ball in the urn. The question is: "What can we say about the colour of that final ball when we are given the initial contents of the urn?".

1

Well, we can try all possible games! The games that start with one ball in the urn are very simple. Because they involve no move at all, we might call them "the empty games", and could represent them as

$$\bigcirc$$

and

$$\bullet$$

respectively.

The games of one move are not very complicated either: we can represent them by

$$\bigcirc\ \bigcirc\ \rightarrow\ \bullet$$
$$\bigcirc\ \bullet\ \rightarrow\ \bigcirc$$
$$\bullet\ \bullet\ \rightarrow\ \bullet$$

respectively.

But with games of two moves, life already becomes more complicated. We might represent them as follows (note that there are six possible games):

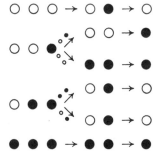

It is clear that such a tabulation becomes extremely tedious. Besides that, one is never fully prepared with such a tabulation: suppose that we have made the tabulation of games up to 100 moves, then we still know nothing when faced with an urn that initially contains 300 balls.

Looking at the three single moves possible, we observe that the last two ($\bigcirc\ \bullet\ \rightarrow\ \bigcirc$ and $\bullet\ \bullet\ \rightarrow\ \bullet$) leave the number of white balls in the urn unchanged, while the first move ($\bigcirc\ \bigcirc\ \rightarrow\ \bullet$) reduces the number of white balls in the urn by two. In other words, each move leaves the so-called "parity" of the number of white balls in the urn unchanged: an even number of white balls in the urn remains even, and an odd number of white balls in the urn remains odd. In short: if the initial number of white balls is even, the final ball is black, and if the initial number of white balls is odd, the final ball is white. And that answers the question!

Note that this single argument settles the question for *all* initial contents of the urn, and per intial contents for *all* of the perhaps many possible games.

The above illustrates the following features of mathematics:

(a) the answer to our question was a very general one in the sense that it

is pertinent to an unlimited number of different cases (here: possible games);
(b) the answer to our question was very precise; this in contrast to the soft
sciences, such as sociology, in which generality is traditionally achieved by
vagueness, i.e. the opposite of precision;
(c) the answer to our question has been justified by a convincing argument,
i.e. the type of proof that makes mathematical statements more trustworthy
than anything else we utter.

In a very elementary, but fundamental sense the example is also typical of
some of the mathematical arguments that are relevant to automatic computing.
Replace the initial contents of the urn by "the input", the rules of the game
by "the program", the game as it evolves by "the computation", and the
colour of the final ball by "the result", and the above example gives you in a
nutshell the bare structure of one of the most effective ways we know of
reasoning about programs. (Thanks to the fact that in each move the player
draws two arbitrary balls, our example even reflects the characteristics of
so-called "non-deterministic algorithms", in which the computational
history need not be uniquely determined by the input that has been supplied
explicitly.)

A while ago I mentioned as a leading characteristic of mathematical
statements their "generality" in the sense that they are applicable to a very
large, often even unlimited number of cases. And it is a good thing to realize
that almost all computer applications are "general" in that very same sense.
In a banking application one does not design a system that can *only* transfer
$100 from the account of a certain Mr Smith to that of a certain Mr Brown!
On the contrary, the banking system should be able to cope with the transfer
of almost *any* amount from *any* account to *any other* account. So much for
the generality.

The next characteristic of mathematics that I mentioned was precision.
And it is a good thing to realize that almost all computer applications, to be
worthwhile, have to have that characteristic of precision as well. Again the
banking application may serve as an illustration. It is not only that all accounts
are kept track of accurately to the dollar and cent, it is much more: for it to
be useful, the system as a whole must have a number of very precise properties. As far as the internal transfers from one account to another are concerned,
the system must reflect the Law of Conservation of Money: the sum of the
accounts must remain constant because each deduction from one account
must be compensated by an equal increase of another account.

The last characteristic I mentioned was trustworthiness. And it is a good
thing to realize that to be worthwhile almost all computer applications
must be trustworthy. What is the purpose of designing a banking system with
the best intentions when in actual practice it fails to keep track correctly of
the flow of money? Not only does it have to do so correctly, but before

installing it and switching over to it we must have solid grounds for believing that it will do so correctly. Installing the system without such solid grounds would, in view of the risks involved, be an act of sheer irresponsibility.

Having thus shown that each worthwhile computer application shares with mathematics the latter's three leading characteristics, I hope to have convinced you that by its very nature responsible systems design and development—in short: programming reliably—*must* be an activity of an undeniably mathematical nature. And having chosen the banking application as illustration, I hope to have convinced you that this conclusion is not confined to the application of computers to science and technology.

Though the conclusion seems inescapable, I should mention for the sake of completeness that not everybody is willing to draw it. You see, mathematics is about thinking, and doing mathematics is always trying to think as well as possible. By an unfortunate accident of history, however, programming became an industrial activity in the United States at a moment that the American manager was extremely fearful of relying on the education and the intelligence of his company's employees. Then management tried to organize the industrial programming task in such a way that each individual programmer would need to think as little as possible. This has been a sad mistake, but the more management, with this conception of programming, failed to meet its deadlines and to achieve reasonable quality standards, the more has been invested in these ill-directed efforts. And now we have reached the paradoxical situation that, while the evidence for the intrinsic difficulty of the programming task has become more and more convincing each year, the recognition of the difficulty has become, both politically and socially, more and more unpalatable. It should be noted that under these circumstances, foresight and courage, if not also the tenacity of a bull-terrier, are required for the foundation of an international chair of informatics at which programs and programming are considered to be worthy of our serious scientific attention.

Let me next indicate, in the broadest outline possible, what this serious scientific attention could cover. I shall keep this outline broad for two reasons: first this is not the occasion to bore you with technicalities, secondly I hope to give an explanation with which the subsequent occupants of this chair won't disagree too much.

It is now the time to confess that my example of the game with the urn filled with a finite number of balls, each of which is white or black, though in one respect absolutely typical, is very misleading in another respect: compared to the actual situation in programming it is such a gross oversimplification, that the use of this example in an expository lecture is almost an intellectual dishonesty.

So that you may understand how terribly gross the oversimplification really is, I would like you to realize that something as trivial as "a factor of ten"—something we usually treat as a gradual difference from which we can abstract—makes in practice an almost essential difference. Once I was called to explain to a housewife what tremendous difference a mere factor of ten makes. I asked her how many children she had, knowing that she had six. The lady saw the point. Compared to the programming problem, the urn example is an oversimplification that is orders of magnitude worse than merely ignoring a factor of ten.

In the urn example, the initial state is fully characterized by two integers, viz. the number of white balls and the number of black balls respectively. That specification of the input is ridiculously simple compared to, for instance, the class of possible inputs a compiler must be able to process, viz. all texts that are legal or illegal program texts in the programming language concerned.

In the urn example the final state, i.e. the colour of the final ball, represents only a single bit of information. That, again, is ridiculously simple compared to the output required from standard programs such as compilers, for which the representation of the result often requires millions of bits.

And finally, in the urn example I could state "the rules of the game" in one or two sentences, whereas in the practice of automatic computing the program—i.e. "the rules of the computational game"—often requires many thousands, and sometimes apparently even millions of lines of text.

In the urn example, a single argument based on the rules sufficed for *all* possible games. In computing, a single argument based on the program text should analogously suffice for *all* computations that are possible under control of that program. The necessary economy of thought requires as its ultimate consequence that we learn how to reason about programs without mentioning the corresponding computational processes at all. This means no more and no less than that we must learn how to come to grips with the program text as a mathematical object in its own right. We must be able to deal with it directly, rather than via the detour of the class of all corresponding computations.

It is abundantly clear that significant progress in programming, in reasoning about programs, and in the design of programming languages will only materialize, provided we learn how to do this, while temporarily *fully* ignoring that our program texts also admit the interpretation of executable code, because it is precisely that interpretation that clutters up our minds with all the computational processes, which truly baffle the imagination. In short: for the effective understanding of programs we must learn to abstract from the existence of computers.

This abstraction is not easy. For most people trained as electronic engineers it is even impossible, though not for all: it is a pleasure to mention Niklaus Wirth from Zurich as an exception. This is not surprising, for suddenly they find themselves invited to abstract from what they have been taught to regard as the core of their craft. As you might expect, vested interests inhibit a widespread recognition of the obvious conclusion, viz. that as a rule departments of electronic engineering actually deprive their graduates of the ability to understand later in life what computing science is really about.

In the ears of the traditional mathematician the suggestion to abstract from the existence of computers sounds much more natural. He should feel quite at home with the idea of regarding, reading, writing and manipulating program texts just like any other mathematical formulae. But there is one big, big difference: never in his life has he encountered such big formulae! Remember the drastic difference already made by a single factor of ten, and realize that program texts present themselves to the traditional mathematician as formulae that are not one, but several orders of magnitude bigger than the formulae he used to deal with! In relation to our mathematical tradition, it is just a drastic problem of scale, so drastic, as a matter of fact, that quite a few mathematicians, firmly rooted in the past, are quite unable to recognize programming as a mathematical activity. Research and education in computing sciences are, however, more concerned with the mathematicians of the future.

By now you may have some feeling for the type of topics that would be fully appropriate for this international chair of informatics.

The most general topic, and also the one of the widest significance, could be called "the scaling up of mathematics". Such scaling up would imply a different style of mathematical texts in general, and the use of more appropriate notations in particular. By and large, current mathematical style has been determined by fashion, and current mathematical notation by accident.

The degree to which separable concerns are, indeed, separated is, for instance, an aspect of mathematical style, but as far as I know students of mathematics are not taught today to take a conscious decision in this respect.

Similarly, the adequacy of chosen notational conventions can be judged by their suitability to our manipulative needs. Again, as far as I know, students of mathematics are not taught today to screen notational conventions for their suitability before they adopt them.

As a result the style of today's mathematical text is unnecessarily confusing and its notation is unnecessarily clumsy. This is obvious: people tend to commit all the sins they think they can afford to commit. Prior to a commitment to "scaling up" they can hardly be called "sins", but computing's demands on mathematics is sure to cause a "moral" shift between good and bad mathematics. Already one of the common reactions of the well-trained computing scientist to the average mathematical paper is: "Oh gosh, what a lousy programmer the guy who wrote this must be!" Already we could start purging from the practice of mathematics the usual little sins which the computing scientist knows will, at the next level, become capital ones. The scaling up of mathematics in general is, of course, a very ambitious topic.

A more modest topic, closer to the field of automatic computing, would be the following. In the case of a soluble problem, what is essentially the same solution can be realized by very different programs. This observation is well-known, but raises all sorts of questions.

A pretty obvious question would be "Which of the possible programs would be the easiest to understand?", but the question is not as innocent as it seems, for what do we mean by "ease of understanding"? Programs are expressed in (what I may here denote by) linguistic structures, and different linguistic structures require different patterns of reasoning for the justification of their usage. Intuitively people tend to prefer the ones they are most familiar with, but we shouldn't confuse "convenient" with "conventional", and should remember that what we call thinking and understanding are not much more than our personal habits, habits that we can replace by others by training ourselves. Some linguistic structures are known to cause troubles in a sense as objective as the statement that decimal arithmetic is "easier" in Arabic than in Roman numerals, but the area as a whole is still a field for investigation and experiment.

Another question in connection with different possible programs realizing the same solution is the following: "Does a single program suit all our purposes?". The solution might have different relevant aspects, each of which is most manageably reflected in a different program. Who knows? Note that the absence of an example of such a solution does not settle the question: we tend to think about solutions in terms of a program that realizes it, and the mere conception of a solution that requires two or more alternative programs for the adequate reflection of its different aspects might therefore be well beyond our current intellectual abilities! I only raised the last question as an example, in the hope that it may give you some idea of the possible scope of our concerns.

While programming we don't only consider different programs embodying the same solution to a given problem; usually we have to invent the solution as well. Human inventiveness being what it is, we usually invent more than one solution, with the result that we have to choose. When different solutions to the same problem can be shown to be correct by proofs that share part of the argument, is it then possible to realize those solutions by programs that share parts of the text? Those parts of the text could then already be written without completely committing oneself to the solution to be finally adopted; the larger the program, the more important the possibility to postpone such commitments. Equally important is the possibility of postponing the precise choice of the problem to be solved: you really cannot expect your customer— regardless of whether you are your own customer or your customer is someone else—to have fully made up his mind and stick to it.

In the previous paragraph I have sketched in a very informal fashion some of the flexibility requirements. What the manager sees as "keeping options open" is seen by the scientist as "sharing": different programs sharing code, different proofs sharing arguments, different theories sharing subtheories, and different problems sharing aspects. The need for such "sharing" is characteristic of the design of anything big. The control of such "sharing" is at the heart of the problem of "scaling up" and it is the challenge to the computing scientist or mathematician to invent the abstractions that will enable us to exert this control with sufficient precision.

After having seen how much the catch phrase "the scaling up of mathematics" captures of the challenge posed to us by the existence of modern computers, we are quite naturally led to the question to what extent those very machines—the fast symbol manipulators they are—could assist us in meeting that challenge. Like all the questons raised in the second part of this talk, this question will also remain unanswered here. I will confine myself to pointing out that the question has two sides.

First we have questions such as "What mechanizable assistance can we think of besides the well-known program transformation and theorem proving systems, and how useful can we expect them to be?", but also, once such a mechanization has been designed "How does the economics of its usage depend on the size of the application?". Because I did not define "size", the latter question is vague, but remember that we were interested in "scaling up"! Hence, costs growing quadratically (or worse) as a function of something we would like to increase by several orders of magnitude, would disqualify the tool for the very purpose we had in mind.

Secondly, the answer to what extent computers can assist us in meeting the challenge of "scaling up mathematics" also depends on our interpretation of that challenge. For some mathematicians doing mathematics is a mental activity whose primary purpose is understanding. Such a mathematician is inclined to reject an alleged theorem for which the only available alleged proof is millions of steps long, i.e. orders of magnitude too long to be read and, as he calls it, "understood".

The question "What is Mathematics?" is as unavoidable and as unanswerable as the question "What is Life?". In actual fact I think it's almost the same question.

2. A verification condition generator for FORTRAN

R. S. BOYER and J STROTHER MOORE

ABSTRACT

This paper provides both a precise specification of a subset of FORTRAN 66 and FORTRAN 77 and a specification of the verification condition generator we have implemented for that subset. Our subset includes all the statements in FORTRAN 66 except the following: READ, WRITE, REWIND, BACKSPACE, ENDFILE, FORMAT, EQUIVALENCE, DATA and BLOCK DATA. We place some restrictions on the remaining statements; however, our subset includes certain uses of COMMON, adjustable array dimensions, function subprograms, subroutine subprograms with side effects, and computed and assigned GO TOs. Unusual features of our system include a syntax checker that enforces all our syntactic restrictions on the language, the thorough analysis of aliasing, the generation of verification conditions to prove termination, and the generation of verification conditions to ensure against such run-time errors as array bound violations and arithmetic overflow. We have used the system to verify several running FORTRAN programs. We present one such program and discuss its verification.

1. SUMMARY*

Mechanical program verification systems usually consist of two main programs—a verification condition generator and a theorem-prover. The use of such a system involves two steps. (a) The verification condition generator accepts as its input a source program to be verified, an input/output specification for the program, and some inductive invariants; the verification condition generator produces some formulas, called "verification conditions", which imply that the source program behaves as specified. (b) The verification conditions are then submitted to the theorem-prover. If the theorem-prover

* The work reported here was supported in part by ONR Contract N00014-75-C-0816 and NSF Grant MCS-7904081.

9

determines that the verification conditions are theorems, then the source program behaves as specified.

This document describes a verification condition generator for a subset both of FORTRAN 66 [12] and FORTRAN 77 [1]. While we place constraints on the language that are not found in the ANSI specifications, ours is a true subset in the sense that a processor that correctly implements either FOR-TRAN correctly implements our language. Our subset includes certain uses of COMMON, function subprograms, subroutine subprograms with side effects, and computed and assigned GO TOs. The most notable exceptions from our subset are the input/output statements (e.g. READ, WRITE and FORMAT), EQUIVALENCE, DATA and procedural parameters.

The logical language used to specify the FORTRAN programs is that described in [5] and in [6]. The verification conditions produced are suitable for input to the theorem-prover described in [5].

Unusual features of our system—aside from our choice of FORTRAN and our use of a quantifier free specification language—include a syntax checker that enforces all our syntactic restrictions on the language, the thorough analysis of aliasing, the generation of verification conditions to prove termination, and the generation of verification conditions to ensure against such run-time errors as array-bound violations and arithmetic overflow.

Although our syntax checker and verification condition generator handle programs involving finite precision REAL arithmetic, we have not yet formalized the semantics of those operations and hence cannot mechanically verify programs that operate on REALs.

The two step approach to program verification was formalized by Floyd in [8]. King [10] implemented the first mechanical verification condition generator. Since then, many verification condition generators have been implemented for many different programming languages, although we are not aware of any other verification condition generator for FORTRAN. For an introduction to program verification, see Anderson [2] or Manna [11]; both books contain bibliographies.

2. APOLOGIA

The two steps of program verification stem from the fact that conventional (i.e. von Neumann) programming languages are not mathematical languages. The semantics of von Neumann languages are sufficiently messy that it is not possible to derive one truth from another in these languages by the application of simple rules such as "modus ponens" and "substitution of equals for equals". While various methods have been proposed for conducting "proofs" in these von Neumann languages, the methods are all variations of the two-step theme: transform the specified and annotated program into mathematical formulas and prove those formulas.

There exist programming languages that are also mathematical languages. In fact, the last few years have seen so much "flexibility" introduced into the notion of "programming language" that prominent researchers have agreed to call first order predicate calculus and set theory "programming languages" and then proceeded to argue the merits of various "compilers" and "interpreters" (i.e. theorem-provers). No one has yet found a way to execute programs written in such languages as efficiently as programs written in conventional programming languages—at least for most of the usual programming tasks.

However, because of the great effort devoted to programming language design and semantics during the past decade, many students of program semantics will smirk, scowl or choke at the mere mention of the word "FORTRAN". For example, a noted program semanticist remarked to the First International Conference on Reliable Software that if the West hoped to win the next war, it had better stop using COBOL and FORTRAN.* Nevertheless, the use of FORTRAN is widespread, even within first-rate computer science departments. We suspect that the wide use of FORTRAN will continue until someone designs and implements a mathematical programming language that executes as efficiently as FORTRAN. As long as the use of FORTRAN continues, we suspect that it may be profitable to specify and verify FORTRAN programs.

We conclude this apologia with a quotation from Backus's "The History of FORTRAN, I, II, and III" [3].

> To this day I believe that our emphasis on object program efficiency rather than on language design was basically correct. I believe that had we failed to produce efficient programs, the widespread use of languages like FORTRAN would have been seriously delayed. In fact, I believe that we are in a similar, but unrecognized, situation today: in spite of all the fuss that has been made over myriad language details, current conventional languages are still very weak programming aids, and far more powerful languages would be in use today if anyone had found a way to make them run with adequate efficiency. In other words, the next revolution in programming will take place only when *both* of the following requirements have been met: (a) a new kind of programming language, far more powerful than those of today, has been developed and (b) a technique has been found for executing its programs at not much greater cost than that of today's programs.

---

* We leave to the reader the tough choice between (a) the simple semantics of almost-as-efficient modern languages providing such features as variant records and pointers, and (b) the blinding speed of a resolution theorem-prover executing the powerful "there exists x such that p(x)" feature.

3. THE ANSI SPECIFICATIONS OF FORTRAN

Neither specification of FORTRAN ([12], [1]) provides all that is needed to specify a verification condition generator.

(1) The rules that define the syntax of FORTRAN are clearly stated, but they are intermixed with those that define the execution of a FORTRAN program. Because the specification of the syntax and semantics are intertwined, the reader of this document might have some difficulty interpreting a remark by us such as "suppose we are given a syntactically correct program". Therefore, we specify in detail the syntax of our subset of FORTRAN.

(2) The results of arithmetic operations on types REAL, DOUBLE PRECISION, and COMPLEX are not specified in [12] or [1] (or, for that matter, in more fashionable language definitions). The absence of such specifications makes it difficult to verify much about programs that use such operations. It may be possible to specify such operations in a way that is applicable to a variety of existing machines and useful for mechanical theorem-proving; see, for example, Brown [7]. We have not yet incorporated any such specifications into our system. We repeat an early warning of Goldstine and von Neumann [9] on just this issue:

> The floating binary point represents an effort to render a thorough mathematical understanding of at least part of the problem unnecessary, and we feel that this is a step in a doubtful direction.

(3) The definitions of FORTRAN do not provide a method for specifying in a formal language the effects or results of FORTRAN subprograms. (For example, there is no specified nomenclature for referring to entities of a COMMON block not declared in a program unit even though the program unit might be specified to redefine those entities via CALLs to other subprograms.) We have invented some nomenclature for specifying input/output assertions, invariants, and so forth.

(4) Some concepts used in [12] and [1] (e.g. "entity", "by value", and "by name") are not defined and some statements are bafflingly vague (e.g. "It is not necessary for a processor to evaluate all of the operands of an expression if the value of the expression can be determined otherwise". Section 6.6.1 [1]). We believe it is possible to produce paraphrases of [12] and [1] that are formal and that reflect the intentions of the authors, but no such documents exist as far as we know. We have relied upon common sense and our understanding of informal English to imagine a formal definition of FORTRAN with respect to which our verification condition generator might be formally proved correct.

4. AN INFORMAL DESCRIPTION OF OUR FORTRAN SUBSET

In this section we describe informally the subset of FORTRAN with which our system deals.

In selecting our subset, we omitted many features. That we have omitted a feature of FORTRAN does not indicate that we think that feature is logically intractable. We have no doubt that a verification condition generator could be implemented to include some of the FORTRAN features we have omitted.

For the rest of this section and the next, we assume that the reader has a rough idea of FORTRAN syntax.

The input to our verification condition generator must include not only the subprogram (function or subroutine) to be verified, but also all subprograms referenced somehow by the candidate subprogram. Each referenced subprogram must have been previously specified and verified. For example, some of our restrictions depend upon the types and dimensions of the "dummy arguments" (i.e. formal parameters) of the referenced subprograms and upon how those subprograms modify their arguments.

4.1. Statements in our subset

The FORTRAN statements in our subset are:

Arithmetic assignment	DO
logical assignment	DIMENSION
GO TO assignment	COMMON
Unconditional GO TO	INTEGER
Assigned GO TO	REAL
Computed GO TO	DOUBLE PRECISION
Arithmetic IF	COMPLEX
CALL	LOGICAL
RETURN	EXTERNAL
CONTINUE	Statement function
STOP	FUNCTION
PAUSE	SUBROUTINE
Logical IF	END

Our subset does not include the following FORTRAN 77 statements:

BACKSPACE	FORMAT
BLOCK DATA	IMPLICIT
Block IF	INQUIRE
CHARACTER	INTRINSIC
Character assignment	OPEN
CLOSE	PARAMETER

DATA   PRINT
ELSE   PROGRAM
ELSEIF   READ
ENDFILE   REWIND
ENDIF   SAVE
ENTRY   WRITE
EQUIVALENCE

4.2. Restrictions

For those statements in our subset we enforce all of the restrictions of both FORTRAN 66 and 77; furthermore, we enforce some additional restrictions.

To state our restrictions precisely we introduce some nomenclature. We do so formally later. One such notion is that a variable or array is "possibly smashed" by a subprogram. Roughly speaking, this means that the subprogram contains an assignment statement which alters the variable or array, or the subprogram calls another subprogram that possibly smashes the variable or array.

We now informally enumerate the major restrictions we impose, beyond those imposed by the ANSI specifications. While some of the restrictions may appear radical, many of the most severe are in fact closely related to ANSI restrictions. In the next section we comment on the relations between our restrictions and those of ANSI.

Every expression using infix operators must be fully parenthesized. For example, either $(A + (B + C))$ or $((A + B) + C)$ is permitted, but $A + B + C$ is not.

We countenance no implicit coercion. In an arithmetic assignment statement or a statement function statement, $v = e$, the type of e must be the type of v. In $(e_1 + e_2)$ the types of e_1 and e_2 must be the same.

No Hollerith constants are permitted.

No COMMON statement may declare a variable or array to be in blank COMMON, and the components of each labeled COMMON block x must be specified in exactly the same order and with exactly the same names, types, and dimensions in each subprogram in which x is a labeled COMMON block.

The names of intrinsic functions cannot be used except to denote those functions. For example, ABS may not be used as the name of a user-defined function subprogram.

No variable used in a GO TO assignment or an assigned GO TO statement of a subprogram may be used in any statement of the subprogram except a type, assigned GO TO, or GO TO assignment statement.

Subroutines and functions may not be passed as arguments to subprograms.
In a CALL statement or function reference, if the formal argument is an
   array, then the corresponding actual must be an array of the same size
   and number of dimensions.
Function subprograms may not possibly smash any of their arguments or
   anything in COMMON. That is, function subprograms may not have
   side effects.
No subroutine call may "possibly" violate the strict aliasing restrictions of
   FORTRAN. For example, if a subroutine has two arguments and possibly
   smashes the first, then that subroutine may not be called with the same
   array passed in both arguments nor may an array in COMMON be passed
   as the first argument if the subroutine "knows" about the COMMON
   block, even via subprograms. Furthermore, an array element may not be
   passed to a subroutine in an argument position that is possibly smashed.
An adjustable array dimension may not be possibly smashed, and the
   control variable and parameters of a DO may not be possibly smashed
   within the range of the DO.
DOs may not have extended ranges.

4.3. Tokens

Suppose we have written and verified a subprogram in which a local array
is declared to be of size 256. Suppose that we later wish to use the subprogram
in another application and wish the local array to be of size 128. Then, if we
wish to have confidence in the correctness of the modified program, we must
verify it "again". For example, the new program may not have enough space
to perform as specified, array bounds may be violated (either positively or
negatively), and a new analysis of overflow and underflow is necessary.

Since twiddling the built-in constants in a program is a fairly common
activity, especially when moving the program from one site to another, it is
convenient if it can be done without incurring the cost of verifying the modified program. To that end we permit the simultaneous verification of a large
class of programs by the addition to our language of what we call "tokens".
From the programmer's point of view, tokens are similar to INTEGER
variables, except that they may be used wherever FORTRAN permits
INTEGER constants. Furthermore, before the subprogram is compiled, the
user must specify positive INTEGER constants to be substituted for the
tokens. Such a substitution into a syntactically correct program (as we define
it) produces a syntactically correct FORTRAN program.

To prove the correctness of subprograms containing tokens, it is often
necessary to include hypotheses about the values of the tokens in one's
input assertions. For example, in one program we have verified we required

that one token be a power of two and another be its base two logarithm. Not only do tokens make it easier to obtain two slightly different versions of a correct program, they usually make it easier to verify a single program because they make obvious the key relationships between the constants without bringing in unnecessary detail (such as 8192 and 13). In addition, the explicit statement of the crucial relationships between the constants makes it easier to modify the program in the future. Of course, failure to instantiate the tokens with values satisfying the input assertions will produce programs that execute correctly whenever unsatisfiable input assertions are satisfied.

5. COMMENTS ON THE RESTRICTIONS

In this section we offer partial explanations for the major restrictions enumerated in the previous section.

5.1. Full parenthesization

FORTRAN permits one to write $A + B + C$. The order in which the subexpressions of unparenthesized expressions are combined is left up to the processor. However, $(A + B) + C$ may cause an overflow when $A + (B + C)$ does not (e.g. let A and B be very large INTEGERs and let C be the negation of B). By insisting upon full parenthesization, we reduce the number of orders of combination. However, even if an expression is fully parenthesized, a processor may use the facts that addition and multiplication are commutative.

5.2. Coercion

FORTRAN permits one to write $R + D$, where R is of type REAL and D is of type DOUBLE PRECISION. The result is of type DOUBLE PRECISION. Similarly, one may write the assignment $D = R$, which converts the value of R into a DOUBLE PRECISION number and smashes the result into D. For simplicity, we prohibit such implicit coercion. Since our subset includes the intrinsic functions for explicit coercion (e.g. DBLE converts a REAL value into a DOUBLE PRECISION one) no expressive power is lost (e.g. we permit $DBLE(R) + D$ and $D = DBLE(R)$).

5.3. Hollerith data

FORTRAN 66 makes some provisions for manipulating "Hollerith data". However, FORTRAN 77 does not.

5.4. Common

FORTRAN permits two subprograms to declare different organizations for the same COMMON block. Thus, one subprogram may declare that the first "storage unit" contains a REAL while the other subprogram declares that the first storage unit contains an INTEGER. The two declarations need not have the same number of names, sizes or types. For labeled COMMON they must, however, describe the same number of storage units. For blank COMMON, one may be arbitrarily longer than the other.

Such organization of storage complicates the determination of whether a variable is defined and what its value is. For example, if the INTEGER variable I and the REAL variable R share the same storage location, then I becomes undefined when R is defined (e.g. assigned to), and vice versa. We made our restrictions on the use of COMMON to eliminate such complications.

5.5. Intrinsic functions

FORTRAN permits the user to define a function with the same name as an intrinsic function. But FORTRAN 66 and 77 have different rules for obtaining the right to call such user-defined functions.

5.6. Label variables

We enforce a strict syntactic segregation between INTEGER variables used to hold statement labels and INTEGER variables used in normal arithmetic expressions.

FORTRAN achieves much the same effect but makes a semantic requirement. In particular, if an INTEGER variable is assigned a label, subsequent reference to the variable as an INTEGER is prohibited unless there is an intervening arithmetic assignment. Similarly, an assigned GO TO is prohibited if the label variable has an arithmetic rather than label value. Our restriction does not decrease the expressive power of the language, but may require the introduction of a second variable name to be used in those contexts requiring a "statement label type" variable.

5.7. Functional parameters

Our verification condition generator assumes that each time a CALL statement or function reference is encountered it can determine exactly which subroutine or function subprogram is being invoked so that it can obtain the specification of the referenced subprogram and produce the necessary verification conditions. If we had permitted subroutines or functions to be passed as arguments, then verification condition generation would have been severely complicated.

5.8. Agreement of dimension

FORTRAN permits the passing of an n-dimensional array to a subprogram "expecting" an m-dimensional array. Since the ANSI specifications spell out the order in which array elements are stored, such abuse of array indexing is well defined and can be used to implement unusual overlays and access patterns.

FORTRAN also permits passing an array element to a subprogram expecting an array. We have omitted both features because of their complexity.

5.9. Functions

Our requirement that function subprograms do not have side effects stems from the fact that a FORTRAN processor may evaluate (or not evaluate) the parts of an expression in an unpredictable order.

Let us illustrate the problems this causes. Suppose that N is an INTEGER variable in COMMON, that function subprogram R has the side effect of setting N to $N + 1$ and that function subprogram S has the side effect of setting N to 2*N. Finally, suppose that just before executing the assignment statement

$$X = (R(X)*S(X))$$

N has the value 5. Then after the execution of the assignment statement, N may have the value 11 or may have the value 12.

Worse, if the value returned by S(X) is 0, then the value of N after the evaluation of (R(X)*S(X)) would be 10 if the processor were smart enough not to evaluate R(X) once it spotted that S(X) returned 0, since an expression part need not be evaluated unless the processor finds it necessary. In fact, a really smart processor might be able to determine that S(X) always returns 0. Then after the evaluation of (R(X)*S(X)), the value of N might still be 5! Of course, the reason FORTRAN permits such flexibility in evaluation is so that good optimizing compilers can be written. In fact, the ANSI definitions of FORTRAN specify that the value of N is "undefined" if either the call to R or S might not be evaluated. (See section 10.2.9 of [12] and section 6.6.1 of [1]). It is interesting to speculate on the number of times correct optimising compilers have introduced "bugs" into programs written by programmers unfamiliar with the ANSI specifications.

Another reason for prohibiting side effects in function calls is the complexity

of the rules concerning what is perhaps the most bizarre concept in [12]—
"second level definition" (see sections 10.2.7 and 10.2.8). It is perhaps not
widely known that if X is of type REAL, A is an array, and R and N are as
above, then the following sequence of two instructions is illegal:

$$X = R(X)$$
$$B = A(N)$$

After the first statement, in which N is redefined, N is no longer defined at
the second level and may not be used as a subscript.

5.10. Aliasing

Presumably to permit the implementation of parameter passing by either
a "call by reference" or "call by return value" scheme, and because of its
concern with optimizing compilers, the FORTRAN 66 specification took a
dim view of aliasing.

For example, suppose subroutine SUBR takes two arguments, I and J,
and assigns to I. Then a CALL of the form

$$CALL\ SUBR(K, K)$$

is illegal. In a "call by reference" implementation, the assignment to I would
also smash J inside the subprogram. (Consider the difficulty of writing an
optimizing compiler for such an implementation of parameter passing unless
the specification rules out CALLs such as the one exhibited. For example, it
would be impossible to take advantage of the information that the current
value of J is in an accumulator.) In a "call by return value" implementation
the assignment to I would not smash J, but the final effect of the CALL on
K would depend upon the order in which the final values of the formal
parameters were assigned to K.

Without mentioning the word "aliasing," FORTRAN 66 prohibits it in
some cases. "If a subroutine reference causes a dummy argument (i.e. formal
parameter) in the referenced subroutine to become associated with (i.e. be
allocated the same storage location as) another dummy argument in the
same subroutine or with an entity in common, a definition of (i.e. assignment
to) either entity within the subroutine is prohibited". (Section 8.4.2 of [12],
bracketed definitions of unconventional terms added by us.) FORTRAN 77
has a similar prohibition.

We enforce this restriction by requiring that if a subprogram "possibly
smashes" an argument, then it is illegal to associate that argument with any
other argument or entity in COMMON. (A less syntactic interpretation is
possible. One might choose to permit CALLs that "possibly smash" aliased
arguments provided it could be shown that at runtime no such smashing
occurs.)

5.11. DO loop controls

FORTRAN 66 specifies that variables that represent adjustable array dimensions in a subprogram may not be modified during execution of the subprogram. In addition the control variable and parameters of a DO statement may not be modified by the statements in the range of the DO. Oddly, FORTRAN 77 permits both kinds of modifications but specifies that such modifications do not affect the size of the array or the number of times the DO loop is executed. This permits compilers to optimize the control of DO loops by storing the initial values of those variables in registers and using hardware increment and test instructions.

Again, we use our syntactically defined concept of "possibly smashed" to interpret this. For example, if SUBR is a subroutine that possibly smashes its first argument and I is the control variable of a DO statement, then the range of the DO statement may not contain:

CALL SUBR(I, X)

because it appears to modify I illegally. It is possible that particular invocation of SUBR does not in fact modify I so that such a CALL is technically permitted by the ANSI FORTRAN standards.

5.12. Extended DOs

Although FORTRAN 66 permits "extended DOs," FORTRAN 77 prohibits them.

6. THE FORMAL SYNTAX

In this and the next five sections we make precise the preceding statements about our FORTRAN subset and what we mean when we say a subprogram is "correct" with respect to an input/output specification. Then, in Section 8, we present a sample program in our subset and some of the verification conditions generated for it. The example has been organized so as to illustrate some of the formal notions about to be presented. However, some readers may wish to inspect the example before entering the formal sections of this document.

Lasciate ogni speranza, voi ch' entrate.

We adopt from [1] the definitions of the following: symbolic name, INTEGER constant, REAL constant, DOUBLE PRECISION constant, COMPLEX constant, LOGICAL constant and unsigned constant.

For example, MATRIX is a symbolic name. −127 is an INTEGER constant and 1.25E−5 is a REAL constant.

Notation. sequences. We shall write
$\langle\rangle$ for the empty sequence;
$\langle a \rangle$ for the sequence of length 1 whose only member is a;
$\langle a\ b \rangle$ for the sequence of length 2 whose first member is a and whose second member is b;
$\langle a\ b\ c \rangle$ for the sequence of length 3 whose first member is a, whose second member is b, and whose third member is c, and so on.

Definition. token. A *token* is a sequence of from 2 to 7 characters that satisfies the constraints on variable symbols in our logic (see [5] and [6]) and that begins with the character @.

Definition. constant. x is a *constant* if and only if x is an INTEGER, REAL, DOUBLE PRECISION, COMPLEX or LOGICAL constant.

Definition. label. A *label* is a sequence of from 1 to 5 digits the first of which is not 0.

Definition. types. x is a *type* if and only if x is one of the character sequences INTEGER, DOUBLE, COMPLEX, REAL or LOGICAL.

Definition. type of a constant. The *type of* an INTEGER, REAL, DOUBLE PRECISION, COMPLEX or LOGICAL constant is respectively INTEGER, REAL, DOUBLE, COMPLEX or LOGICAL.

Definition. variable pattern. x is a *variable pattern* if and only if for some symbolic name n and some type t, x is $\langle n\ t \rangle$. If $\langle n\ t \rangle$ is a variable pattern, then n is its *name* and t is its *type*.

Note. We have invented the concept of variable pattern, which is not employed in the usual specifications of FORTRAN syntax, to help in our definition of FORTRAN syntax (e.g. in the syntax of well-formed FORTRAN expressions). The presence of the variable pattern $\langle v\ t \rangle$ in the "syntactic environment" (to be defined) of a FORTRAN program indicates that the symbolic name v is to be used as a variable of type t.

Definition. array pattern. x is an *array pattern on* s if and only if s is a set of symbolic names, and for some n, t, i, j and k, each of the following is true:
(1) x is one of the sequences $\langle n\ t\ i \rangle$, $\langle n\ t\ i\ j \rangle$, or $\langle n\ t\ i\ j\ k \rangle$.
(2) n is a symbolic name.
(3) t is a type.
(4) Each of i, j, and k is either a positive, unsigned INTEGER constant, a token, or a member of s.

The *name* of an array pattern is its first member, its *type* is its second member. The *dimension list* of an array pattern p is the terminal subsequence of p starting with the third member of p.

Note. An array pattern is used to encode the type, number of dimensions, and size of each dimension of a symbolic name used as an array name in a FORTRAN subprogram. Those elements of the dimension list that are symbolic names are the so-called "adjustable" dimensions of the array. For example, if JMAX is in the set of symbolic names s, then $\langle$MATRIX REAL 10 JMAX$\rangle$ is an array pattern on s and encodes the information that MATRIX is a two-dimensional array of type REAL, measuring 10 by JMAX.

Definition. sort. s is a *sort* if and only if for some t, i, j and k, t is a type, each of i, j and k is a positive INTEGER, a token, or a symbolic name, and s is one of the sequences

$\langle t \rangle$
$\langle t\ i \rangle$
$\langle t\ i\ j \rangle$
$\langle t\ i\ j\ k \rangle$.

The *sort of* a variable pattern $\langle v\ t \rangle$ is $\langle t \rangle$, the *sort of* an array pattern $\langle v\ t\ i \rangle$, $\langle v\ t\ i\ j \rangle$, or $\langle v\ t\ i\ j\ k \rangle$ is, respectively, $\langle t\ i \rangle$, $\langle t\ i\ j \rangle$, or $\langle t\ i\ j\ k \rangle$.

Definition. function pattern. p is a *function pattern* if and only if for some fn, some t, and some nonempty sequence $\langle v_1 \ldots v_n \rangle$ each of the following statements is true:

(1) p is the sequence $\langle fn\ t\ v_1 \ldots v_n \rangle$;

(2) fn is a symbolic name;

(3) t is a type;

(4) Each member of $\langle v_1 \ldots v_n \rangle$ is either a variable pattern or an array pattern on the set of names of the v_i with type INTEGER;

(5) fn is not the name of any member of $\langle v_1 \ldots v_n \rangle$;

(6) For each choice of v_i and v_j from $\langle v_1 \ldots v_n \rangle$, the name of v_i is different from that of v_j, provided i and j are different.

The *name* of a function pattern is its first member. The *type* of a function pattern is its second member. If p is a function pattern of length $n + 2$, then (a) p *has* n *arguments*, (b) if i is an integer greater than 0 and less than or equal to n, then the ith *argument of* p is the $i + 2$nd member of p, and (c) the *argument list* of p is the sequence of length n whose ith member is the ith argument of p.

Note. A function pattern is used to encode the number, names, and sorts of dummy arguments to a function subprogram and the type of the result.

Definition. statement function pattern. p is a *statement function pattern* if and only if p is a function pattern and each member of the argument list of p is a variable pattern.

Note. A statement function pattern is used to encode the number and types of the arguments of a statement function and the type of the result. The names of the variable patterns in a statement function pattern are actually irrelevant. See the definition of the "statement function statement".

Definition. intrinsic function pattern. The *intrinsic function patterns* are:

⟨ABS REAL ⟨I REAL⟩⟩
⟨IABS INTEGER ⟨I INTEGER⟩⟩
⟨DABS DOUBLE ⟨I DOUBLE⟩⟩
⟨AINT REAL ⟨I REAL⟩⟩
⟨INT INTEGER ⟨I REAL⟩⟩
⟨IDINT INTEGER ⟨I DOUBLE⟩⟩
⟨AMOD REAL ⟨I REAL⟩ ⟨J REAL⟩⟩
⟨MOD INTEGER ⟨I INTEGER⟩ ⟨J INTEGER⟩⟩
⟨AMAX0 REAL ⟨I INTEGER⟩ ⟨J INTEGER⟩⟩
⟨AMAX1 REAL ⟨I REAL⟩ ⟨J REAL⟩⟩
⟨MAX0 INTEGER ⟨I INTEGER⟩ ⟨J INTEGER⟩⟩
⟨MAX1 INTEGER ⟨I REAL⟩ ⟨J REAL⟩⟩
⟨DMAX1 DOUBLE ⟨I DOUBLE⟩ ⟨J DOUBLE⟩⟩
⟨AMIN0 REAL ⟨I INTEGER⟩ ⟨J INTEGER⟩⟩
⟨AMIN1 REAL ⟨I REAL⟩ ⟨J REAL⟩⟩
⟨MIN0 INTEGER ⟨I INTEGER⟩ ⟨J INTEGER⟩⟩
⟨MIN1 INTEGER ⟨I REAL⟩ ⟨J REAL⟩⟩
⟨DMIN1 DOUBLE ⟨I DOUBLE⟩ ⟨J DOUBLE⟩⟩
⟨FLOAT REAL ⟨I INTEGER⟩⟩
⟨IFIX INTEGER ⟨I REAL⟩⟩
⟨SIGN REAL ⟨I REAL⟩ ⟨J REAL⟩⟩
⟨ISIGN INTEGER ⟨I INTEGER⟩ ⟨J INTEGER⟩⟩
⟨DSIGN DOUBLE ⟨I DOUBLE⟩ ⟨J DOUBLE⟩⟩
⟨DIM REAL ⟨I REAL⟩ ⟨J REAL⟩⟩
⟨IDIM INTEGER ⟨I INTEGER⟩ ⟨J INTEGER⟩⟩
⟨SNGL REAL ⟨I DOUBLE⟩⟩
⟨REAL REAL ⟨I COMPLEX⟩⟩
⟨AIMAG REAL ⟨I COMPLEX⟩⟩
⟨DBLE DOUBLE ⟨I REAL⟩⟩
⟨CMPLX COMPLEX ⟨I REAL⟩ ⟨J REAL⟩⟩
⟨CONJG COMPLEX ⟨I COMPLEX⟩⟩
⟨EXP REAL ⟨I REAL⟩⟩
⟨DEXP DOUBLE ⟨I DOUBLE⟩⟩

⟨CEXP COMPLEX ⟨I COMPLEX⟩⟩
⟨ALOG REAL ⟨I REAL⟩⟩
⟨DLOG DOUBLE ⟨I DOUBLE⟩⟩
⟨CLOG COMPLEX ⟨I COMPLEX⟩⟩
⟨ALOG10 REAL ⟨I REAL⟩⟩
⟨DLOG10 DOUBLE ⟨I DOUBLE⟩⟩
⟨SIN REAL ⟨I REAL⟩⟩
⟨DSIN DOUBLE ⟨I DOUBLE⟩⟩
⟨CSIN COMPLEX ⟨I COMPLEX⟩⟩
⟨COS REAL ⟨I REAL⟩⟩
⟨DCOS DOUBLE ⟨I DOUBLE⟩⟩
⟨CCOS COMPLEX ⟨I COMPLEX⟩⟩
⟨TANH REAL ⟨I REAL⟩⟩
⟨SQRT REAL ⟨I REAL⟩⟩
⟨DSQRT DOUBLE ⟨I DOUBLE⟩⟩
⟨CSQRT COMPLEX ⟨I COMPLEX⟩⟩
⟨ATAN REAL ⟨I REAL⟩⟩
⟨DATAN DOUBLE ⟨I DOUBLE⟩⟩
⟨ATAN2 REAL ⟨I REAL⟩ ⟨J REAL⟩⟩
⟨DATAN2 DOUBLE ⟨I DOUBLE⟩ ⟨J DOUBLE⟩⟩
⟨DMOD DOUBLE ⟨I DOUBLE⟩ ⟨J DOUBLE⟩⟩
⟨CABS REAL ⟨I COMPLEX⟩⟩

Note. In the spirit of FORTRAN 77, our intrinsic function patterns include patterns for the basic external functions of FORTRAN 66.

Our FORTRAN subset includes operations on types REAL, DOUBLE and COMPLEX, and our verification condition generator (to be described) will generate correct verification conditions for those operations provided their input/output relations are specified. However, we have not yet specified any of the operations involving finite precision REAL arithmetic and consequently have no mechanical means of proving anything about FORTRAN programs that use such operations.

Our patterns for the maximum and minimum functions have only two arguments. Consequently, syntactically correct programs in our subset may not apply the maximum and minimum functions to an arbitrary number of arguments as permitted in FORTRAN. The maximum and minimum functions are the only FORTRAN 66 functions with an indefinite number of arguments.

Definition. subroutine pattern. p is a *subroutine pattern* if and only if for some fn and some (possibly empty) sequence $v_1, \ldots, v_n$ each of the following statements is true:
(1) p is the sequence ⟨fn $v_1 \ldots v_n$⟩;
(2) fn is a symbolic name;

(3) Each member of $\langle v_1 \ldots v_n \rangle$ is either a variable pattern or an array pattern on the set of names of the v_i with type INTEGER;

(4) fn is not the name of any member of $\langle v_1 \ldots v_n \rangle$;

(5) For each possible choice of v_i and v_j from $\langle v_1 \ldots v_n \rangle$, the name of v_i is different from that of v_j provided i is different from j.

The *name* of a subroutine pattern is its first member. If p is a subroutine pattern of length $n + 1$, then (a) p *has* n *arguments*, (b) if i is an integer greater than 0 and less than $n + 1$, then the ith *argument of* p is the $i + 1$st member of p, and (c) the *argument list* of p is the sequence of length n whose ith member is the ith argument of p.

Note. We next define the notion of a "syntactic environment". Intuitively, such an environment is implicitly associated with a given FORTRAN sub-program (e.g. subroutine) and specifies the names of all entities known to the subprogram: arrays, variables (artificially divided into two sets according to whether they will be used to store labels for assigned GO TO statements), functions (divided into statement functions and others), subroutines and COMMON block names. A syntactic environment also specifies other syntactic information about these entities, such as their type, number of dimensions or arguments, and so on.

Definition. syntactic environment. s is a *syntactic environment* if and only if s is a sequence of seven sets (called the array patterns, variable patterns, label variable patterns, statement function patterns, function patterns, sub-routines patterns, and block names of s) such that each of the following statements is true:

(1) Each member of the array patterns is an array pattern on the names of the variable patterns of type INTEGER, and no two members of the array patterns have the same name;

(2) Each member of the variable patterns is a variable pattern, and no two members of the variable patterns have the same name;

(3) Each member of the label variable patterns is a variable pattern of type INTEGER;

(4) Each member of the statement function patterns is a statement function pattern, and no two members of the statement function patterns have the same name;

(5) Each member of the function patterns is a function pattern, and no two members of the function patterns have the same name;

(6) Each member of the subroutine patterns is a subroutine pattern, and no two members of the subroutine patterns have the same name;

(7) Each member of block names is a symbolic name;

(8) If n is the name of a member of one of the first six sets (i.e. the array,

variable, label variable, statement function, function or subroutine patterns of s), then n is not the name of a member of any other member of the first six sets nor is n a member of the block names;

(9) If n is the name of an intrinsic function pattern, the n is not a member of the block names of s nor is it the name of any member of the array, variable, label variable, statement function, or subroutine patterns of s;

(10) If n is the name of an intrinsic function pattern and n is the name of a member of the function patterns of s, then the intrinsic function pattern of which n is the name is a member of the function patterns of s.

Note. Most of the restrictions above regarding the use of names of various types follow from the ANSI FORTRAN specifications. Here are the major additional requirements we impose:

(1) the strict segregation of "normal" variables from those variables involved in assigned GO TO or GO TO assignment statements;

(2) the limitation of the use of intrinsic function names, and

(3) the disjointness requirements on the names in the seven sets above. (FORTRAN permits a limited amount of overlapping, e.g. the variable names must be disjoint from the array names, but not necessarily from the block names.)

Notation. has the form. x *has the form* y if and only if x and y are sequences of characters and x is the result of replacing each maximal, contiguous subsequence of y composed of lower case alphanumeric characters with the current meaning of each of those subsequences. For example, if a is "XY", ab is "UV", and z is "ABC", then "IF UV(XY) = ABC" has the form

$$\text{IF ab(a)} = z$$

Definition. subscript. x *is a subscript with respect to* s if and only if s is a syntactic environment and x is an unsigned INTEGER constant, a token, or the name of some variable pattern of type INTEGER in the variable patterns of s.

Definition. expression, sort of, proper subexpression, variable reference, array reference, array element reference, subscript sequence, arithmetic expression, operation symbol, argument sequence, relational expression, logical expression, function reference. Suppose s is a syntactic environment. We define inductively the concept c *is an expression with respect to* s. Simultaneously, we define certain auxiliary concepts. In some cases the entire definition of "expression" must be read to find all the clauses of these auxiliary concepts. We shall omit the phrase "with respect to" through this definition and wherever the appropriate s is obvious from context.

(1) If c is an unsigned constant of type t, then c is an expression, $\langle t \rangle$ is the sort of c, and c has no proper subexpressions.

(2) If c is a token, then c is an expression, $\langle INTEGER \rangle$ is the sort of c, and c has no proper subexpressions.

(3) If c is the name of a member of the variable patterns of s, then c is an expression, the sort of c is the sort of the variable pattern with name c in the variable patterns of s, and c has no proper subexpressions. [Such a c is called a *variable reference with respect to* s.]

(4) If c is the name of a member of the array patterns of s, then c is an expression, the sort of c is the sort of the array pattern with name c in the array patterns of s, and c has no proper subexpressions. [Such a c is called an *array reference with respect to* s.]

(5) For all a, t, i, j and k, and for all subscripts e_1, e_2 and e_3,
(a) if $\langle a\ t\ i \rangle$ is a member of the array patterns of s, and c has the form

$$a(e_1)$$

then c is an expression, the sort of c is $\langle t \rangle$, and the proper subexpressions of c are e_1 and the proper subexpressions of e_1;
(b) if $\langle a\ t\ i\ j \rangle$ is a member of the array patterns of s and c has the form

$$a(e_1, e_2)$$

then c is an expression, the sort of c is $\langle t \rangle$, and the proper subexpressions of c are e_1, e_2, the proper subexpressions of e_1, and the proper subexpressions of e_2; and
(c) if $\langle a\ t\ i\ j\ k \rangle$ is a member of the array patterns of s and c has the form

$$a(e_1, e_2, e_3)$$

then c is an expression, the sort of c is $\langle t \rangle$, and the proper subexpressions of c are e_1, e_2, e_3, the proper subexpressions of e_1, the proper subexpressions of e_2, and the proper subexpressions of e_3.
[Such a c is called an *array element reference to* a *with respect to* s. The *subscript sequence of* c is $\langle e_1 \rangle$, $\langle e_1\ e_2 \rangle$, or $\langle e_1\ e_2\ e_3 \rangle$, according to whether case (a), (b) or (c) above obtains.]

(6) For all e_1, e_2 and t, if e_1 and e_2 are expressions, t is a type other than LOGICAL, the sort of both e_1 and e_2 is $\langle t \rangle$, and c has one of the forms

$$(e_1 + e_2)$$
$$(e_1 - e_2)$$
$$(e_1 * e_2)$$
$$(e_1 / e_2)$$

then c is an expression, the sort of c is $\langle t \rangle$, and the proper subexpressions of c are e_1, e_2, the proper subexpressions of e_1, and the proper subexpressions of e_2. [Such a c is called an *arithmetic expression with respect to* s, the *operation symbol of* c is +, −, *, or / according to which of the above four forms describes c, and the *argument sequence of* c is $\langle e_1\ e_2 \rangle$.]

(7) For all e_1, e_2, t_1, t_2 and t_3, if e_1 and e_2 are expressions, the sort of e_1 is $\langle t_1 \rangle$, the sort of e_2 is $\langle t_2 \rangle$, the sequence $\langle t_1\ t_2\ t_3 \rangle$ is one of the sequences:

⟨INTEGER INTEGER INTEGER⟩
⟨REAL INTEGER REAL⟩
⟨DOUBLE INTEGER DOUBLE⟩
⟨COMPLEX INTEGER COMPLEX⟩
⟨REAL REAL REAL⟩
⟨REAL DOUBLE DOUBLE⟩
⟨DOUBLE REAL DOUBLE⟩
⟨DOUBLE DOUBLE DOUBLE⟩

and c has the form

$$(e_1\ ** \ e_2)$$

then c is an expression, the sort of c is $\langle t_3 \rangle$, and the proper subexpressions of c are e_1, e_2, the proper subexpressions of e_1, and the proper subexpressions of e_2. [Such a c is called an *arithmetic expression with respect to* s, the *operation symbol of* c is **, and the *argument sequence of* c is $\langle e_1\ e_2 \rangle$.]

(8) For all e_1, e_2 and t, if e_1 and e_2 are expressions, t is a type, t is not LOGICAL, t is not COMPLEX, both e_1 and e_2 have sort $\langle t \rangle$, and c has one of the forms

$$(e_1\ .LT.\ e_2)$$
$$(e_1\ .LE.\ e_2)$$
$$(e_1\ .EQ.\ e_2)$$
$$(e_1\ .NE.\ e_2)$$
$$(e_1\ .GT.\ e_2)$$
$$(e_1\ .GE.\ e_2)$$

then c is an expression, the sort of c is $\langle$LOGICAL$\rangle$, and the proper subexpressions of c are e_1, e_2, the proper subexpressions of e_1, and the proper subexpressions of e_2. [Such a c is called a *relational expression with respect to* s, the *operation symbol of* c is .LT., .LE., .EQ., .NE., .GT., or .GE. according to which of the above six forms describes c, and the *argument sequence of* c is $\langle e_1\ e_2 \rangle$.]

(9) For all e_1 and e_2, if e_1 and e_2 are expressions of sort $\langle$COMPLEX$\rangle$, and c has the form

$$(e_1\ .EQ.\ e_2)$$

or

$$(e_1\ .NE.\ e_2)$$

then c is an expression, the sort of c is ⟨LOGICAL⟩, and the proper sub-expressions of c are e_1, e_2, the proper subexpressions of e_1, and the proper subexpressions of e_2. [Such a c is called a *relational expression with respect to* s, the *operation symbol of* c is .EQ. or .NE. according to which of the two forms above describes c, and the *argument sequence of* c is ⟨e_1 e_2⟩.]

(10) For all e_1 and e_2, if e_1 and e_2 are expressions and the sort of both e_1 and e_2 is ⟨LOGICAL⟩, then if c has the form

$$(e_1 \text{ .OR. } e_2)$$

or

$$(e_1 \text{ .AND. } e_2)$$

then c is an expression, the sort of c is ⟨LOGICAL⟩, and the proper sub-expressions of c are e_1, e_2, the proper subexpressions of e_1, and the proper subexpressions of e_2. [Such a c is called a *logical expression with respect to* s, the *operation symbol of* c is .OR. or .AND. according to which of the above two forms describes c, and the *argument sequence of* c is ⟨e_1 e_2⟩.]

(11) For all e, if e is an expression, the sort of e is ⟨LOGICAL⟩, and c has the form

$$(\text{.NOT. } e)$$

then c is an expression, the sort of c is ⟨LOGICAL⟩, and the proper sub-expressions of c are e and the proper subexpressions of e. [Such a c is called a *logical expression with respect to* s, the *operation symbol of* c is .NOT., and the *argument sequence of* c is ⟨e⟩.]

(12) For each symbolic name fn, type t, integer n greater than 0, and for all sequences ⟨e_1 ... e_n⟩ and ⟨v_1 ... v_n⟩, if
(a) ⟨fn t v_1 ... v_n⟩ is a member of the statement function or the function patterns of s,
(b) for each integer i greater than 0 and less than or equal to n, e_i is an expression and
(i) the type of e_i is the type of v_i,
(ii) the length of the sort of e_i is the length of the sort of v_i, and
(iii) for k greater than 1 and less than or equal to the length of the sort of v_i, if the kth element of the sort of v_i is an INTEGER constant or token, then the kth element of the sort of e_i is that constant or token, and otherwise, for the m such that the name of v_m is the kth element of the sort of v_i, e_m is the kth element of the sort of e_i, and
(c) c has the form

$$fn(e_1, \ldots, e_n)$$

then c is an expression, the sort of c is ⟨t⟩, and the proper subexpressions of c are the members of ⟨e_1 ... e_n⟩ together with the proper subexpressions of each member of $\langle e_1 \ldots e_n \rangle$. [Such a c is called a *function reference to* fn *with respect to* s, and the *argument sequence of* c is $\langle e_1 \ldots e_n \rangle$.]

Note. In Section 5 we comment on some of the differences between our definition of an expression and the slightly more relaxed FORTRAN definitions (e.g. our prohibition of implicit coercion, our requirement of full parenthesization, and our requirement that arguments passed to functions have exactly the right dimension and size).

Definition. subexpressions. x is a member of the *subexpressions* of y if and only if for some syntactic environment s, x and y are expressions with respect to s and either x is y, or x is a proper subexpression of y.

Definition. used as a subscript. x is *used as a subscript in* y *with respect to* s if and only if s is a syntactic environment, y is an expression with respect to s, and for some z, z is a subexpression of y, z is an array element reference with respect to s, and x is a symbolic name and a member of the subscript sequence of z.

Example. Suppose $\langle$ A INTEGER 10$\rangle$ and $\langle$ B INTEGER 10$\rangle$ are members of the array patterns of a syntactic environment s and that $\langle$ I INTEGER$\rangle$ and $\langle$ J INTEGER$\rangle$ are members of the variable patterns of s. Then I and J are the only expressions used as subscripts in ((A(I) + B(J))*A(3)).

Note. We now define the statements in our FORTRAN subset. Our subset includes the FORTRAN "DO statement", which is the standard iterative construct. However, because the semantics of the DO statement is naturally specified in terms of more primitive statements, we ignore the DO statement in our definition of syntactic and semantic correctness. After the definition of semantic correctness we describe how we handle the syntax and semantics of DO statements.

Definition. statements: COMMON, DIMENSION, type, EXTERNAL, assignment, GO TO assignment, unconditional GO TO, assigned GO TO, computed GO TO, arithmetic IF, CALL, RETURN, CONTINUE, STOP, PAUSE, logical IF, statement function, FUNCTION, SUBROUTINE, END; declare; used as a label. st is a *statement with respect to* s if and only if s is a syntactic environment and one of the following statements is true:

(1) For some member n of the block names of s and some nonempty sequence $\langle a_1 \ldots a_k \rangle$ of distinct symbolic names, each member of which is the name of a member of the array or the variable patterns of s, st has the form

$$\text{COMMON } /n/a_1, a_2, \ldots, a_k$$

(Such a statement is called a *COMMON statement*. In such a statement, n is said to be *declared as a COMMON block* and each a_i is said to be *declared to be in the COMMON block* n.)

(2) For some v, t, i, j and k, one of $\langle v\ t\ i \rangle$, $\langle v\ t\ i\ j \rangle$, or $\langle v\ t\ i\ j\ k \rangle$ is a member of the array patterns of s, and st has (respectively) the form

$$\text{DIMENSION } v(i)$$
$$\text{DIMENSION } v(i, j)$$
$$\text{DIMENSION } v(i, j, k)$$

(Such a statement is called a *DIMENSION statement*. In such a statement, v is *declared to be an array*.)

(3) For some v, v is the name of a variable, label variable, array, statement function, or function pattern of s whose type is INTEGER, REAL, DOUBLE, COMPLEX or LOGICAL and st has (respectively) the form

$$\text{INTEGER } v$$
$$\text{REAL } v$$
$$\text{DOUBLE PRECISION } v$$
$$\text{COMPLEX } v$$
$$\text{LOGICAL } v$$

(Such a statement is said to be a *type statement*. In such a statement, v is *declared to have type* INTEGER, REAL, DOUBLE, COMPLEX or LOGICAL, respectively.)

(4) For some v, v is the name of a nonintrinsic function pattern of s, and st has the form

$$\text{EXTERNAL } v$$

(Such a statement is said to *declare* v *to be EXTERNAL*.)

(5) For some t, v, and exp, t is a type, v and exp are both expressions of sort $\langle t \rangle$, v is an array element reference or a variable reference, and st has the form

$$v = exp$$

(Such a statement is called an *assignment statement*.)

(6) For some i and k, i is the name of a label variable pattern of s, k is a label, and st has the form

$$\text{ASSIGN } k \text{ TO } i$$

(Such a statement is called a *GO TO assignment statement*. k and only k is *used as a label* in such a statement.)

(7) For some label k, st has the form

$$GO\ TO\ k$$

(Such a statement is called an *unconditional GO TO statement*. k and only k is *used as a label* in such a statement.)

(8) For some label variable pattern of s with name i and for some non-empty sequence of labels $\langle k_1 \ldots k_n \rangle$, st has the form

$$GO\ TO\ i,\ (k_1, \ldots, k_n)$$

(Such a statement is called an *assigned GO TO statement*. k is *used as a label* in such a statement if and only if k is a member of $\langle k_1 \ldots k_n \rangle$.)

(9) For some variable pattern of s with name i and type INTEGER and for some nonempty sequence of labels $\langle k_1 \ldots k_n \rangle$, st has the form

$$GO\ TO\ (k_1, \ldots, k_n),\ i$$

(Such a statement is called a *computed GO TO statement*. k is *used as a label* in such a statement if and only if k is a member of $\langle k_1 \ldots k_n \rangle$.)

(10) For some labels k_1, k_2 and k_3, and for some expression x of sort $\langle INTEGER \rangle$, $\langle REAL \rangle$ or $\langle DOUBLE \rangle$, st has the form

$$IF\ (x)\ k_1,\ k_2,\ k_3$$

(Such a statement is called an *arithmetic IF statement*. k_1, k_2 and k_3, and only k_1, k_2 and k_3, are *used as labels* in such a statement.)

(11) For some subroutine pattern of s with name sub and (possibly empty) argument list $\langle v_1 \ldots v_n \rangle$, for some sequence $\langle a_1 \ldots a_n \rangle$ of expressions, and for all i greater than 0 and less than or equal to n, each of the following statements is true:

(a) the type of a_i is the type of v_i,

(b) the length of the sort of a_i is the length of the sort of v_i, and

(c) for k greater than 1 and less than or equal to the length of the sort of v_i, if the kth element of the sort of v_i is an INTEGER constant or token, then the kth element of the sort of a_i is that constant or token, and otherwise, for the m such that the name of v_m is the kth element of the sort of v_i, a_m is the kth element of the sort of a_i, and

(d) st has either the form

$$CALL\ sub$$

or the form

$$CALL\ sub(a_1, \ldots, a_n)$$

(according to whether n is 0 or greater than 0).
(Such a statement is a *CALL of* sub.)

(12) st has one of the forms

RETURN
CONTINUE
STOP
PAUSE

(Such a statement is called a *RETURN, CONTINUE, STOP* or *PAUSE statement*, respectively.)

(13) For some sequence of digits, n, whose length is greater than 0 and less than 6, none of whose members is 8, and none of whose members is 9, st has the form

STOP n

or

PAUSE n

(Such a statement is called a *STOP* or *PAUSE* statement, respectively.)

(14) For some expression x of sort ⟨LOGICAL⟩ and for some st_2, st_2 is an assignment, GO TO assignment, unconditional GO TO, assigned GO TO, computed GO TO, arithmetic IF, CALL, RETURN, CONTINUE, STOP or PAUSE statement with respect to s, and st has the form

IF (x) st_2

(Such a statement is called a *logical IF statement* and *contains* st_2. k is *used as a label* in such a statement if and only if st_2 is an unconditional, computed, or assigned GO TO, arithmetic IF, or GO TO assignment statement and k is used as a label in st_2.)

(15) For some member ⟨fn t ⟨v_1 t_1⟩ ... ⟨v_n t_n⟩⟩ of the statement function patterns of s, for some nonempty sequence ⟨⟨a_1 t_1⟩ ... ⟨a_n t_n⟩⟩ of distinct members of the variable patterns of s, and for some expression x, not a variable reference, whose sort is ⟨t⟩ and which has no subexpression that is an array reference or an array element reference, st has the form

$$f(a_1, \ldots, a_n) = x$$

(Such a statement is called a *statement function statement* and is a *definition* of f. x is the *body* of such a statement and $a_1, \ldots, a_n$ are the *arguments* of such a statement.)

(16) For some variable pattern of s with name f and type t and for some nonempty sequence $\langle a_1 \ldots a_n \rangle$ of names of distinct members of the variable or array patterns of s, f is not one of the a_i, and either (a) t is not DOUBLE and st has the form

$$t \text{ FUNCTION } f(a_1, \ldots, a_n)$$

or (b) t is DOUBLE and st has the form

$$\text{DOUBLE PRECISION FUNCTION } f(a_1, \ldots, a_n)$$

(Such a statement is called a *FUNCTION statement*. The *arguments* of the statement are $a_1, \ldots, a_n$. The *name* of the statement is f and the *type* of the statement is t.)

(17) For some symbolic name sub that is not a member of the block names of s and is not the name of any member of the array, variable, label variable, statement function, function, or subroutine patterns of s, and is not the name of any intrinsic function pattern, and for some (possibly empty) sequence $\langle a_1 \ldots a_n \rangle$ of names of distinct members of the variable and array patterns of s, st has the form

$$\text{SUBROUTINE sub}$$

or

$$\text{SUBROUTINE sub}(a_1, \ldots, a_n)$$

according to whether the sequence $\langle a_1 \ldots a_n \rangle$ is empty or not. (Such a statement is called a *SUBROUTINE statement*. sub is the *name* of the statement. In the first case, the statement has no arguments. In the second case the *arguments* of the statement are $a_1, \ldots, a_n$.)

(18) st has the form

$$\text{END}$$

(Such a statement is called an *END statement*.)

Note. In Section 5 we compare the syntax of statements in our subset with the syntax of FORTRAN statements.

Definition. executable statment. st is an *executable statement with respect to* s if and only if st is an assignment, GO TO assignment, unconditional GO TO, computed GO TO, assigned GO TO, arithmetic IF, CALL, RETURN, CONTINUE, STOP, PAUSE or logical IF statement with respect to s.

Definition. used as a label variable. x is *used as a label variable in* st *with respect to* s if and only if s is a syntactic environment, x is a symbolic name, st is a statement with respect to s, and one of the following statements is true:

(1) For some labels $lab_1, \ldots, lab_n$, st has the form:

$$GO\ TO\ x, (lab_1, \ldots, lab_n)$$

(2) For some label lab, st has the form:

$$ASSIGN\ lab\ TO\ x$$

(3) For some statement st_2 with respect to s, st is a logical IF statement containing st_2 and x is used as a label variable in st_2.

Definition. used on the second level. x is *used on the second level in* st *with respect to* s if and only if s is a syntactic environment, x is a symbolic name, st is a statement with respect to s, and one of the following statements is true:

(1) For some v and exp, st is an assignment statement of the form

$$v = exp$$

and x is used as a subscript in v or in exp.

(2) For some labels $lab_1, \ldots,$ and lab_k, st has the form

$$GO\ TO\ (lab_1 \ldots, lab_n), x$$

(3) For some labels lab_1, lab_2, and lab_3 and for some expression exp, st is an arithmetic IF statement of the form:

$$IF\ (exp)\ lab_1, lab_2, lab_3$$

and x is used as a subscript in exp.

(4) For some symbolic name subr and expressions $a_1, \ldots, a_n$, st has the form

$$CALL\ subr(a_1, \ldots, a_n)$$

and x is used as a subscript in some a_1.

(5) For some statement st_2 and expression exp, st is a logical IF statement of the form

$$IF\ (exp)\ st_2$$

and either x is used as a subscript in exp or x is used on the second level in st_2.

Definition. label function. f is a *label function for* seq *with respect to* s if and only if for some integer n, seq is a sequence of n statements with respect to s, f is a one-to-one function, each member of the domain of f is a label, each member of the range of f is an integer greater than 0 and less than or equal to n, and for each label x in the domain of f, the (f x)th member of seq is an executable statement with respect to s.

Note. A label function is the formal device by which we associate statement labels with some of the executable statements in a program. For example, imagine that we have in mind a FORTRAN function or subroutine (i.e. a "procedure subprogram"). Suppose that the 10th, 20th and 30th statements of the program are the only statements labeled and that the labels are 1000, 2000 and 3000 respectively. Then this FORTRAN subprogram is conveniently characterized by three mathematical objects: the syntactic environment s with respect to which the expressions and statements in the program are formed, the sequence of statements seq comprising the program, and the label function that maps 1000 to 10, 2000 to 20, and 3000 to 30, and is undefined elsewhere. We will use such triples to characterize the subprograms in our subset.

Definition. subprogram. A triple ⟨s seq labs⟩ is a *subprogram* if and only if each of the following statements is true:

(1) s is a syntactic environment.

(2) seq is a sequence of statements with respect to s.

(3) labs is a label function for seq with respect to s.

(4) The first statement of seq is a SUBROUTINE or FUNCTION statement and no other statement of seq is a SUBROUTINE or FUNCTION statement.

(5) For all ap, a, i and d, if ap is a member of the array patterns of s, a is the name of ap, i is 1, 2, or 3, the ith member of the dimension list of ap is d, and d is a symbolic name, then both a and d are arguments of the first statement of seq.

(6) If the first statement of seq is a SUBROUTINE statement, then for each pattern p in the array, variable, label variable, statement function or function patterns of s, the name of p is declared in exactly one type statement of seq.

(7) If the first statement of seq is a FUNCTION statement, then for each pattern p in the array, label variable, statement function, or function patterns of s, or in the variable patterns of s except for the pattern whose name is the name of the first statement of seq, the name of p is declared in exactly one type statement of seq and the name of the first statement of seq is not declared in any type statement of seq.

(8) The name of each member of the variable patterns of s is used as a variable (other than as an actual) in some statement of seq other than a type or FUNCTION statement.

(9) The name of each member of the variable patterns of s that is an argument of the first statement of seq is used as a variable (other than as an actual

in a function reference) in some statement of seq other than a type, CALL, FUNCTION or SUBROUTINE statement of seq.

(10) The name of each intrinsic member of the function patterns of s occurs in some nontype statement of seq.

(11) If f is the name of a member of the function patterns of s and f is not the name of an intrinsic function pattern, then f is declared to be EXTERNAL in exactly one statement of seq.

(12) Each member of the block names of s is declared as a COMMON block in exactly one statement of seq.

(13) No symbolic name is declared to be in a COMMON block in two COMMON statements of seq.

(14) No argument of the first statement of seq is declared to be in a COMMON block by a COMMON statement of seq.

(15) If the first statement of seq is a FUNCTION statement, then the name of that statement is not declared to be in a COMMON block by a COMMON statement of seq.

(16) The name of each member of the statement function patterns of s is defined in exactly one statement function statement of seq.

(17) The name of each member of the array patterns of s is declared in exactly one DIMENSION statement of seq.

(18) Every label used in a GO TO assignment, unconditional GO TO, computed GO TO, assigned GO TO, arithmetic IF or logical IF statement of seq is a member of the domain of labs.

(19) The name of each member of the subroutine patterns of s is called in at least one CALL statement of seq.

(20) The name of each member of the label variable patterns of s is used as a label variable in at least one statement of seq.

(21) At least one member of seq is a RETURN statement.

(22) The subsequence of seq obtained by deleting the first and last statements of seq satisfies the following conditions: (a) the type statements precede the other statements, (b) the COMMON, EXTERNAL and DIMENSION statements precede the statement function and executable statements, and (c) the statement function statements precede the executable statements.

(23) For each stmt and fn, if stmt is a statement function statement of seq with respect to s, the body of the statement has a subexpression that is a function reference to fn with respect to s, and fn is the name of a statement function pattern of s, then the statement function statement of seq that defines fn precedes stmt in seq.

(24) The next to last statement of seq is an unconditional GO TO, computed GO TO, assigned GO TO, arithmetic IF, RETURN or STOP statement.

(25) The last statement of seq is an END statement and no other statement of seq is an END statement.

If ⟨s seq labs⟩ is a subprogram, then the *name* of ⟨s seq labs⟩ is the name of the first statement of seq and the *arguments* of ⟨s seq labs⟩ are the arguments of the first statement of seq.

Definition. subroutine subprogram. ⟨s seq labs⟩ is a *subroutine subprogram* if and only if ⟨s seq labs⟩ is a subprogram and the first member of seq is a SUBROUTINE statement.

Definition. function subprogram. ⟨s seq labs⟩ is a *function subprogram* if and only if ⟨s seq labs⟩ is a subprogram and the first member of seq is a FUNCTION statement.

Note. We now define "superficial context". Intuitively, a superficial context is a sequence of subprograms such that each of the functions and subroutines used by any of them is defined earlier in the sequence, and such that certain "interprogram" relationships exist between the subprograms.

Definition. superficial context. c is a *superficial context* if and only if c is a (possibly empty) sequence of subprograms ⟨⟨s_1 seq_1 $labs_1$⟩ ... ⟨s_n seq_n $labs_n$⟩⟩ and each of the following statements is true:

(1) For each s_i and for each ⟨sub v_1 ... v_n⟩ in the subroutine patterns of s_i, there exists an integer j greater than 0 and less than i such that the first statement of seq_j is a SUBROUTINE statement, sub is the name of the first statement of seq_j, the first statement of seq_j has n arguments, and for each integer k greater than 0 but less than or equal to n, the kth argument of the first statement of seq_j is the name of v_k, and v_k is a member of either the array or variable patterns of s_j.

(2) For each s_i and for each ⟨f t v_1 ... v_n⟩ in the function patterns of s_i, either the pattern is an intrinsic function pattern or there exists an integer j greater than 0 and less than i such that the first statement of seq_j is a FUNCTION statement, f is the name of the statement, t is the type of the statement, the statement has n arguments, and for all k greater than 0 but less than or equal to n, the kth argument of the first statement of seq_j is the name of v_k, and v_k is a member of either the array or variable patterns of s_j.

(3) If sub_i and sub_j are members of c and i is not j, then the name of sub_i is not the name of sub_j or the name of any intrinsic function pattern.

(4) If ⟨s seq labs⟩ is a member of c, then for no member sub_j of c is the name of sub_j a member of the block names of s.

(5) If ⟨s_i seq_i $labs_i$⟩ and ⟨s_j seq_j $labs_j$⟩ are distinct members of c, and if n is a member of the block names of s_i and s_j, then the COMMON statement of seq_i that declares n to be a COMMON block is identical to the COMMON statement of seq_j that declares n to be a COMMON block. Furthermore, if

a is a symbolic name that is declared in seq_i to be in the COMMON block n, then there exists a pattern whose name is a that is either both a member of the variable patterns of s_i and the variable patterns of s_j or is both a member of the array patterns of s_i and the array patterns of s_j.

(6) If $\langle s_i \ seq_i \ labs_i \rangle$ and $\langle s_j \ seq_j \ labs_j \rangle$ are members of c and a is a symbolic name that is declared to be in a COMMON block n by a member of seq_i and is declared to be in a COMMON block m by a member of seq_j, then n is m. Furthermore, a is not the name of any member of c nor a member of the block names of any member of c.

Note. In Section 5 we comment upon some of the interprogram relationships we impose in addition to those of FORTRAN.

Note. In order to specify subprograms it is necessary to be able to refer unambiguously to variables and arrays—even variables and arrays not declared in the subprogram itself. For example, suppose subroutine MULT declares A as a "local" array (i.e. A is declared in MULT but not in a COMMON). Suppose that MULT CALLs the subroutine TEST, which declares A to be in COMMON block BLK and modifies that "global" A. A reference to A in a FORTRAN statement in MULT is understood to be a reference to the "local" A. It is not possible for a FORTRAN statement in MULT to refer to the "global" A of TEST. However, since the value of the "global" A may affect the computation of TEST and thus the computation of MULT, it may be necessary in specifying MULT to refer to the "global" A. To permit clear talk about matters we now define the "local" and "global" names of a subprogram and introduce the notion of the "long" and "short" names of variables and arrays. An assertion in MULT can refer to the value of the A in COMMON block BLK by using the name BLK-A, which is the "long" name of the "global" A.

Definition. local names. n is a *local name* of a subprogram $\langle$ s seq labs $\rangle$ if and only if n is the name of a member of the array, variable, or label variable patterns of s, and n is not declared by any COMMON statement of seq to be in any COMMON block.

Definition. COMMON names. n is a *COMMON name* of a subprogram $\langle$ s seq labs $\rangle$ if and only if for some b and some v, b is a member of the block names of s, v is declared by some COMMON statement of seq to be in the COMMON block b, and n has the form

b–v

Definition. short name. n is the *short name* of m if and only if n is a symbolic name and either (a) m is a symbolic name and n is m, or (b) for some symbolic name b, m has the form b–n.

Definition. long name. n is the *long name of* m *with respect to* sub if and only if sub is a subprogram and either (a) n is a local name of sub and n is m, or (b) n is a COMMON name of sub and m is the short name of n.

Example. Suppose we have in mind a subprogram sub in which ARRAY is declared as an array but is not in COMMON, and SIZE is declared as a variable in the COMMON block named BLK. Then ARRAY is a local name of sub. BLK-SIZE is a COMMON name of sub. The short name of ARRAY is ARRAY. The short name of BLK–SIZE is SIZE. The long name of ARRAY with respect to sub is ARRAY. The long name of SIZE with respect to sub is BLK–SIZE.

Note. We now define the "global names" of a subprogram and the "global sort" of a long name. Intuitively, the global names of a subprogram are the global variables and arrays of the subprogram and all the subprograms it CALLs. Of course, the unambiguous long names of the variables are used.

Definition. global names. If c is a superficial context and sub is a member of c, then the *global names of* sub *with respect to* c are the COMMON names of sub together with the global names of each sub_j of c such that the name of sub_j is the name of a nonintrinsic function of subroutine pattern of sub.

Definition. global sort. t is the *global sort of* n *in* sub *with respect to* c if and only if c is a superficial context, sub is a member of c, and one of the following is true:

(1) n is a local name of sub and t is the sort of the array, variable, or label variable pattern in sub with name n.

(2) n is a global name of sub with respect to c, n has the form b–v for some b and v, and t is the sort of the array or variable pattern with name v in any member of c in which v is declared to be in block b.

Note. We next define the notion that a variable or an array is "possibly smashed" by a subprogram. The intuitive idea is that v is possibly smashed in a subprogram if execution of the subprogram appears sometimes to alter the value of v either by assigning to it or by CALLing a subroutine that possibly smashes it. The notion of "possibly smashed" is used in a variety of places in this document. For example, it is involved in the question of whether a subroutine CALL violates the FORTRAN prohibition against aliasing. The notion is also used to extend the output assertion of a subprogram by the implicit assertion that variables not possibly smashed are unmodified by CALLs of the subprogram.

There is one subtle aspect to the definition of "possibly smashed". Although we check that a variable might be smashed by the execution of a subroutine subprogram, we do not check that it is possibly smashed by the execution of a function subprogram. The reason is that when we define a "syntactically correct context" we will require that function subprograms not possibly smash any variables except locals that are not arguments (i.e. functions have no side effects). Thus, provided one is dealing with a "syntactically correct context," our definition of "possibly smashed" indeed guarantees that no variable of the calling program is modified by the execution of a function subprogram.

Definition. possibly smashed. v is *possibly smashed by* $\langle s_i \; seq_i \; labs_i \rangle$ *in* c *through* st if and only if (a) c is a superficial context, (b) $\langle s_i \; seq_i \; labs_i \rangle$ is a member of c, (c) st is a statement of seq_i, and (d) for some u, u is the short name of v, v is a global name or a local name of $\langle s_i \; seq_i \; labs_i \rangle$, and one of the following statements is true:

(1) v is a local or COMMON name of $\langle s_i \; seq_i \; labs_i \rangle$, and for some expressions x_1, x_2, x_3, and e with respect to s_i, st has one of the forms

$$u = e$$
$$u(x_1) = e$$
$$u(x_1, x_2) = e$$
$$u(x_1, x_2, x_3) = e$$

(2) v is a local name of $\langle s_i \; seq_i \; labs_i \rangle$, and for some k, st has the form

ASSIGN k TO u

(3) For some symbolic name sub, and expressions $e_1, \ldots,$ and e_n with respect to s_i, st has the form

CALL sub

or

CALL sub($e_1, \ldots, e_n$)

and for the member $\langle s_j \; seq_j \; labs_j \rangle$ of c with the name sub, either (a) v is a global name of $\langle s_j \; seq_j \; labs_j \rangle$ and v is possibly smashed by $\langle s_j \; seq_j \; labs_j \rangle$ through some member of seq_j, or (b) v is a local or COMMON name of $\langle s_i \; seq_i \; lab_i \rangle$, and for some i greater than 0 and less than n + 1, e_i is a variable reference or array reference to u, and the ith argument of $\langle s_j \; seq_j \; labs_j \rangle$ is possibly smashed by $\langle s_j \; seq_j \; labs_j \rangle$ in c through some member of seq_j.

(4) For some statement st_2 and expression exp, st is a logical IF statement of the form

IF (exp) st_2

and v is possibly smashed by $\langle s_i \; seq_i \; labs_i \rangle$ in c through st_2.

(If we say "v is possibly smashed by sub in c" (omitting "through st"), we mean "for some st, v is possibly smashed by sub in c through st".)

Note. We complete the syntactic characterization of our FORTRAN subset by defining a "syntactically correct context" to be a sequence of subprograms that, in addition to being a superficial context, contains no function subprogram that causes side effects and no CALL statement that violates certain aliasing restrictions. In Section 5 we comment upon these restrictions and their relationship to FORTRAN.

Definition. syntactically correct context. c is a *syntactically correct context* if and only if c is a superficial context and each of the following statements is true:

(1) For each function subprogram sub of c, no global name of sub nor argument of sub is possibly smashed by sub in c.

(2) In each subroutine subprogram $\langle s$ seq labs$\rangle$ of c, no argument of $\langle s$ seq labs$\rangle$ that is a member of the dimension list of an array pattern of s is possibly smashed by $\langle s$ seq labs$\rangle$ in c.

(3) For each $\langle s$ seq labs$\rangle$ and sub_j in c, for each sub, for each sequence of expressions $\langle e_1 \ldots e_n \rangle$ with respect to s, and for each statement in seq of the form

$$\text{CALL sub}(e_1, \ldots, e_n)$$

if sub is the name of sub_j, then for each integer i greater than 0 and less than or equal to n, if the ith argument of sub_j is possibly smashed by sub_j in c, then for some symbolic name v each of the following is true:

(a) e_1 is either a variable reference to v or an array reference to v,

(b) the long name of v with respect to $\langle s$ seq labs$\rangle$ is not a global name of sub_j, and

(c) for each integer j greater than 0, not equal to i, and less than or equal to n, e_j is not a variable, array, or array element reference to v.

(4) For each $\langle s$ seq labs$\rangle$ and sub_j in c, for each m, sub, and sequence of expressions $\langle e_1 \ldots e_n \rangle$ with respect to s, and for each statement in seq of the form

$$\text{CALL sub}(e_1, \ldots, e_n)$$

if sub is the name of sub_j and m is a COMMON name of $\langle s$ seq labs$\rangle$ that is possibly smashed by sub_j in c, then for k greater than 0 and less or equal to n, e_k is not a variable, array, or array element reference to the short name of m.

(5) For each $\langle s$ seq labs$\rangle$ in c, if x is a COMMON or local name of $\langle s$ seq labs$\rangle$ and the short name of x is used on the second level in some statement of seq, then x is not possibly smashed by $\langle s$ seq labs$\rangle$ in c through any CALL statement of $\langle s$ seq labs$\rangle$.

7. FLOW GRAPHS

In this section we describe the flow of control through a FORTRAN subprogram.

Informally, the flow is specified by an "ordered, directed graph" whose nodes are associated with the statements of the subprogram. A proof of correctness involves the consideration of all "paths" through the graph. To aid the consideration of the possibly infinite number of paths created by loops, the exploration process utilizes a "cover" of the graph, which is a subset of the nodes sufficient to "cut" every loop. Given a graph and a cover for it, it is then possible to identify a finite number of paths through the graph, called the "Floyd paths", such that the correctness of these paths implies the correctness of all paths through the graph*. We make these graph theoretic terms precise before discussing the graphs for subprograms.

Definition. ordered, directed graph; edge; head; tail. $\langle n\ e \rangle$ is an *ordered directed graph* if and only if n is a set and e is a function whose range is a subset of n and whose domain is a subset of the Cartesian product of n with the positive integers. Each member $\langle \langle x\ i \rangle\ z \rangle$ of e is an *edge* of the graph, x is the *head* of the edge, z is the *tail* of the edge, and $\langle \langle x\ i \rangle\ z \rangle$ is the ith *edge leading from* x.

Definition. path. If g is an ordered, directed graph, then p is a *path* in g if and only if p is a (possibly empty and possibly infinite) sequence $\langle e_1\ e_2\ ... \rangle$ of edges of g and for each member e_{i+1} of p, if $i \rangle 0$ then the tail of e_i is the head of e_{i+1}.

Definition. cover. If g is an ordered, directed graph, then c is a *cover* for g if and only if c is a subset of the nodes of g and for each infinite path p in g the tail of some element of p is a member of c.

Definition. Floyd path. p is a *Floyd path of g for* c if and only if g is an ordered directed graph, c is a cover for g, p is a nonempty, finite path in g, the head of the first and the tail of the last members of p are members of c, and for each integer i greater than 1 and less than or equal to the length of p, the head of the ith member of p is not a member of c.

Definition. flow graph. The *flow graph* of a subprogram $\langle s$ seq labs$\rangle$ is the pair $\langle n\ e \rangle$ such that each of the following is true:

(1) n is the set of all integers j such that the absolute value of j is less than or equal to the length of seq and either j is positive and the jth member of seq is an executable statement or j is negative and the -jth member of seq is a logical IF statement.

(2) e is the set of all $\langle \langle i\ j \rangle\ k \rangle$ such that for some st

(a) i and k are members of n, and

(b) either i is positive and st is the ith statement of seq or i is negative and the -ith statement of seq contains st, and (in either case) one of the following statements is true:

---

* Readers interested in a more tutorial sketch of the application of the Floyd method should see [5].

(i) st is an assignment, GO TO assignment, CALL, CONTINUE, or PAUSE statement, j is 1, and k is $|i| + 1$;
(ii) for some label m, st has the form:

$$GO\ TO\ m$$

j is 1, and k is (labs m);
(iii) for some labels $m_1, \ldots,$ and m_n, st has the form:

$$GO\ TO\ i,\ (m_1, \ldots, m_n)$$

or

$$GO\ TO\ (m_1, \ldots, m_n),\ i$$

j is greater than 0 but less than or equal to n, and k is (labs m_j);
(iv) for some labels m_1, m_2 and m_3, and for some expression e, st has the form:

$$IF\ (e)\ m_1,\ m_2,\ m_3$$

and j is 1, 2 or 3, and k is, respectively, (labs m_1), (labs m_2), or (labs m_3); or
(v) for some expression e and some statement st', st has the form:

$$IF\ (e)\ st'$$

j is 1 or 2, and k is, respectively, $-i$ or $i + 1$.

Definition. statement of. If ⟨s seq labs⟩ is a subprogram and n is a member of the nodes of the flow graph of ⟨s seq labs⟩, then *the statement of* n is the nth member of seq if n is positive and the statement contained in the −nth member of seq if n is negative.

Note. A node n of the flow graph g of a subprogram is the head of some edge of g if and only if the statement of n is neither a RETURN or a STOP statement.

Definition. reachable. m is *reachable* from n in g if and only if g is an ordered, directed graph, m and n are nodes of g, and there exists a finite path p of g such that the head of the first edge of p is n and the tail of the last edge of p is m.

Note. To enforce the ANSI 66 requirement that every executable statement in a subprogram "can" sometimes be executed, we will require that every node in the flow graph of the subprogram be reachable from the node corresponding to the first executable statement.

8. TERMS

Before we discuss the specification of subprograms we define the logical theory in which we are operating. For example, there is an intuitive feeling that for every FORTRAN expression (e.g. (X + A(I))) there must be a term in the logic that in some sense denotes the value of that expression. The verification condition generator must construct for each FORTRAN expression the corresponding term of the logic. Therefore, at the very least we must define the well-formed terms of the logic and specify the correspondence between FORTRAN expressions and terms.

Notation. expressions versus terms. Some logicians use the words "expression" and "term" interchangeably. In this document we use the word "expression" exclusively to refer to FORTRAN expressions with respect to a given syntactic environment, as previously defined. We use the word "term" exclusively to refer to well-formed terms in the mathematical logic in which we operate.

Note. We first specify the "basic FORTRAN theory", which is a logic produced by extending the logic described in [5] and [6]. The syntax of the logic is the prefix syntax used by Church's lambda-calculus. For example, we write (MOD X Y) to denote the term that others might denote by MOD(X, Y), mod(X, Y), or X mod Y.

In addition to a version of the propositional calculus with function symbols and equality, the logic provides a principle under which new types of inductively constructed objects may be introduced, a principle under which new recursive functions may be defined, and a principle of induction.

The logic does not provide the usual notion of predicates or relations. Without loss of generality we use functions exclusively; a property is expressed by writing down a term that is either equal to the object (FALSE) or not equal to the object (FALSE) according to whether the property fails to hold or holds. (The constant (TRUE) is a commonly used object not equal to (FALSE).) For example, the function ZLESSP, of two arguments, returns (TRUE) or (FALSE) according to whether its first argument is less than its second.

The logic does not provide explicit quantification. Variables in formulas are implicitly universally quantified. To express certain forms of quantification it is necessary to define new recursive functions. For example, to assert that some members of a finite sequence have a given property one may introduce the recursive function that maps over the sequence and checks for the property.

The basic FORTRAN theory contains some of the function symbols used in the transcription of FORTRAN expressions into mathematical terms. For example, it contains the function ZPLUS that returns the sum of its two integer arguments, and the previously mentioned ZLESSP.

Definition. basic FORTRAN theory. The *basic FORTRAN theory* is the logical theory obtained by extending the theory defined in [5] and [6] as specified in Appendix A.

Note. We now make some definitions that make it easier to refer to certain function symbols of the basic FORTRAN theory.

Definition. FORTRAN recognizers. The *FORTRAN recognizer* for a type INTEGER, REAL, DOUBLE, COMPLEX or LOGICAL is (respectively) the function symbol ZNUMBERP, RNUMBERP, DNUMBERP, CNUMBERP or LOGICALP.

Definition. function symbol for t and op. For the combinations of type t and operator symbol op given below, the *function symbol* for t and op is defined by the following table:

| op/t | INTEGER | Function symbol for t and op | | |
		REAL	DOUBLE	COMPLEX
+	ZPLUS	RPLUS	DPLUS	CPLUS
−	ZDIFFERENCE	RDIFFERENCE	DDIFFERENCE	CDIFFERENCE
*	ZTIMES	RTIMES	DTIMES	CTIMES
/	ZQUOTIENT	RQUOTIENT	DQUOTIENT	CQUOTIENT
.LT.	ZLESSP	RLESSP	DLESSP	
.LE.	ZLESSEQP	RLESSEQP	DLESSEQP	
.EQ.	ZEQP	REQP	DEQP	CEQP
.NE.	ZNEQP	RNEQP	DNEQP	CNEQP
.GE.	ZGREATEREQP	RGREATEREQP	DGREATEREQP	
.GT.	ZGREATERP	RGREATERP	DGREATERP	

Definition. exponentiation function symbol. The *exponentiation function symbol* for certain combinations of types t_1 and t_2 is defined by the following table:

t_1	t_2	Exponentiation function symbol
INTEGER	INTEGER	ZEXPTZ
REAL	INTEGER	REXPTZ
DOUBLE	INTEGER	DEXPTZ
COMPLEX	INTEGER	CEXPTZ
REAL	REAL	REXPTR
REAL	DOUBLE	REXPTD
DOUBLE	REAL	DEXPTR
DOUBLE	DOUBLE	DEXPTD

Note. The next five definitions make it easier to describe certain terms in our logic.

Definition. list term, LENGTH. We define the *list term* for a sequence of terms $\langle s_1 \ldots s_n \rangle$ to be the term (LIST $s_1 \ldots s_n$). If t is the list term for a sequence of length n, then the *LENGTH* of t is n.

Definition. conjunction. The *conjunction* of the terms s_1, s_2, ..., s_n is the term (AND $s_1 s_2 \ldots s_n$).

Definition. disjunction. The *disjunction* of the terms s_1, s_2, ..., s_n is the term (OR $s_1 s_2 \ldots s_n$).

Definition. implication. If u and v are formulas, the *implication from* u *to* v is the formula (IMPLIES u v).

Definition. lexicographic comparison. If t_1 and t_2 are terms then the *lexicographic comparison of* t_1 *with* t_2 is (LEX $t_1 t_2$).

Note. The specification of a given FORTRAN subprogram begins with the production by the user of a "FORTRAN theory" rather than the basic FORTRAN theory. As a rule the basic FORTRAN theory is too primitive to permit the expression of the specifications of interesting programs without first being extended by the definition of new functions. For example, to specify a matrix multiplication subroutine, the user might first extend the basic FORTRAN theory by the definition of the usual mathematical operations and relations on vectors and matrices.

Definition. FORTRAN theory. A *FORTRAN theory* is an extension of the basic FORTRAN theory. The extension may add no axiom (e.g. definition) in which the function symbol START is used.

Note. The user supplied FORTRAN theory must be extended by the addition of several new function symbols before we arrive at the theory in which the verification conditions will be proved. For example, for each function subprogram referenced in the subprogram being verified, we will add an undefined function symbol whose value is as specified by the (previously accepted) input/output assertions for the function subprogram. These function symbols are used in the terms representing the values of FORTRAN expressions. To ensure that this extension makes sense (e.g. does not attempt to "redefine" an existing function) we make the next definition.

Definition. appropriate. T is *an appropriate theory* for c if and only if each of the following statements is true:
    (1) T is a FORTRAN theory.
    (2) c is a syntactically correct context.
    (3) NEXT and BEGIN are not function symbols of T.
    (4) For all $\langle$s seq labs$\rangle$ in c, if v is the long name of a member of the

variable, label variable, or array patterns of s, then v is not the name of a function symbol of T, nor is v NEXT or BEGIN.

(5) If v is the name of a function subprogram of c, then v is not the name of a function symbol of T, nor is v NEXT or BEGIN.

Note. For reasons indicated previously, we require that no function subprogram of c have as its name the name of a function symbol of T. But certain specific function symbols are required to be in T (e.g. EQUAL, ZPLUS, ZEXPTZ) and these symbols are acceptable FORTRAN names. Thus, this restriction technically prevents the use of our system to verify FORTRAN programs involving functions with those "built-in" names because no "appropriate theory" exists. Such problems are easily avoided by systematic renaming of the mathematical functions used to denote the values of FORTRAN entities. However, to avoid making this document even more obscure, we here agree to live with the naming limitations imposed above.

Given a theory T appropriate for a syntactically correct context c, we now describe three incremental extensions of T, the last of which is the theory in which one must prove the verification conditions for a subprogram of c. The three extensions are obtained by adding certain new function symbols, including one for each global name and argument, local name, and nonintrinsic function subprogram used in the subprogram being verified. By producing the final theory incrementally and giving names to the intermediate versions we make it possible to say "x is a term" of one of these intermediate theories, which is a convenient way of saying that x contains no function symbols except those in the specified theory.

Definition. primary verification extension. T_2 is the *primary verification extension* of T_1 *for* c *and* sub$_j$ if and only if T_1 is an appropriate theory for c, sub$_j$ is a member of c, and T_2 is the extension of T_1 that results from adding as a function symbol of one argument each of the global names of sub$_j$ and each of the arguments of sub$_j$.

Definition. secondary verification extension. T_2 is the *secondary verification extension* of T_1 *for* c *and* sub$_j$ if and only if T_1 is an appropriate theory for c, sub$_j$ is a member of c, and T_2 is the extension of the primary verification extension of T_1 that results from adding as a function symbol of one argument each of the local names of sub$_j$ that is not an argument of sub$_j$.

Definition. tertiary verification extension. T_2 is the *tertiary verification extension* of T_1 *for* c *and* sub$_j$ if and only if T_1 is an appropriate theory for c, sub$_j$ is a member of c, and T_2 is the extension of the secondary verification extension of T_1 that results from both of the following:

(1) Adding NEXT and BEGIN as function symbols of 1 and 0 arguments respectively.

(2) Adding as a function symbol the name of each function pattern of the syntactic environment of sub_j that is not an intrinsic function pattern and by providing each such function symbol f with the number of arguments that is the sum of (a) the number of arguments of the function pattern with name f and (b) the number of global names of the member of c whose name is f.

Note. If ARRAY is a local name of a subprogram, our convention is to denote the value of ARRAY at a given point in the execution of the subprogram by a term of the form (ARRAY state), where state is a constant term that may be thought to denote (in a completely arbitrary way) the state of the processor. The only use of states is to permit us to use terms such as (ARRAY state) to refer to the various values taken on by program variables during execution. We formalize the notion of "state term" later. To refer to the current value of ARRAY in an invariant, the user writes (ARRAY STATE). It is understood that the current state term will be substituted for STATE when the invariant is encountered by the verification condition generator. It is important that STATE not occur arbitrarily within an invariant since that would permit the invariant to exploit the structure of what amounts only to a naming convention. The next definition provides us with a succinct way of saying that some particular set of terms occur only as arguments to those functions denoting the values of program variables.

Definition. incarcerates. p *incarcerates* v *with respect to* c *and* sub_j if and only if c is a syntactically correct context, sub_j is member of c, v is a set, and for some theory T appropriate for c, p can be obtained from some term p' of T that does not have any member of v as a subterm by simultaneously replacing variables with terms of the form (f v') where f is a global or local name of sub_j and v' is a member of v.

Example. Suppose T is a theory appropriate for c and c contains some subprogram sub_j and CNT is a local name of sub_j. Then the term

$$\text{(ZEQP (CNT NEWSTATE)}$$
$$\text{(ZPLUS 1 (CNT STATE)))}$$

incarcerates {NEWSTATE, STATE} with respect to c and sub_j, because the term can be obtained by instantiating

$$\text{(ZEQP U}$$
$$\text{(ZPLUS 1 V))}$$

by replacing U with (CNT NEWSTATE) and V with (CNT STATE). Since the following term cannot be obtained by such an instantiation, it does not incarcerate {NEWSTATE STATE}:

$$\text{(ZEQP (CNT NEWSTATE)}$$
$$\text{(ZPLUS STATE (CNT STATE)))}$$

Note. We now formally define the mapping from FORTRAN expressions to terms in a FORTRAN theory.

Definition. statification. If c is a syntactically correct context, ⟨s seq labs⟩ is a member of c, and e is an expression with respect to s, then the *statification* of e (denoted [e] when c and ⟨s seq labs⟩ are obvious from context) is defined, inductively, as follows.

(1) If e is a constant then
if e is .TRUE., then [e] is (TRUE),
if e is .FALSE., then [e] is (FALSE),
and otherwise [e] is e.

(2) If e is a token, then [e] is (e).

(3) If e is a variable or array reference, then [e] is the term (e' STATE), where e' is the long name of e with respect to ⟨s seq labs⟩.

(4) If e is an array element reference, then
for each v and expression x_1, if e has the form $v(x_1)$,
then [e] is (ELT1 [v] [x_1]),
for each v and for all expressions x_1 and x_2,
if e has the form $v(x_1, x_2)$,
then [e] is (ELT2 [v] [x_1] [x_2]), and
for each v and for all expressions x_1, x_2 and x_3,
if e has the form $v(x_1, x_2, x_3)$,
then [e] is (ELT3 [v] [x_1] [x_2] [x_3]).

(5) If e is an arithmetic or relational expression with argument sequence ⟨x_1 x_2⟩ and operation symbol op, op is not **, the sort of x_1 and x_2 is ⟨t⟩, and f is the function symbol for t and op, then [e] is (f [x_1] [x_2]).

(6) If e is an arithmetic expression with operation symbol ** and argument sequence ⟨x_1 x_2⟩, the sort of x_1 is ⟨t_1⟩, the sort of x_2 is ⟨t_2⟩, and f is the exponentiation function symbol for t_1 and t_2, then [e] is (f [x_1] [x_2]).

(7) For all expressions x_1 and x_2, if e has one of the forms

$$(x_1 \text{ .AND. } x_2)$$
$$(x_1 \text{ .OR. } x_2)$$
$$(.NOT. x_1)$$

then [e] is

$$(AND [x_1] [x_2])$$
$$(OR \quad [x_1] [x_2])$$
$$(NOT [x_1])$$

respectively.

(8) For each f that is the name of a statement function pattern of s and for all expressions $x_1, \ldots,$ and x_n, if e has the form:

$$f(x_1, \ldots, x_n)$$

then [e] is the statification of the result of simultaneously replacing each of the arguments of the definition of f in seq with the corresponding x_i in the body of the definition of f in seq.

(9) For each f that is the name of an intrinsic function pattern and for all expressions $x_1, \ldots,$ and x_n, if e has the form:

$$f(x_1, \ldots, x_n)$$

then [e] is $(f\ [x_1] \ldots [x_n])$

(10) Finally, for each f that is the name of some nonintrinsic function pattern of s and for all expressions $x_1, \ldots,$ and x_n, if e has the form:

$$f(x_1, \ldots, x_n),$$

then [e] is

$$(f\ [x_1] \ldots [x_n]\ (k_1\ \text{STATE}) \ldots (k_m\ \text{STATE}))$$

where the k_i are the global names, in alphabetical order, of the member of c whose name is f.

Example. Suppose PROD is the name of a REAL valued function subprogram, subfn, of c. Suppose that subfn takes one argument and declares A1 and A2 to be in COMMON block BLK. Suppose further that BLK-A1 and BLK-A2 are the only global names of subfn. Finally, suppose that VECT is a one-dimensional array declared as a local name in some other subprogram, sub, of c, that I is declared in sub to be an INTEGER variable in COMMON block TEMP, that MAX is a local name of sub, and that

$$(\text{PROD(MAX)} + \text{VECT(I)})$$

is an expression with respect to the syntactic environment of sub. Then the statification of the above expression is:

```
(RPLUS (PROD (MAX STATE)
             (BLK-A1 STATE)
             (BLK-A2 STATE))
       (ELT1 (VECT STATE) (TEMP-I STATE))))
```

Notation. [e, st] is the result of replacing the variable STATE with st in the statification of e.

Definition. term substitution. A finite set s of ordered pairs is said to be a *term substitution* provided that for each ordered pair $\langle u\ v \rangle$ in s, u and v are

terms and no other member of s has u as its first component. The *result of applying* a term substitution s *to* a term t is recursively defined as follows:
> For each v, if ⟨t v⟩ is a member of s,
> the result is v;
> else if t is a variable, the result is t;
> else t is of the form (f t_1 ... t_n)
> and the result is (f t_1' ... t_n'),
> where t_i' is the result of applying
> the term substitution s to t_i.

Example. The result of applying the term substitution ⟨⟨X (G)⟩ ⟨(F X) (H X)⟩⟩ to the term (PLUS X (F X)) is the term (PLUS (G) (H X)). In particular, the result is not (PLUS (G) (F (G))).

9. SPECIFIED CONTEXTS

We now begin discussing the specification of the subprograms of a syntactically correct context. We first formalize the notion of specifying the input and output assertions of the subprograms. Intuitively, if a subprogram has been proved correct, then whenever it is legally invoked (e.g. by a CALL statement we consider syntactically and semantically correct) and the input assertion is true just before the execution of the first statement (that is, after the association of the actuals with the formals), then in the execution of the subprogram a RETURN will eventually be executed, and at the inception of the RETURN statement the output assertion will be true.

Definition. specification for a context. A pair of functions ⟨inpt outpt⟩ is a *specification for* c *and* T if and only if each of the following statements is true:
   (1) T is an appropriate theory for c.
   (2) The domain of inpt is the set of members of c and for each member sub of c, the value, v, of inpt on sub is a term in the primary extension of T for c and sub, and v incarcerates {STATE} with respect to c and sub.
   (3) The domain of outpt is the set of members of c, and for each member sub of c, the value, v, of outpt on sub is a term in the primary extension of T for c and sub, and
(a) if sub is a subroutine subprogram, then v incarcerates {STATE, NEWSTATE} with respect to c and sub, and for every subterm of v of the form (f NEWSTATE), f is possibly smashed by sub in c, and
(b) if sub is a function subprogram, then v contains no variables except STATE and ANS and v incarcerates {STATE} with respect to c and sub.

Definition. input assertion, output assertion. Suppose we have in mind a given inpt, outpt, c and T, such that ⟨inpt outpt⟩ is a specification for c and T. If sub is a member of c, we define the *input assertion of* sub to be the formula that is the value of inpt on sub, and we define the *output assertion of* sub to be the formula that is the value of outpt on sub.

Note. We now formalize the notion of attaching to certain statements in a subprogram the "Floyd invariants". Intuitively, these invariants are assertions about the values of program variables and are supposed to be true every time the processor encounters the statement.

In addition to proving that each subprogram meets its input/output specification, provided it terminates, we desire to prove that each subprogram terminates when called in an environment satisfying its input assertion. To do this we require the user to specify the amount of "time" the program will run by attaching "clocks" to various statements. Intuitively, the "input clock" says how long the program will run (as a function of the initial environment) and the interior clocks say how much time remains (as a function of the variables in the current state). The verification conditions force us to prove that each time a clock is encountered, strictly less "time" remains on it than on the previously encountered clock. Provided the "less than" relation used is well founded, proof of the clock verification conditions is sufficient to imply termination of the program.

It is often convenient for clocks to be functions into the natural numbers and to be compared with the well-founded Peano "less than" relation. However, such a scheme makes it difficult to prove termination for programs involving nested loops because the necessary clocks often involve multiplication, exponentiation, and so on. To mitigate this problem somewhat we make the convention that each clock be an n-tuple of natural numbers (for some value of n fixed by the user for a given subprogram), and we compare these n-tuples with the function LEX, defined in the basic FORTRAN theory.

For example, to prove the termination of a nested loop, the outer of which counts I down somehow while changing J arbitrarily, and the inner of which counts J down while holding I fixed, the clock (LIST (I STATE) (J STATE)) suffices.

Definition. annotation. A sequence of three elements ⟨inpclk 1pinv 1pclk⟩ is called an *annotation with respect to* T, c, *and* sub if and only if each of the following statements is true:

(1) T is an appropriate theory for c.

(2) sub is a member of c.

(3) inpclk is the list term for some sequence of terms in the primary extension of T for c and sub, inpclk has no variable subterm, and inpclk incarcerates {(START)} with respect to c and sub.

(4) 1pinv is a function and for some w, w is the domain of 1pinv, w is a subset of the nodes of the flow graph of sub, the statement of each member of w is a CONTINUE statement, w covers the flow graph of sub, and for each member r of the range of 1pinv, r is a term of the secondary extension of T for c and sub and r incarcerates {STATE, (START)} with respect to c and sub.

(5) 1pclk is a function whose domain is the domain of 1pinv and for each member r of the range of 1pclk, r is the list term of a sequence of terms in the secondary extension of T for c and sub, r and inpclk have the same LENGTH, r incarcerates {STATE, (START)} with respect to c and sub, and has no variable subterm except STATE.

Convention. For the remainder of this section, let us fix upon a T, c, sub, s, seq, labs, inpt, outpt, inpclk, 1pinv, and 1pclk such that each of the following statements is true:

(1) T is an appropriate theory for c.
(2) ⟨s seq labs⟩ is a member of c and sub is ⟨s seq labs⟩.
(3) ⟨inpt outpt⟩ is a specification of c.
(4) ⟨inpclk 1pinv 1pclk⟩ is an annotation for sub.

Definition. input clock, loop invariant, loop clock. The *input clock* is inpclk. If node is a member of the domain of 1pinv, then the *loop invariant* for node is the value of the function 1pinv applied to node, and the *loop clock* for node is the value of the function 1pclk applied to node.

Note. We now introduce the ideas of the "partially instantiated" input and output assertions. These assertions are attached to the entrances and exits of the subprogram.

Definition. partially instantiated input assertion. If sub is a function subprogram, then the *partially instantiated input assertion* is the conjunction of (a) the result of substituting (START) for STATE in the input assertion of sub and (b) the term (DEFINEDP (a (START))) for each a that is an argument of sub and is not the name of an array pattern in s. If sub is a subroutine subprogram, then the *partially instantiated input assertion* is the conjunction of (a) the result of substituting (START) for STATE in the input assertion of sub and (b) the term (DEFINEDP (a (START))) for each a that is both an argument of sub and a member of the dimension list of some array pattern of s.

Note. (START) is the arbitrarily chosen constant denoting the state at the beginning of the execution of the subprogram being verified.

We require that all nonarray arguments to function subprograms be defined, and we automatically extend the user's input assertion to that effect. FORTRAN does not have such a requirement. We have already adopted the requirement that no function subprogram have side effects, including side effects on arguments. Thus, an undefined argument is useless: it cannot be referenced in the subprogram until it is smashed by an assignment or CALL, and it cannot be smashed. The question of the definedness of arrays never comes up. Instead, one is interested in the definedness of particular elements of arrays. Rather than automatically extend every function's input assertion with the draconian requirement that every element of every array be defined, we put no built-in requirements on arrays and thus force the user to state in his input assertions whatever hypotheses are needed about particular array elements.

Definition. partially instantiated output assertion. If sub is a function subprogram, fn is the name of the first statement of seq, and p is the output assertion of sub, then the *partially instantiated output assertion* is the result of substituting (START) for STATE and (fn STATE) for ANS in

$$\text{(AND (DEFINEDP ANS)}$$
$$\text{p)}$$

If sub is a subroutine subprogram, then the *partially instantiated output assertion* is the result of substituting (START) for STATE and STATE for NEWSTATE in the output assertion of sub.

Note. NEWSTATE in an output assertion of a subprogram being verified is understood to refer to the state at the inception of the RETURN statement. That is, on each exit path from the subprogram the verification condition produced will conclude with the partially instantiated output assertion, further instantiated by the replacement of NEWSTATE by the state term at the end of the path.

The user writes the variable ANS in the output assertion of a function subprogram when he wishes to refer to the value delivered by the subprogram. The FORTRAN convention for defining the value of a function is to assign the desired result to the variable with the same name as the function. Thus, in the theory in use when we verify a function subprogram with name fn, fn is a function of one argument, the state of the processor, and denotes the value of a FORTRAN variable. For the verification of fn we replace ANS in the output assertion by (fn NEWSTATE).

Consider what happens when we have verified fn and are now producing the verification conditions for a subprogram that calls fn. In the theory in use when we verify a program that calls fn, fn is a function of $n + m$ arguments (where n is the number of arguments of the FORTRAN subprogram fn and m is the number of its global names). When we use the output assertion of fn to constrain the value delivered by the expression $fn(e_1, \ldots, e_n)$, we replace ANS by [fn(e_1, ..., e_n)] and then replace STATE by the current state term.

The next definition makes it more convenient to describe the verification condition generator. It is useful to extend the flow graph of the subprogram by imagining the insertion into the program of a CONTINUE statement immediately preceding what was previously the first executable statement of the program. We then attach to this statement the input assertion and input clock of the subprogram.

Definition. extended flow graph. The *extended flow graph* of sub is the ordered, directed graph whose nodes are the nodes of the flow graph of sub together with one additional node, 0, and whose edges are the edges of the flow graph of sub together with the edge $\langle\langle 0\ 1\rangle\ i\rangle$, where i is the least positive integer such that the ith member of seq is an executable statement.

Definition. statement of 0. The *statement of 0* is CONTINUE.

Note. Given the extended flow graph, we can now combine the notions of the input assertion and loop assertions and input clock and loop clocks to get, simply, the "assertions" and "clocks".

Definition. assertion, clock, decorated nodes. Let g be the extended flow graph of sub. Below we define the *decorated nodes* of g, the *assertion* for a a decorated node, and the *clock* for some of the decorated nodes. A node n of g is in the *decorated nodes* of g if and only if one of the following is true:

(1) n is 0, in which case the *assertion* for n is the partially instantiated input assertion and the *clock* for n is the input clock.

(2) n is a member of the domain of 1pinv, in which case the *assertion* for n is the loop invariant for n and the *clock* for n is the loop clock for n.

(3) The statement of n is a STOP statement, in which case the *assertion* for n is (FALSE), and the clock for n is undefined.

(4) The statement of n is a RETURN statement, in which case the *assertion* for n is the partially instantiated output assertion and the clock for n is undefined.

10. THE VERIFICATION CONDITIONS

We are finally ready to describe what one has to prove to verify a FORTRAN subprogram. First we formally define the arbitrary constants used to denote "states". Then we spell out the "global assumptions" that may be used in the proof of the verification conditions (e.g. the input assertion and the type of values taken on by the functions denoting variables). Next we discuss the handling of FORTRAN expressions: what may be assumed about the value of an expression (e.g. that the output assertion is true of the value returned by a function subprogram) and what must be proved about an expression (e.g. that the input assertion for a function subprogram holds). Then we turn to FORTRAN statements: what may be assumed about the change of state induced by the execution of a statement (e.g. that a CALL statement changes the state as specified by its output assertion) and what must be proved about a statement (e.g. that the input assertion for a subroutine holds). Finally, we combine all these concepts to say what must be proved about the paths through the program.

Convention. For the remainder of this section, let us fix upon the T, c, sub, s, seq, labs, inpt, outpt, inpclk, 1pinv and 1pclk agreed upon in the previous section.

Definition. PATHS. Suppose g is the extended flow of sub. Then *PATHS* is the set of Floyd paths of g for the decorated nodes of g.

Definition. state term. For each path p in PATHS and for each edge e in p, we define the *state term* of e inductively, as follows. For the first edge of p, the state term is (START) if the head of the first edge is 0; otherwise the state term of the edge is (BEGIN). For each noninitial edge e of p, let stp be the state term of the preceding edge. The state term of e is the term (NEXT stp) if the head of e is an assignment, GO TO assignment, or CALL statement and is stp otherwise.

Note. Thus, as previously noted, (START) is the term denoting the state at the beginning of the execution of sub. (BEGIN) is the arbitrarily chosen term denoting the state at the beginning of any interior path. Every time we move past an assignment or CALL statement (the only two statement types that cause state changes) the state is "bumped" by applying the undefined function NEXT. Thus, on an interior path containing two assignments and a CALL statement, the state at the beginning is (BEGIN) and the state at the end is (NEXT (NEXT (NEXT (BEGIN)))). The only information relating stp and (NEXT stp) is that provided by the semantics of assignment and the output assertions of subroutines.

We next define the set of assumptions that may be used in the proofs of all of the verification conditions.

Definition. global assumptions. a is a member of the *global assumptions* if and only if one of the following is true:
(1) a is the partially instantiated input assertion.
(2) For some local or global name n of sub and for some $\langle t\ d_1 \ldots d_k \rangle$,

$\langle t\ d_1 \ldots d_k \rangle$ is the global sort of n, t' is the FORTRAN recognizer for t, and a has one of the forms

> (IMPLIES (DEFINEDP (n STATE))
>   (t' (n STATE)))),
> (IMPLIES (DEFINEDP (ELT1 (n STATE) I))
>   (t' (ELT1 (n STATE) I)))),
> (IMPLIES (DEFINEDP (ELT2 (n STATE) I J))
>   (t' (ELT2 (n STATE) I J)))),
> (IMPLIES (DEFINEDP (ELT3 (n STATE) I J K))
>   (t' (ELT3 (n STATE) I J K))))

according to whether $\langle t\ d_1 \ldots d_k \rangle$ is of length 1, 2, 3 or 4.

Example. If ARRAY is a local name of sub and is declared as a two-dimensional array of type INTEGER, then one of the global assumptions is that if the I,Jth element of ARRAY is DEFINEDP, then it is an integer (e.g. recognized by ZNUMBERP).

Note. Now we spell out what may be assumed about the value of a FORTRAN expression. For example, in proving that the input assertion for a subroutine CALL is satisfied, we get to assume the "output assumptions" for the arguments of the CALL.

Definition. output assumption. We now define inductively the concept of the *output assumption for* an expression e *with respect to* a state term stp. Throughout the definition, all output assumptions are understood to be with respect to stp.

(1) If e is a constant, a token, or a variable or array reference, the output assumption for e is (TRUE).

(2) If e is an array element reference, the output assumption for e is the conjunction of the output assumption for each member of the subscript sequence of e.

(3) If e is an arithmetic, relational, or logical expression, or a function reference to an intrinsic function, the output assumption for e is the conjunction of the output assumption for each member of the argument sequence of e.

(4) If e is a function reference to a statement function f with argument sequence $\langle x_1 \ldots x_n \rangle$ then the output assumption for e is the output assumption for the expression that results from substituting into the body of the definition of f the expressions $x_1, \ldots, x_n$ for the corresponding arguments of the definition of f.

(5) If e is a function reference to a function, f, other than a statement or intrinsic function, the argument sequence of e is $\langle x_1 \ldots x_n \rangle$, and subn is the

element of c whose name is f and whose arguments are $\langle a_1 \ldots a_n \rangle$, then the output assumption for e is the conjunction of the output assumptions for $x_1, \ldots, x_n$, conjoined with the result of applying the following term substitution to the output assertion of subn:

term	to be replaced with
STATE	stp
$(a_1$ STATE)	$[x_1,$ stp]
. . .	. . .
$(a_n$ STATE)	$[x_n,$ stp]
ANS	[e, stp]

Example. Suppose SUM is a function subprogram of two arguments, A and MAX, that SUM has no global names, and that the output assertion of SUM is (EQUAL ANS (SIGMA 1 (MAX STATE) (A STATE))). Suppose that I and J are local INTEGER names in sub and that VCT is an array in COMMON block BLK in sub. Then the statification, with respect to (BEGIN), of the FORTRAN expression (I + SUM(VCT, J)) is

(ZPLUS (I (BEGIN))
      (SUM (BLK-VCT (BEGIN)) (J (BEGIN))))),

and the output assumption, with respect to (BEGIN), for (I + SUM(VCT, J)) is

(EQUAL (SUM (BLK-VCT (BEGIN)) (J (BEGIN)))
      (SIGMA 1 (J (BEGIN)) (BLK-VCT (BEGIN)))).

In particular, the output assumption for an expression tells us what we may assume about the values returned by the user-defined function subprograms in the expression.

Definition. conjoined output assumptions. If $\langle x_1 \ldots x_n \rangle$ is a sequence of expressions and stp is a state term, then the *conjoined output assumptions for* $\langle x_1 \ldots x_n \rangle$ *with respect to* stp is the formula obtained by conjoining the output assumption (with respect to stp) for each x_i in $\langle x_1 \ldots x_n \rangle$.

Note. The next two definitions introduce the notions of the "definedness condition" for an expression and the "input condition" for an expression. Intuitively, the input condition for an expression must hold when the expression is evaluated by the processor. For example, the input condition for the reference of a function subprogram is an instantiation of its input assertion. Built-in operations, such as "/", also have input conditions. For example, part of the input condition for (X/Y) is that the value of Y be non-0.

There are two subtleties to the definition of input condition: the first is our recognition of the finite precision of arithmetic; the second is our enforcement of the rule that certain entities must be defined in order to be used.

Part of the input condition for the expression $(X + Y)$ is that the sum of the values of X and Y be expressible on the machine. The reader ought to ask: "Is it known that X and Y are expressible?" The answer is yes. We require that every constant mentioned in an expression be expressible and that every built-in operation produce expressible results.

FORTRAN requires that certain entities be defined when they are used in certain ways. For example, e_1 and e_2 must both be defined in $(e_1 + e_2)$. One's first impression is that we should require that all expressions (except array references) produce defined results. Since all function subprograms will be proved to return defined results, and since the built-in functions and operations return defined results, it is only necessary to ensure that variable and array element references are defined. We could therefore define the "input condition" for variable and array element references to require the definedness of the resulting value.

However, one's first impression is often incorrect down to the nitty gritty. We must not require that all variable references produce defined results. The classic example is the use of such an expression in a subroutine argument position that is smashed before it is first referenced—as happens when one is using the argument position to return results from the subroutine.

Therefore, the treatment of the definedness issue in the definition of "input condition" is not quite what one might expect. Instead of simply making all variable references have a definedness requirement as their input condition and letting $(e_1 + e_2)$ inherit that requirement naturally from its subexpressions, we make the input condition for variable references be (TRUE), and we make each composite expression explicitly require the definedness of its immediate variable subexpressions.

Definition. definedness condition. The *definedness condition for* an expression e *with respect to* a state term stp is defined as follows:

(1) If e is a variable reference or array element reference, the definedness condition for e is (DEFINEDP [e, stp]).

(2) Otherwise, the definedness condition for e is (TRUE).

Definition. input condition. We now define inductively the concept of the *input condition for* an expression e *with respect to* a state term stp. Throughout the definition, all input conditions, definedness conditions, and output assumptions are understood to be with respect to stp.

(1) If e is a constant of type t, the input condition for e is (TRUE) if t is LOGICAL and otherwise is

$$(\text{EXPRESSIBLE.uNUMBERP e})$$

where u is Z, R, D or C according as t is INTEGER, REAL, DOUBLE or COMPLEX.

(2) If e is a token or a variable or array reference, the input condition for e is (TRUE).

(3) If e is an array element reference to a with subscript expressions $\langle x_1 \ldots x_n \rangle$, $\langle a\ t\ d_1 \ldots d_n \rangle$ is the member of the array patterns of s with name a, and hyp is the conjoined output assumptions for $\langle x_1 \ldots x_n \rangle$, then the input condition for e is the conjunction of the following:

(a) the conjunction of the input condition for each x_i in $\langle x_1 \ldots x_n \rangle$, and

(b) the conjunction, for i from 1 to n, of

$$\text{(IMPLIES hyp}$$
$$\text{(AND (ZLESSEQP 1 } [x_i, \text{stp}])$$
$$\text{(ZLESSEQP } [x_i, \text{stp}] [d_i, \text{stp}])))$$

(which asserts that each array subscript is within the appropriate bounds).

(4) If e is an arithmetic, relational, or logical expression, or e is a function reference to an intrinsic function, the argument sequence of e is $\langle x_1 \ldots x_n \rangle$, and hyp is the conjoined output assumptions for $\langle x_1 \ldots x_n \rangle$, then the input condition for e is the conjunction of the following:

(a) the conjunction of the input condition for each x_i in $\langle x_1 \ldots x_n \rangle$,

(b) the conjunction of the definedness condition for each x_i in $\langle x_1 \ldots x_n \rangle$, and

(c) the implication from hyp to the result of applying the term substitution that replaces (I STATE) by $[x_1, \text{stp}]$ and (J STATE) by $[x_2, \text{stp}]$ in the "input condition formula" given in Appendix B for the function symbol of the term [e].

(5) For all f and for all expressions $x_1, \ldots, x_n$, if e has the form

$$f(x_1, \ldots, x_n)$$

and f is the name of a statement function pattern of s, and hyp is the conjoined output assumptions for $\langle x_1 \ldots x_n \rangle$, then the input condition for e is the conjunction of:

(a) the conjunction of the input condition for each x_i in $\langle x_1 \ldots x_n \rangle$,

(b) the conjunction of the definedness condition for each x_i in $\langle x_1 \ldots x_n \rangle$, and

(c) the input condition for the expression that results from substituting into the body of the definition of f the expressions $x_1, \ldots, x_n$ for the corresponding arguments of the definition of f.

(6) For each f, for all expressions $x_1, \ldots, x_n, a_1, \ldots, a_n$, and for each subn, if e has the form

$$f(x_1, \ldots, x_n)$$

and f is the name of a function pattern of s, subn is the member of c whose name is f, $a_1, \ldots, a_n$ are the arguments of subn, and hyp is the conjoined output assumptions for $\langle x_1 \ldots x_n \rangle$, then the input condition for e is the conjunction of each of the following:

(a) the conjunction of the input condition for each x_i in $\langle x_1 \ldots x_n \rangle$,

(b) the conjunction of the definedness condition for each x_i in $\langle x_1 \ldots x_n \rangle$, and

(c) the implication from hyp to the result of applying the following term substitution to the input assertion of subn:

term	to be replaced with
STATE	stp
$(a_1$ STATE)	$[x_1,$ stp]
...	...
$(a_n$ STATE)	$[x_n,$ stp]

We are now ready to begin considering the paths through the subprogram being verified. Consider an edge e on such a path and imagine we have just executed the statement in the head of the edge. How is the state produced by executing that statement related to the state immediately preceding it? We make this clear by defining the "assumptions" for the edge. When we find ourselves faced with proving the input assertions, say, of the next statement (the one in the tail of the edge), we get to assume the assumptions for the edge and all the preceding edges on the path.

Definition. assumption. For each path p in PATHS and for each edge e in p, we define the *assumption* for e as follows. For the first edge of p the assumption is the result of replacing STATE with (BEGIN) in the assertion for the head of e. For the other edges e of p, the assumption is defined according to the kind of instruction of the statement, st, of the head of e. Let stp and stn be respectively the state term of the edge preceding e and the state term of e. All output assumptions mentioned are with respect to stp.

(1) For each symbolic name v and for each exp, if st has the form

$$v = exp$$

then the assumption for e is the conjunction of the output assumption for exp, the equation

$$(EQUAL\ [v,\ stn]\ [exp,\ stp])$$

and the equations

$$(EQUAL\ (u\ stn)\ (u\ stp)),$$

for each of the local and global names u of sub except the long name of v.

(2) For each symbolic name v and for all expressions i and exp, if st has the form

$$v(i) = exp$$

then the assumption for e is the conjunction of the output assumption for i, the output assumption for exp, the formulas

$$(EQUAL \ (ELT1 \ [v, \ stn] \ [i, \ stp])$$
$$[exp, \ stp]),$$

$$(IMPLIES \ (NOT \ (EQUAL \ I \ [i, \ stp]))$$
$$(EQUAL \ (ELT1 \ [v, \ stn] \ I)$$
$$(ELT1 \ [v, \ stp] \ I))),$$

and the equations

$$(EQUAL \ (u \ stn) \ (u \ stp)),$$

for each of the local and global names u of sub except the long name of v.

(3) For each symbolic name v and for all expressions i, j and exp, if st has the form

$$v(i, \ j) = exp$$

then the assumption for e is the conjunction of the output assumption for i, the output assumption for j, the output assumption for exp, the formulas

$$(EQUAL \ (ELT2 \ [v, \ stn] \ [i, \ stp] \ [j, \ stp])$$
$$[exp, \ stp]),$$

$$(IMPLIES \ (NOT \ (AND \ (EQUAL \ I \ [i, \ stp])$$
$$(EQUAL \ J \ [j, \ stp])))$$
$$(EQUAL \ (ELT2 \ [v, \ stn] \ I \ J)$$
$$(ELT2 \ [v, \ stp] \ I \ J))),$$

and the equations

$$(EQUAL \ (u \ stn) \ (u \ stp)),$$

for each of the local and global names u of sub except the long name of v.

(4) For each symbolic name v and for all expressions i, j, k and exp, if st has the form

$$v(i, \ j, \ k) = exp$$

then the assumption for e is the conjunction of the output assumption for i, the output assumption for j, the output assumption for k, the output assumption for exp, the formulas

(EQUAL (ELT3 [v, stn] [i, stp] [j, stp] [k, stp])
[exp, stp]),

(IMPLIES (NOT (AND (EQUAL I [i, stp])
(EQUAL J [j, stp])
(EQUAL K [k, stp])))
(EQUAL (ELT3 [v, stn] I J K)
(ELT3 [v, stp] I J K))),

and the equations

(EQUAL (u stn) (u stp)),

for each of the local and global names u of sub except the long name of v.

(5) For each symbolic name v and for each k, if st has the form

ASSIGN k TO v

then the assumption for e is the conjunction of the equation

(EQUAL [v, stn] k)

and the equations

(EQUAL [u, stn] [u, stp])

for each of the local and global names u of sub except v.

(6) For each symbolic name i, for each j, and for all labels $k_1, \ldots,$ and k_n, if e is the jth edge leading from its head and st has the form

GO TO i, $(k_1, \ldots, k_n)$

then the assumption for e is (EQUAL [i, stp] k_j).

(7) For each symbolic name i, for each j, and for all labels $k_1, \ldots,$ and k_n, if e is the jth edge leading from its head and st has the form

GO TO $(k_1, \ldots, k_n)$, i

then the assumption for e is (EQUAL [i, stp] j).

(8) For each type t, for each u, for each expression exp, and for all labels l_1, l_2 and l_3, if st has the form

IF (exp) l_1, l_2, l_3

and exp is an expression of sort ⟨t⟩, and u is the letter Z, R or D according as t is INTEGER, REAL or DOUBLE, then the assumption for e is the conjunction of the output assumption for exp and the term

$$(\text{uLESSP [exp, stp] (uZERO)}),$$

$$(\text{uEQP [exp, stp] (uZERO)}),$$

or

$$(\text{uGREATERP [exp, stp] (uZERO)}),$$

according to whether e is the first, second or third edge leading from its head.

(9) For each member subn of c (with name subr), and for all expressions $e_1, \ldots,$ and e_n, if st has the form:

$$\text{CALL subr}(e_1, \ldots, e_n)$$

or

$$\text{CALL subr}$$

and if the argument names of subn are $a_1, \ldots, a_n$, and $\langle b_1 \ldots b_m \rangle$ is the subsequence of $\langle a_1 \ldots a_n \rangle$ containing just the members of $\langle a_1 \ldots a_n \rangle$ that are possibly smashed by subn in c, and $\langle c_1 \ldots c_m \rangle$ is the corresponding subsequence of $\langle e_1 \ldots e_n \rangle$, then the assumption for e is the conjunction of each of the following:

(a) the conjoined output assumptions for $\langle e_1 \ldots e_n \rangle$ (provided st has the first form above),

(b) the result of applying the following term substitution to the output assertion of subn:

term	to be replaced with
STATE	stp
NEWSTATE	stn
$(a_1 \text{ STATE})$	$[e_1, \text{stp}]$
. . .	. . .
$(a_n \text{ STATE})$	$[e_n, \text{stp}]$
$(b_1 \text{ NEWSTATE})$	$[c_1, \text{stn}]$
. . .	. . .
$(b_m \text{ NEWSTATE})$	$[c_m, \text{stn}]$

and

(c) each equation eq such that for some k, eq has the form

$$(\text{EQUAL (k stn) (k stp)})$$

and each of the following is true: (i) k is a local or global name of sub, (ii) if k is a global name of sub, then k is not possibly smashed by subn in c, and (iii) k is not the long name of any member of $\langle c_1 \ldots c_m \rangle$.

(10) For each expression exp and statement stm, if st has the form

IF (exp) stm

then the assumption for e is the conjunction of the output assumption for exp and the term (EQUAL [exp, stp] (TRUE)) or (EQUAL [exp, stp] (FALSE)) according as e is the first or the second edge leading from its head.

(11) If st has any other form (i.e. st is an unconditional GO TO statement, RETURN, CONTINUE, STOP or PAUSE statement) the assumption for e is (TRUE).

Note. We next define what must be proved when the statement in the tail of an edge is encountered.

Definition. verification condition. For each path p in PATHS and for each edge e in p, we now define the *verification condition* for e. Let n be the node that is the tail of e. Let st be the statement of n. Let stp be the state term of e.

(1) If e is the last member of p, the verification condition for e is the conjunction of (a) the result of substituting stp for STATE in the assertion for n and (b) (TRUE) if st is a RETURN or STOP statement, and otherwise the lexicographic comparison of (i) the result of substituting stp for STATE in the clock for n with (ii) the result of substituting (BEGIN) for STATE in the clock for the first node of p.

(2) For all expressions v and x, if st has the form

v = x

then the verification condition for e is the conjunction of the definedness condition for x with respect to stp, the input condition for x with respect to stp, and the input condition for v with respect to stp.

(3) For each symbolic name v and for all labels $k_1, \ldots,$ and k_n, if st has the form

GO TO v, $(k_1, \ldots, k_n)$

then the verification condition for e is the disjunction of the terms (EQUAL [v, stp] k_j) for each j from 1 to n.

(4) For each symbolic name v and for all labels $k_1, \ldots,$ and k_n, if st has the form

GO TO $(k_1, \ldots, k_n)$, v

then the verification condition for e is the formula

(AND (ZLESSEQP 1 [v, stp])
(ZLESSEQP [v, stp] n))

(5) For each expression x, for all labels l_1, l_2 and l_3, and for each statement stm, if st has the form

$$IF (x) \; l_1, \; l_2, \; l_3$$

or

$$IF (x) \; stm$$

then the verification condition for e is the conjunction of the definedness condition for x with respect to stp and the input condition for x with respect to stp.

(6) For each symbolic name subr, for all expressions $x_1, \ldots ,$ and x_n, and for all subn, $a_1, \ldots , a_n$, and hyp, if subn is the subroutine subprogram of c with name subr, $a_1, \ldots , a_n$ are the arguments of subn, hyp is the conjoined output assumptions for $\langle x_1 \ldots x_n \rangle$ with respect to stp, and st has the form

$$CALL \; subr(x_1, \ldots , x_n)$$

or

$$CALL \; subr$$

then the verification condition for e is the conjunction of:
(a) the implication from hyp to the result of applying the following term substitution to the input assertion of subn:

term	to be replaced with
STATE	stp
$(a_1 \; STATE)$	$[x_1, stp]$
$\ldots$	$\ldots$
$(a_n \; STATE)$	$[x_n, stp]$

and
(b) the conjunction of the input conditions for each x_i in $\langle x_1 \ldots x_n \rangle$.

(7) If st is a GO TO assignment, unconditional GO TO, CONTINUE or PAUSE statement, the verification condition for e is (TRUE).

Note. We now combine all the foregoing concepts to define what we mean when we say that a syntactically correct collection of subprograms is "semantically correct" with respect to some input/output specifications and a FORTRAN theory. Semantically correct contexts are constructed incrementally from the empty context by adding a single new subprogram, specifying and annotating it, and then proving it correct by proving each of its verification conditions, under the assumptions governing each verification condition.

Definition. semantically correct. We define recursively the notion that a context is semantically correct with respect to an input/output specification ⟨i o⟩ and a theory. Let phi be the empty function. Recall that we have fixed upon a T, c, sub, s, seq, labs, inpt, outpt, inpclk, 1pinv and 1pclk.

(1) The empty context is semantically correct with respect to ⟨phi phi⟩ and T.

(2) Suppose that c' is semantically correct with respect to ⟨inpt' outpt'⟩ and T. Suppose further that the restrictions of inpt and outpt to c' are, respectively, inpt' and outpt', and that c is obtained by adding sub to the end of c'. Then c is semantically correct with respect to ⟨inpt outpt⟩ and T if

(a) every node in the extended flow graph of sub is reachable from 0, and

(b) for each path p in PATHS and for each edge e in p, the verification condition for e is a logical consequence (in the tertiary verification extension of T for c and sub) of the global assumptions and the assumptions for e and for all of the edges that precede e in p.

11. THE DO STATEMENT

We now describe how we handle the FORTRAN DO statement. Our description is informal but complete.

We define the *DO statement* to be a statement of the form:

$$DO\ lab\ v = i, j, k$$

or

$$DO\ lab\ v = i, j$$

where lab is a label, v is an INTEGER variable name, and each of i, j and k is an INTEGER variable name, a positive INTEGER constant, or a token. The second form of DO is an abbreviation for an instance of the first in which k is 1. We will henceforth restrict our attention to the first form.

We extend the definition of "possibly smashed" so that the DO statement:

$$DO\ lab\ v = i, j, k$$

possibly smashes the long name of v.

We permit a subprogram ⟨s seq labs⟩ to contain DO statements among the executable statements provided the following additional syntactic constraints are met.

(1) If seq contains a statement, $stmt_1$, of the form:

$$DO\ lab\ v = i, j, k$$

then lab must be the statement label of some statement, $stmt_2$, after $stmt_1$ in seq. $stmt_2$ must be an assignment, GO TO assignment, or CONTINUE statement, or a logical IF containing one of the three preceding kinds of statements. The sequence of statements from and including the first statement after $stmt_1$ through and including $stmt_2$ is called the *range* of $stmt_1$.

(2) All DOs must be "nested" in the sense that if the ranges of two DO statements are not disjoint, then the range of one contains the range of the other.

(3) No label used in an unconditional, computed or assigned GO TO, or in an arithmetic or logical IF statement, stmt, may be attached to a statement within the range of a DO not containing stmt.

(4) No statement within the range of a DO statement of the form:

$$\text{DO lab } v = i, j, k$$

may possibly smash the long name of any of the variables among v, i, j and k.

After we have accepted a subprogram as syntactically well formed, we translate the subprogram to an equivalent one that does not contain DO statements. All concepts relating to the "semantic correctness" of the original subprogram are defined in terms of the semantic correctness of the translated program. For example, the flow graph for the original subprogram is defined to be the flow for the translation of the subprogram.

To *translate* a subprogram we replace each DO statement and its range by a new sequence of statements. Let the DO statement and its range be described schematically by:

$$\text{nnn DO lab } v = i, j, k$$
$$\text{stmt}_1$$
.
.
.
$$\text{lab stmt}_n$$

For generality, we suppose that the DO statement itself has a statement label nnn, so that we can describe how the statement labels in the new program are related to those in the original program. We replace the above sequence of statements with:

$$\text{nnn IF } (((i.GT.j).OR.((i.LT.1).OR.(k.LT.1)))) \text{ STOP}$$
$$v = i$$
$$\text{top CONTINUE}$$
$$\text{IF } ((v.GT.j)) \text{ GO TO fin}$$
$$\text{stmt}_1$$
.
.
.
$$\text{lab stmt}_n$$
$$v = (v + k)$$
$$\text{GO TO top}$$
$$\text{fin CALL UNDEFINER}(v)$$

The two statement labels top and fin generated for a given DO statement are different from the labels generated for any other DO statement of the subprogram and are different from all labels in the original subprogram. The old statement label nnn is attached to the logical IF statement indicated above. Labels on statements $stmt_1$ through $stmt_n$ in the original subprogram are attached to statements $stmt_1$ through $stmt_n$ in the translated subprogram.

The logical IF at nnn is generated in accordance with the ANSI FORTRAN 66 requirement that the initial values of i, j and k be such that i is greater than j (so the DO is allowed to cycle at least once), and all be greater than 0. We enforce the ANSI restriction by testing its negation and executing STOP if the ANSI restriction is not met. The path on which the ANSI restriction is assumed not to hold requires that we prove (FALSE), the assertion for STOP. Thus, we must be able to establish that the ANSI restriction holds at nnn.

ANSI requires that the variables among i, j and k must be defined upon the execution of the DO statement. In addition, the constants among i, j and k must be expressible integers. Both these requirements are enforced by the normal processing of the logical expression in the logical IF at nnn.

The CONTINUE statement labeled top is provided as a node which may be annotated with an assertion.*

At the statement labeled fin we CALL the subroutine (named, in this document) UNDEFINER, giving it the DO statement's control variable, v. UNDEFINER is built into the verification condition generator and is known to "possibly smash" its argument and have no effect on any other name. Both the input and output assertion for UNDEFINER are (TRUE). Thus, in accordance with ANSI FORTRAN 66, the value of v upon the normal completion of the DO loop is unknown. This clause in the ANSI specification permits different compilers to implement the loop control differently.

12. USING SEMANTICALLY CORRECT CONTEXTS

We have formally defined what it means for a FORTRAN subprogram to be semantically correct with respect to an input/output specification and a theory. We have not related our formal notions to the real world of FORTRAN computing. In particular, if the FORTRAN programmer has a semantically correct context (e.g. a "library" of "correct" subroutines), how does he use its subprograms and what do they do?

---

* We do not spell out in this document the precise means we provide for the user to annotate his program. However, we provide a mechanism by which the user can write a loop invariant for the DO, and that invariant is attached to the CONTINUE statement at top.

It would be necessary to formalize all of FORTRAN to answer this question with the same level of precision and formality with which we have defined "semantic correctness". However, we can describe vaguely how semantically correct contexts may be used. Because of its vagueness, the following description must be taken with a grain of salt.

To obtain a useable FORTRAN program from a context c that is semantically correct with respect to some input and output specification and a theory T, the following steps are performed:

(1) The theory T is extended so as to specify the values of certain undefined functions. In particular, for each token, token, an axiom is added equating (token) with some expressible positive integer. In addition, axioms are added that equate (LEAST.INEXPRESSIBLE.POSITIVE.INTEGER) and (GREATEST.INEXPRESSIBLE.NEGATIVE.INTEGER) with integers satisfying the axiom INTEGER.SIZE of Appendix A.

(2) The user then checks that, in the light of the extended theory, the input and output specifications suit his needs. (For example, given the newly specified values of the tokens, do the input specifications permit the desired applications of the subprograms?)

(3) The user checks that the FORTRAN processor on which he intends to operate executes the built-in arithmetic, logical, and intrinsic functions in accordance with the definitions of Appendix A and the input conditions of Appendix B. (For example, does the processor's integer addition mechanism really return the mathematical sum of two integers whenever that sum is in the interval between (LEAST.INEXPRESSIBLE.POSITIVE.INTEGER) and (GREATEST.INEXPRESSIBLE.NEGATIVE.INTEGER)?)

(4) All occurrences of tokens in the subprograms of c are replaced by their axiomatized values and the subprograms are printed according to the standard FORTRAN rules regarding lines and columns.

(5) The printed subprograms are then combined with unverified subprograms and a main program. The main program must include a COMMON declaration of each COMMON block of c. Each such COMMON block must be declared in the main program precisely as it is declared in any member of c (including type and dimension information).

(6) The user checks that the combined executable program does not exceed the "capacity" of his processor (see section 1.2.1 of [12] and section 1.3.2 of [1]). This will include checking that there is enough "room" to store the arrays and subprograms. It could conceivably involve more bizarre interpretations of "capacity" such as restrictions on the number of formal arguments or subroutine CALLs. What is actually required here is a formal characterization of the "capacity" of the processor in question.

Subprograms in the verified context may be called from unverified programs and are guaranteed to terminate without run-time error and produce results consistent with their input/output specifications. Of course, such calls must satisfy the FORTRAN rules for invoking subprograms (e.g. the types of the actuals must correspond to the types of the formals, adjustable array dimensions must be properly defined, and so on).

13. AN EXAMPLE

In a 1977 *Communications of the ACM* article [4], we described an algorithm for finding the first occurrence of one character string, PAT, in another, STR. The algorithm is currently the fastest known way to solve this problem on the average. Our algorithm has two unusual properties. First, in verifying that PAT does not occur within the first i characters of STR the algorithm will typically fetch and look at fewer than i characters. Second, as PAT gets longer the algorithm speeds up. That is, the algorithm typically spends less time to find long patterns than short ones.

In Chapter XVIII of [5] we present a version of the algorithm coded in a simple "toy" programming language that—like many languages used in program verification—ignores many issues raised by conventional programming languages. In this section we discuss the verification of the same version of the algorithm, but this time coded in our FORTRAN subset. Our subroutine finds the first occurrence of one array of "character codes" in another array of "character codes". By "character codes" we mean INTEGERs in the range 1 to @ASIZE, a token understood to be the size of the alphabet (e.g. 128 for ASCII).

String searching is not FORTRAN's forte. However, we chose this example for four reasons. First, the algorithm is of interest both theoretically and practically and is in day-to-day use in certain text processing systems. Secondly, the algorithm has been published, illustrated and carefully explained elsewhere. Thirdly, the algorithm presents certain interesting features from the point of view of verification. Finally, it is interesting to contrast the verification of a "toy" version with the verification of exactly the same algorithm in a real language.

13.1. The implementation in FORTRAN

The whole idea behind the algorithm is illustrated by the following example. Suppose we are trying to find PAT in STR and, having scanned some initial part of STR and failed to find PAT, are now ready to ask whether PAT occurs at the position marked by the arrow below:

```
PAT:                    EXAMPLE
STR:    LET_US_CONSIDER_A_SIMPLE_EXAMPLE
                            ↑
```

Instead of focusing on the left-hand end of the pattern (i.e., on the "E" indicated by the arrow) the algorithm considers the right-hand end of the pattern. In particular, the alogorithm fetches the "I" in the word "SIMPLE." Since "I" does not occur in PAT, the algorithm can slide the pattern down by seven (the length of PAT) without missing a possible match. Afterwards, it focuses on the end of the pattern again, as marked by the arrow below.

PAT: EXAMPLE
STR: LET_US_CONSIDER_A_SIMPLE_EXAMPLE

In general, as the next step would suggest, the algorithm slides PAT down by the number of characters that separate the end of the pattern from the last occurrence in PAT of the character, c, just fetched from STR (or the length of PAT if c does not occur in PAT). In the configuration above, PAT would be moved forward by five characters, so as to align the "X" in PAT with the just fetched "X" in STR.

If the algorithm finds that the character just fetched from STR matches the corresponding character of PAT, it moves the arrow backwards and repeats the process until it either finds a mismatch and can slide PAT forward, or matches all the characters of PAT.

The algorithm must be able to determine efficiently for any character c, the distance from the last occurrence of c in PAT to the right-hand end of PAT. But since there are only a finite number of characters in the alphabet we can preprocess PAT and set up a table that answers this question in a single array access.

The reader is referred to [4] for a thorough description of an improved version of the algorithm that can be implemented so as to search for PAT through i characters of STR and execute less than i machine instructions, on the average. In addition, [4] contains a statistical analysis of the average case behavior of the algorithm and discusses several implementation questions.

A FORTRAN version of the algorithm is exhibited below. The subroutine FSRCH is the search algorithm itself; it takes five arguments, PAT, STR, PATLEN, STRLEN and X. PAT and STR are one-dimensional adjustable arrays of length PATLEN and STRLEN respectively. X is the dummy argument into which the answer is smashed. The answer is either the index into STR at which the winning match is found, or else it is STRLEN + 1 indicating no match exists.

FRSCH starts by CALLing the subroutine SETUP, which preprocesses PAT and smashes the COMMON array DELTA1. DELTA1 has one entry for each character code in the alphabet. SETUP executes in time linear in PATLEN. It initializes DELTA1 as though no character occurred in PAT and then sweeps PAT once, from left to right, filling in the correct value of

DELTA1 for each character occurrence, as though that occurrence were the last occurrence of the character in PAT. Thus, if the same character occurs several times in PAT (as "E" does in "EXAMPLE") then its DELTA1 entry is smashed several times and the last value is the correct one.

```
        SUBROUTINE FSRCH(PAT, STR, PATLEN, STRLEN, X)
        INTEGER DELTA1
        INTEGER PATLEN
        INTEGER STRLEN
        INTEGER PAT
        INTEGER STR
        INTEGER I
        INTEGER J
        INTEGER C
        INTEGER NEXTI
        INTEGER X
        INTEGER MAX0
        DIMENSION DELTA1 (@ASIZE)
        DIMENSION PAT(PATLEN)
        DIMENSION STR(STRLEN)
        COMMON /BLK/DELTA1
        CALL SETUP(PAT, PATLEN)
        I = PATLEN
200     CONTINUE
        IF ((I.GT.STRLEN)) GO TO 500
        J = PATLEN
        NEXTI = (1 + I)
300     CONTINUE
        C = STR(I)
        IF ((C.NE.PAT(J))) GO TO 400
        IF ((J.EQ.1)) GO TO 600
        J = (J - 1)
        I = (I - 1)
        GO TO 300
400     I = MAX0((I + DELTA1(C)), NEXTI)
        GO TO 200
500     X = (STRLEN + 1)
        RETURN
600     X = I
        RETURN
        END
```

```
        SUBROUTINE SETUP (A, MAX)
        INTEGER DELTA1
        INTEGER A
        INTEGER MAX
        INTEGER I
        INTEGER C
        DIMENSION DELTA1(@ASIZE)
        DIMENSION A(MAX)
        COMMON /BLK/DELTA1
        DO 50 I = 1, @ASIZE
        DELTA1(I) = MAX
   50   CONTINUE
        DO 100 I = 1, MAX
        C = A(I)
        DELTA1(C) = (MAX − I)
  100   CONTINUE
        RETURN
        END
```

As described in this document, our subset allows only one variable to be declared in each INTEGER statement, requires the declaration of implicitly typed INTEGER variables such as I and J, and requires full parenthesization of expressions. These restrictions could be relaxed somewhat. The statements labeled 200 and 300 in FSRCH are CONTINUE statements to permit the attachment of loop assertions at those points.

Chapter XVIII of [5] discusses the "toy" version of the algorithm implemented above and fully illustrates the algorithm at work. We highly recommend that the reader see Chapter XVIII before continuing with this discussion. In particular, that chapter contains a description of the algorithm in which we devote a paragraph to virtually every statement in the code for FSRCH. Furthermore, we carefully derive the input/output assertions for the algorithm, discuss, from an intuitive point of view, the invariants that are being maintained, express those invariants formally, derive the verification conditions (ignoring such things as aliasing, overflow, and array bounds violations), and prove the verification conditions. In the following discussion we assume the reader understands how the algorithm works.

13.2. The FORTRAN theory

To specify the input and output assertions for these two subroutines we must extend the basic FORTRAN theory by the introduction of the mathematical concepts of (a) a sequence being a "character string" on a given sized alphabet, (b) the initial segments of two strings "matching", (c) the leftmost match of PAT in STR, and (d) the distance from the last occurrence of C in PAT to the end of PAT. Below we give the definitions of these mathematical functions.

Definition.

```
(STRINGP A I SIZE)
=
(IF (ZEROP I)
    T
    (AND (NUMBERP (ELT1 A I))
         (NOT (EQUAL (ELT1 A I) 0))
         (NOT (LESSP SIZE (ELT1 A I)))
         (STRINGP A (SUB1 I) SIZE)))
```

Definition.

```
(MATCH PAT J PATLEN STR I STRLEN)
=
(IF (LESSP PATLEN J)
    T
    (IF (LESSP STRLEN I)
        F
        (AND (EQUAL (ELT1 PAT J) (ELT1 STR I))
             (MATCH PAT
                    (ADD1 J)
                    PATLEN STR
                    (ADD1 I)
                    STRLEN))))
```

Definition.

```
(SEARCH PAT STR PATLEN STRLEN I)
=
(IF (LESSP STRLEN I)
    (ADD1 STRLEN)
    (IF (MATCH PAT 1 PATLEN STR I STRLEN)
        I
        (SEARCH PAT STR PATLEN STRLEN
                (ADD1 I))))
```

Definition.

```
(DELTA1 A C MAX)
=
(IF (ZEROP MAX)
    0
    (IF (EQUAL C (ELT1 A MAX))
        0
        (ADD1 (DELTA1 A C (SUB1 MAX)))))
```

For example, (MATCH PAT J PATLEN STR I STRLEN) determines whether the characters of PAT in positions J through PATLEN are equal to the corresponding characters of STR starting at position I and not exceeding STRLEN. MATCH is recursive. That is, provided J $<$ PATLEN and I $<$ STRLEN, MATCH checks that the Jth character of $\overline{\text{PAT}}$ is equal to the Ith character of STR and, if so, requires that there be a MATCH starting at positions I $+$ 1 and J $+$ 1. The recursive function SEARCH is the mathematical expression of the naive string searching algorithm. (SEARCH PAT STR PATLEN STRLEN I) asks, for each position in STR between I and STRLEN, whether a MATCH with PAT occurs at that position.

We extend the *basic FORTRAN theory* by adding the definitions above. The result is a *FORTRAN theory* theory *appropriate* for a context containing SETUP and FSRCH.

13.3. The specification of SETUP

To verify SETUP we must first *specify* it with *input* and *output assertions*. These assertions must be expressed in terms of the formal arguments to SETUP and its global names. Note that our implementation of SETUP used the formal arguments A and MAX. In the actual CALL of SETUP from FSRCH A will be PAT and MAX will be PATLEN. We chose different names to make instantiations of the input and output assertions more obvious.

The input assertion for SETUP is:

```
(AND (STRINGP (A STATE) (MAX STATE) (@ASIZE))
     (NOT (EQUAL (MAX STATE) 0))
     (NUMBERP (MAX STATE))
     (LESSP (ADD1 (@ASIZE))
            (LEAST.INEXPRESSIBLE.POSITIVE.INTEGER))
     (LESSP (ADD1 (MAX STATE))
            (LEAST.INEXPRESSIBLE.POSITIVE.INTEGER)))
```

The assertion requires that the elements of A from 1 to MAX be character codes in the alphabet of size @ASIZE, and that MAX be a positive INTEGER. In addition, it requires that both @ASIZE $+$ 1 and MAX $+$ 1 be expressible.

The reader may ask "Why the $+$1s? Why not simply require that @ASIZE and MAX be expressible?" An inspection of the ANSI FORTRAN 66 semantics for DO-loops reveals that

$$\text{DO } 100 \text{ I} = 1, \text{MAX}$$

causes I to be set to MAX $+$ 1 immediately before the termination condition is checked for the last time. Thus, unless MAX $+$ 1 is expressible, the last increment will either cause an overflow error or cause I to be set to garbage.

The reader may also ask "Why do you prohibit a MAX of 0? Doesn't that just correspond to the empty string?" One's first considered reaction might be that the condition is present because MAX is the dimension of an array declared in SETUP. However, that aspect of MAX's use does not show up in the verification conditions generated for SETUP; so why is it in the input assertion for SETUP? The answer is because of the

$$\text{DO } 100 \text{ I} = 1, \text{ MAX}$$

statement. FORTRAN 66 requires that on entry to the DO loop the maximum, i.e. MAX, be greater than or equal to the initial value, 1. Should MAX ever be 0, a program with the above DO statement in it will cause unpredictable behavior on some correct FORTRAN 66 processors.

The *output assertion* for SETUP is:

```
(IMPLIES (AND (NUMBERP C)
              (NOT (EQUAL C 0))
              (NOT (LESSP (@ASIZE) C)))
         (EQUAL (ELT1 (BLK-DELTA1 NEWSTATE) C)
                (DELTA1 (A STATE)
                        C
                        (MAX STATE)))))
```

The assertion relates NEWSTATE (the state at the conclusion of the execution of SETUP) to STATE (the state at the beginning of the execution). Informally, it says that for every character C in the alphabet, the Cth element of the DELTA1 array in COMMON block BLK (at the conclusion of the execution) is equal to the distance from the last occurrence of C in A to the end of A, where that distance is defined by the mathematical function DELTA1.

Note that, as required of an output assertion, the term above is a term in the primary verification extension of our theory. That is, it is well-formed and mentions no function symbols other than those in our extension of the basic FORTRAN theory and the arguments and global names of SETUP. Note also that it incarcerates STATE and NEWSTATE: they appear only as arguments to the arguments and globals of SETUP.

The system has proved SETUP correct as specified above. To describe the verification of SETUP we would have to *annotate* it with an *input clock*, *loop invariants*, and *loop clocks* for the two DO loops. Since we go into the verification of FSRCH in some detail, we will now skip over the details of SETUP. Assume SETUP has been proved and that we now have a semantically correct context that contains it.

Let us jump ahead for a moment and consider the following questions. What do we have to prove when we encounter

CALL SETUP(PAT, PATLEN)

in another subprogram (e.g. FSRCH)? Suppose the state term before the CALL is (START). Then we must prove the *verification condition* generated for the CALL, which is the conjunction of:
(a) a term substitution instance of the input assertion for SETUP:

(AND (STRINGP (PAT (START))
          (PATLEN (START))
          (@ASIZE))
    (NOT (EQUAL (PATLEN (START)) 0))
    (NUMBERP (PATLEN (START)))
    (LESSP (ADD1 (@ASIZE))
          (LEAST.INEXPRESSIBLE.POSITIVE.INTEGER))
    (LESSP (ADD1 (PATLEN (START)))
          (LEAST.INEXPRESSIBLE.POSITIVE.INTEGER))), and

(b) the conjunction of the input conditions for the actual expressions, which is (TRUE) since they are variables.

On the other side, what do we get to assume after the CALL of SETUP? The new state term is (NEXT (START)). The *assumption* arising from the CALL is the conjunction of the following:
(a) the conjoined output assumptions for the actual expressions, which is (TRUE) in this case,
(b) a term substitution instance of the output assertion of SETUP:

(IMPLIES (AND (NUMBERP C)
         (NOT (EQUAL C 0))
         (NOT (LESSP (@ASIZE) C)))
    (EQUAL (ELT1 (BLK-DELTA1 (NEXT (START)))
         C)
       (DELTA1 (PAT (START))
         C
         (PATLEN (START)))))

which tells us that the elements of DELTA1 in the new state are correctly set,
(c) the assumption that PAT and PATLEN (and all the other local and global names of the calling subprogram not *possibly smashed* by the CALL of SETUP) are unchanged in the new state:

(EQUAL (PAT (NEXT (START)))
    (PAT (START)))

(EQUAL (PATLEN (NEXT (START)))
(PATLEN (START))).

In short, in the state after the CALL, DELTA1 is correctly set and no other names have been affected.

13.4. The specification of FSRCH

Assuming we have a semantically correct context containing SETUP we now proceed to specify FSRCH. The *input assertion* for FSRCH is:

```
(AND (LESSP (ADD1 (@ASIZE))
            (LEAST.INEXPRESSIBLE.POSITIVE.INTEGER))
     (STRINGP (PAT STATE) (PATLEN STATE) (@ASIZE))
     (NUMBERP (PATLEN STATE))
     (LESSP 0 (PATLEN STATE))
     (STRINGP (STR STATE) (STRLEN STATE) (@ASIZE))
     (NUMBERP (STRLEN STATE))
     (LESSP 0 (STRLEN STATE))
     (LESSP (PLUS (PATLEN STATE) (STRLEN STATE))
            (LEAST.INEXPRESSIBLE.POSITIVE.INTEGER)))
```

Informally, the assertion puts the same restrictions on @ASIZE and PAT as required by our use of SETUP. In addition, it requires that STR be a nonempty character string on the alphabet of size @ASIZE. The most interesting requirement however is the last: the sum of PATLEN and STRLEN must be expressible.

At first sight one might think that FSRCH will work for any sized PAT and STR as long as every character in them can be indexed. Were that true, it would be enough to require that both PATLEN and STRLEN be expressible. But suppose that PAT has been pushed down STR so that the last character of PAT is aligned with the last character of STR. That is, I is set to STRLEN. Suppose that the last character, C, of STR does not occur in PAT. Then we increment I by the contents of the DELTA1 array at C. That value will be PATLEN, since C does not occur in PAT. Thus, I becomes STRLEN + PATLEN. FSRCH then jumps to 200, discovers that I exceeds STRLEN, and quits. But if STRLEN + PATLEN were not expressible, the step in which we increment I the last time would either cause an overflow error or return garbage.

The output assertion for FSRCH is:

$$(EQUAL\ (X\ NEWSTATE)$$
$$(SEARCH\ (PAT\ STATE)$$
$$(STR\ STATE)$$
$$(PATLEN\ STATE)$$
$$(STRLEN\ STATE)$$
$$1))$$

Informally, the assertion says that at the conclusion of FSRCH, X is set to the correct value, as defined by applying the mathematical function SEARCH to the initial values of the arguments.

13.5. The annotation of FSRCH

To prove FSRCH correct we must *annotate* it. We first specify the input clock. Recall that a clock is an n-tuple of natural numbers. The "time" remaining on a clock when it is encountered is supposed to be lexicographically smaller than the "time" remaining on the previously encountered clock. The input clock is attached to the entry and thus puts a limit on the total amount of "time" the program can run, expressed as a function of the initial environment.

By inspecting FSRCH we see that every time we go around the loop through statement label 200, I is bigger than it was before—though this observation requires some understanding of NEXTI and MAX0. I cannot get bigger than STRLEN + PATLEN. So the program can cycle through statement 200 only a finite number of times. However, there is an inner loop, through statement 300. Every time the program cycles through it, J gets smaller and is bounded below by 0. Thus, we have a lexicographic argument that the program terminates. The argument uses clocks with two components. Intuitively, the first component must tick down at least once every time we go through the outer loop. We do not care what the second component does when the first component ticks down. The second component must tick down every time we go through the inner loop—and when that happens the first component must not increase! Here is the *input clock* for FSRCH.

$$(LIST\ (PLUS\ 1$$
$$(STRLEN\ (START))$$
$$(PATLEN\ (START)))$$
$$0)$$

By making the first component large enough in the input clock we do not have to worry about the initial value of the second component.

We now specify the loop invariants and loop clocks for FSRCH. It is at this point that the reader benefits the most from the presentation in Chapter

XVIII of [5] because there we explain the role of many of the conjuncts in the two loop invariants. Here is the *loop invariant* that we attach to the CONTINUE statement at line 200 in FSRCH:

```
(AND (EQUAL (PAT STATE) (PAT (START)))
     (EQUAL (STR STATE) (STR (START)))
     (EQUAL (PATLEN STATE)
            (PATLEN (START)))
     (EQUAL (STRLEN STATE)
            (STRLEN (START)))
     (NUMBERP (I STATE))
     (NOT (LESSP (I STATE) (PATLEN (START))))
     (LESSP (I STATE)
            (PLUS (PATLEN (START))
                  (SEARCH (PAT (START))
                          (STR (START))
                          (PATLEN (START))
                          (STRLEN (START))
                          1)))
     (IMPLIES (AND (NUMBERP C)
                   (NOT (EQUAL C 0))
                   (NOT (LESSP (@ASIZE) C)))
              (EQUAL (ELT1 (BLK-DELTA1 STATE) C)
                     (DELTA1 (PAT (START))
                             C
                             (PATLEN (START)))))))
```

The first seven conjuncts are described in [5] (modulo the translation from indices that start at 0 to indices that start at 1). Intuitively, they say that PAT, STR, PATLEN and STRLEN are not being modified (i.e. they are the same objects in the current state, STATE, as in the initial state (START)), that there are at least PATLEN characters to the left of I (so we may compare them pairwise), and that we have not yet passed the right-hand end of the winning match of PAT in STR. The final conjunct says that the DELTA1 array is not being modified. In particular, it says that its configuration in the current state STATE has the same property that it did immediately after we called SETUP.

Here is the *loop clock* attached to statement 200:

```
(LIST (DIFFERENCE (PLUS 1
                        (STRLEN (START))
                        (PATLEN (START)))
                  (I STATE))
      (ADD1 (PATLEN (START))))
```

Since I is never 0, the first component of this clock is less than that of the input clock. We will have to prove that this clock is bigger than any clock we encounter on a nonexit path leading out of statement 200 (which we can do because the only such path leads to the inner loop where we will hold the first component fixed and count the second down). We will also have to prove that this clock is smaller than any clock we see at the beginning of a path coming into statement 200 (which we can do since, except for the input path, the only such path will come from the inner loop where I will have been increased with the MAX0 expression).

The *loop invariant* to be attached to the CONTINUE statement at statement 300 in FSRCH is:

```
(AND (EQUAL (PAT STATE) (PAT (START)))
     (EQUAL (STR STATE) (STR (START)))
     (EQUAL (PATLEN STATE)
            (PATLEN (START)))
     (EQUAL (STRLEN STATE)
            (STRLEN (START)))
     (NOT (LESSP (NEXTI STATE)
                 (ADD1 (PATLEN (START)))))
     (LESSP (NEXTI STATE)
            (ADD1 (PLUS (PATLEN (START))
                        (SEARCH (PAT (START))
                                (STR (START))
                                (PATLEN (START))
                                (STRLEN (START))
                                1))))
     (IMPLIES (AND (NUMBERP C)
                   (NOT (EQUAL C 0))
                   (NOT (LESSP (@ASIZE) C)))
              (EQUAL (ELT1 (BLK-DELTA1 STATE) C)
                     (DELTA1 (PAT (START))
                             C
                             (PATLEN (START)))))
     (NUMBERP (I STATE))
     (NOT (EQUAL (I STATE) 0))
     (NUMBERP (J STATE))
     (NOT (EQUAL (J STATE) 0))
     (NUMBERP (NEXTI STATE))
     (NOT (LESSP (PATLEN (START)) (J STATE)))
     (NOT (LESSP (STRLEN (START)) (I STATE)))
     (EQUAL (NEXTI STATE)
```

```
              (PLUS (ADD1 (PATLEN (START)))
                    (DIFFERENCE (I STATE) (J STATE)))))
          (NOT (LESSP (ADD1 (STRLEN (START)))
                      (NEXTI STATE)))
          (NOT (LESSP (I STATE) (J STATE)))
          (MATCH (PAT (START))
                 (ADD1 (J STATE))
                 (PATLEN (START))
                 (STR (START))
                 (ADD1 (I STATE))
                 (STRLEN (START)))
          (NUMBERP (ELT1 (BLK-DELTA1 STATE)
                         (ELT1 (STR (START)) (I STATE))))
          (NUMBERP (ELT1 (STR (START)) (I STATE)))
          (NUMBERP (ELT1 (PAT (START)) (J STATE)))))
```

The first seven conjuncts are really just a version of the invariant at 200, which we must maintain because we will have to prove it when we exit the inner loop and jump to 200. The next eleven conjuncts specify the invariant inherently maintained by the inner loop. This invariant is discussed in [5]. Intuitively, it requires that J and I be "corresponding" legal indices into PAT and STR and that we have established that the terminal substrings of PAT and STR starting at J + 1 and I + 1 MATCH. The last three conjuncts are unnecessary but make the verification a little easier. They inform us that the elements of DELTA1, STR and PAT that we will access in any single iteration through the inner loop are nonnegative INTEGERs. These facts can be derived. However, by making them explicit we permit the theorem-prover to simplify certain arithmetic expressions more rapidly because it can immediately rule out the possibilities that negative quantities are involved.

The *loop clock* at statement 300 is:

```
    (LIST (DIFFERENCE (PLUS 1
                            (STRLEN (START))
                            (PATLEN (START)))
                      (SUB1 (NEXTI STATE)))
          (J STATE))
```

When we come into the inner loop from the outer, this clock is less than the clock at 200 because the first component is equal and the second component is smaller. Every time we go around the inner loop this clock will be less than it was the previous time because the first component will not have changed and the second will have been decremented by 1. When we go from the inner loop back out to the outer one, the clock at 200 will be smaller because I will be larger than (SUB1 (NEXTI STATE)).

13.6. The verification of one path through FSRCH

The *global assumption* for the verification of FSRCH is the conjunction of (1) the *partially instantiated input assertion* for FSRCH:

```
(AND (LESSP (ADD1 (@ASIZE))
            (LEAST.INEXPRESSIBLE.POSITIVE.INTEGER))
     (STRINGP (PAT (START))
              (PATLEN (START))
              (@ASIZE))
     (NUMBERP (PATLEN (START)))
     (LESSP 0 (PATLEN (START)))
     (STRINGP (STR (START))
              (STRLEN (START))
              (@ASIZE))
     (NUMBERP (STRLEN (START)))
     (LESSP 0 (STRLEN (START)))
     (LESSP (PLUS (PATLEN (START))
                  (STRLEN (START)))
            (LEAST.INEXPRESSIBLE.POSITIVE.INTEGER))
     (DEFINEDP (STRLEN (START)))
     (DEFINEDP (PATLEN (START))))
```

and (2) the axiom defining the types of the variables in FSRCH, when they are defined:

```
(AND (IMPLIES (DEFINEDP (PATLEN STATE))
              (ZNUMBERP (PATLEN STATE)))
     (IMPLIES (DEFINEDP (J STATE))
              (ZNUMBERP (J STATE)))
     (IMPLIES (DEFINEDP (NEXTI STATE))
              (ZNUMBERP (NEXTI STATE)))
     (IMPLIES (DEFINEDP (C STATE))
              (ZNUMBERP (C STATE)))
     (IMPLIES (DEFINEDP (STRLEN STATE))
              (ZNUMBERP (STRLEN STATE)))
     (IMPLIES (DEFINEDP (X STATE))
              (ZNUMBERP (X STATE)))
     (IMPLIES (DEFINEDP (I STATE))
              (ZNUMBERP (I STATE)))
```

```
        (IMPLIES (DEFINEDP (ELT1 (PAT STATE)
                          I))
             (ZNUMBERP (ELT1 (PAT STATE)
                          I)))
        (IMPLIES (DEFINEDP (ELT1 (STR STATE)
                          I))
             (ZNUMBERP (ELT1 (STR STATE)
                          I)))
        (IMPLIES (DEFINEDP (ELT1 (BLK-DELTA1 STATE)
                          I))
             (ZNUMBERP
                (ELT1 (BLK-DELTA1 STATE)
                          I))))).
```

We now consider the verification conditions along the path from the input to statement 200. The path contains the artificially added *node 0*, the call of SETUP, the initialization of I to PATLEN, and the annotated CONTINUE statement labeled 200.

The initial state term is (START). Consider the first edge, which terminates at the CALL statement:

CALL SETUP (PAT, PATLEN)

We have already exhibited the verification condition for this CALL statement. In particular, we have to prove that the instantiated input assertion for SETUP is satisfied. We get to assume the global assumptions above. The proof is trivial.

The state term after the CALL is (NEXT (START)). We also get to assume the previously discussed assumptions resulting from the CALL of SETUP. Those assumptions relate variables in the (START) state to those in (NEXT (START)). Let us continue down the input path to:

I = PATLEN

The verification condition for the edge leading to this statement is the conjunction of the input condition for I (which is (TRUE)), the input condition for PATLEN (which is (TRUE)), and the definedness condition for PATLEN in the current state (NEXT (START)). That is, we have to prove:

(DEFINEDP (PATLEN (NEXT (START))))

assuming the global assumptions and the assumptions resulting from the CALL of SETUP. Those latter assumptions, recall, tell us that (PATLEN (NEXT (START))) is equal to (PATLEN (START)). But the global assumption tells us (DEFINEDP (PATLEN (START))). Thus, this verification condition is trivial also.

As a result of the assignment statement above, the new state term is (NEXT (NEXT (START))). The assumption for the edge coming out of the assignment tells us that (I (NEXT (NEXT (START)))) is (PATLEN (NEXT (START))), and that, except for I, the value of every variable in (NEXT (NEXT (START))) is equal to its value in (NEXT (START)).

We finally arrive at the CONTINUE statement at label 200—the last node in the path. The verification condition for this statement is the conjunction of (1) the instance of the loop assertion at 200 obtained by replacing STATE by the current state term:

```
(AND (EQUAL (PAT (NEXT (NEXT (START)))) (PAT (START)))
     (EQUAL (STR (NEXT (NEXT (START)))) (STR (START)))
     (EQUAL (PATLEN (NEXT (NEXT (START))))
            (PATLEN (START)))
     (EQUAL (STRLEN (NEXT (NEXT (START))))
            (STRLEN (START)))
     (NUMBERP (I (NEXT (NEXT (START)))))
     (NOT (LESSP (I (NEXT (NEXT (START)))) (PATLEN (START))))
     (LESSP (I (NEXT (NEXT (START))))
            (PLUS (PATLEN (START))
                  (SEARCH (PAT (START))
                          (STR (START))
                          (PATLEN (START))
                          (STRLEN (START))
                          1)))
     (IMPLIES (AND (NUMBER C)
                   (NOT (EQUAL C 0))
                   (NOT (LESSP (@ASIZE) C)))
              (EQUAL (ELT1 (BLK-DELTA1 (NEXT (NEXT (START)))) C)
                     (DELTA1 (PAT (START))
                             C
                             (PATLEN (START))))))))
```

and (2) the lexicographic comparison of the loop clock at 200 (instantiated with the current state term) and the input clock:

```
(LEX (LIST (DIFFERENCE (PLUS 1
                             (STRLEN (START))
                             (PATLEN (START)))
                       (I (NEXT (NEXT (START))))))
           (ADD1 (PATLEN (START))))
     (LIST (PLUS 1
```

(STRLEN (START))
(PATLEN (START)))
0)).

To prove this we get to use the global assumptions, and the assumptions provided by the previously encountered CALL and assignment statements. In particular, the latter assumptions permit the theorem-prover to reduce terms such as (PAT (NEXT (NEXT (START)))) to (PAT (START)), about which we have assumptions provided by the input assertion.

13.7. A comparison with the toy version

Our mechanical theorem-prover has proved the verification conditions for SETUP and FSRCH. We will not discuss the other paths through FSRCH. The discussion of the toy version of the algorithm in [5] sketches the proofs that the assertion at the beginning of each path implies the assertion at the end. However, as we have noted, addressing the limitations of a real programming language requires that one consider more than the simple paths from one assertion to the next.

Let us consider the statement labelled 400:

$$400 \ I = MAX0((I + DELTA1(C)), NEXTI)$$

In our toy version of the problem, the verification condition generator walks through this statement and records the fact that I is the maximum of the present mathematical values of $I + DELTA1(C)$ and NEXTI. The statement requires nothing new for us to prove.

But in a real language, the statement at 400 is a mine field of possible errors. In FORTRAN terms, we have to prove six things to get past this assignment statement:

(1) C is defined.
(2) C is a legal index into DELTA1, i.e., $1 \leq C \leq @ASIZE$.
(3) DELTA1(C) is defined.
(4) I is defined.
(5) $I + DELTA1(C)$ is expressible.
(6) NEXTI is defined.

We will sketch the proofs of these six facts. First, in the state in which we encounter this statement, C is STR(J). Since J is a legal index into STR and since the input assertion tells us that for all such J, STR(J) is a character code between 1 and @ASIZE, we can conclude that C is defined. We can also conclude that C a legal index into DELTA1 since @ASIZE is also the size of the DELTA1 array. (Note that the argument that we can use C as an index into DELTA1 is beyond the scope of a standard compiler or type checker.) We can prove that DELTA1(C) is defined using the invariant about the effect of SETUP on BLK-DELTA1. In particular, DELTA1(C) is equal to the value of the mathematical function DELTA1 applied to certain arguments, and it is easy to show that the function in question always returns a number. We can prove that I and NEXTI are defined from the inner loop invariant. The only remaining problem is to prove that I + DELTA1(C) does not cause an overflow. Here is the proof. The inner invariant tells us that I is positive and less than or equal to STRLEN (ostensibly so that we can use it as an index into STR). As noted above, DELTA1(C) is equal to the value of the mathematical function DELTA1 applied to certain arguments. It is easy to prove by mathematical induction on the size of PAT that the value of the DELTA1 function is nonnegative and less than or equal to PATLEN. Therefore, I + DELTA1(C) is bounded below by 1 and above by STRLEN + PATLEN, which is expressible, by the input assertion.

Thus, we have proved the verification condition required to move past the statement labeled 400. It is encouraging to note that the proof is not deep. Instead, it is merely tedious. But the tedium—and the responsibility for the logical correctness of the proof—is the burden of our mechanical theorem-prover, not the user. When the theorem-prover has proved all of the verification conditions generated for SETUP and FSRCH we have gained something real: when executed by any correct FORTRAN processor in an environment that satisfies our input assertion, FSRCH will always terminate, will never cause a run-time error, and computes the correct answer.

ACKNOWLEDGEMENT

We would like to thank Paul Yans, of the University of Liège, Belgium, for his useful criticisms of an early draft of this document.

APPENDIX A
THE BASIC FORTRAN THEORY

We construct the *basic FORTRAN theory* in two stages. First we build the so-called "integer fragment" containing the formal correspondents of the FORTRAN INTEGER and LOGICAL operations, relations and functions. Then we extend the integer fragment by adding the function symbols required for the REAL, DOUBLE and COMPLEX types.

We completely specify the integer fragment of the basic FORTRAN theory. We only sketch how to extend the integer fragment to produce the basic FORTRAN theory. We have not yet formalized in our theory the mathematics behind type REAL (and thus also behind types DOUBLE and

COMPLEX). However, it is necessary to introduce certain function symbols and assumptions used by the verification condition generator in the handling of REAL, DOUBLE and COMPLEX expressions.

Definition. integer fragment. The *integer fragment* is produced by extending the theory in [5] and [6] by adding the following functions, shells and axioms.

Note. First, we add the function LOGICALP, which recognizes objects of type LOGICAL. The logical operations corresponding to FORTRAN's .AND., .OR. and .NOT. are the functions AND, OR and NOT, which are already in the primitive theory described in [5] and [6].

Definition.
> (LOGICALP X)
>
> =
>
> (OR (EQUAL X (TRUE))
> (EQUAL X (FALSE)))

Note. Next we begin the construction of the mathematical functions that correspond to FORTRAN's built-in operations on type INTEGER.

The primitive theory upon which we construct the basic FORTRAN theory already includes the (Peano-like) shell axioms for the natural numbers (recognized by NUMBERP) and the shell axioms for the negatives. The negative number -n is constructed by applying the "constructor" function MINUS to the Peano number n. The negatives are recognized by the function NEGATIVEP. Given a negative representing − n, the function NEGATIVE. GUTS returns the Peano number n. The primitive theory also includes the Peano sum and less than functions, PLUS and LESSP. We begin by defining the remaining elementary functions on natural numbers.

Definition.
> (DIFFERENCE X Y)
>
> =
>
> (IF (ZEROP X)
> 0
> (IF (ZEROP Y)
> X
> (DIFFERENCE (SUB1 X) (SUB1 Y))))

Definition.
> (TIMES X Y)
>
> =
>
> (IF (ZEROP X)
> 0
> (PLUS Y (TIMES (SUB1 X) Y)))

Definition.

 (QUOTIENT X Y)

 =

 (IF (ZEROP Y)

  0

  (IF (LESSP X Y)

   0

   (ADD1 (QUOTIENT (DIFFERENCE X Y) Y)))))

Definition.

 (EXPT I J)

 =

 (IF (ZEROP J)

  1

  (TIMES I (EXPT I (SUB1 J)))))

Note. Now, using the negatives and the Peano numbers, we "define" the set of positive and negative integers (often called "Z") by defining the Boolean function ZNUMBERP to return T or F according to whether its argument is an integer. We then define the standard functions on the integers. These equations define the usual infinite sets of ordered pairs embodying the traditional mathematical notions of integer sum, product, etc. For example, our definition of integer sum specifies the value of the sum of arbitrarily large integers. Because of the finiteness of actual processors, these mathematical notions, by themselves, do not accurately describe the semantics of the corresponding FORTRAN integer operations, and we do not so use them. Instead, we use these mathematical notions in the input/output specifications of those finite FORTRAN operators.

Definition.

 (ZNUMBERP X)

 =

 (OR (NEGATIVEP X) (NUMBERP X))

Definition.

 (ZZERO)

 =

 (ZERO)

Definition.

 (ZPLUS X Y)

 =

 (IF

```
(NEGATIVEP X)
(IF
 (NEGATIVEP Y)
 (MINUS (PLUS (NEGATIVE.GUTS X)
              (NEGATIVE.GUTS Y)))
 (IF (LESSP Y (NEGATIVE.GUTS X))
     (MINUS (DIFFERENCE (NEGATIVE.GUTS X) Y))
     (DIFFERENCE Y (NEGATIVE.GUTS X))))
(IF
 (NEGATIVEP Y)
 (IF (LESSP X (NEGATIVE.GUTS Y))
     (MINUS (DIFFERENCE (NEGATIVE.GUTS Y) X))
     (DIFFERENCE X (NEGATIVE.GUTS Y)))
 (PLUS X Y)))
```

Definition.

```
(ZDIFFERENCE X Y)
     =
(IF
 (NEGATIVEP X)
 (IF (NEGATIVEP Y)
     (IF (LESSP (NEGATIVE.GUTS Y)
                (NEGATIVE.GUTS X))
         (MINUS (DIFFERENCE (NEGATIVE.GUTS X)
                            (NEGATIVE.GUTS Y)))
         (DIFFERENCE (NEGATIVE.GUTS Y)
                     (NEGATIVE.GUTS X)))
     (MINUS (PLUS (NEGATIVE.GUTS X) Y)))
 (IF (NEGATIVEP Y)
     (PLUS X (NEGATIVE.GUTS Y))
     (IF (LESSP X Y)
         (MINUS (DIFFERENCE Y X))
         (DIFFERENCE X Y))))
```

Definition.

```
(ZTIMES X Y)
     =
(IF (NEGATIVEP X)
    (IF (NEGATIVEP Y)
        (TIMES (NEGATIVE.GUTS X)
               (NEGATIVE.GUTS Y))
```

```
                    (MINUS (TIMES (NEGATIVE.GUTS X) Y)))
                (IF (NEGATIVEP Y)
                    (MINUS (TIMES X (NEGATIVE.GUTS Y)))
                    (TIMES X Y)))
```

Definition.

```
        (ZQUOTIENT X Y)
        =
        (IF (NEGATIVEP X)
            (IF (NEGATIVEP Y)
                (QUOTIENT (NEGATIVE.GUTS X)
                          (NEGATIVE.GUTS Y))
                (MINUS (QUOTIENT (NEGATIVE.GUTS X) Y)))
            (IF (NEGATIVEP Y)
                (MINUS (QUOTIENT X (NEGATIVE.GUTS Y)))
                (QUOTIENT X Y)))
```

Definition.

```
        (ZEXPTZ I J)
        =
        (IF (ZEROP J)
            1
            (ZTIMES I (ZEXPTZ I (SUB1 J))))
```

Note. (ZEXPTZ I J) returns I raised to the Jth power, provided I is a positive or negative integer and J is a nonnegative integer. In particular, the definition of ZEXPTZ does not handle the case that J is negative—which involves real (or at least rational) arithmetic. (In fact, since the Peano function ZEROP returns T on all objects other than those constructed by the Peano ADD1 function, (ZEXPTZ I J) is defined to be 1 for negative J.) This is an acceptable definition for ZEXPTZ, which is used in the formalization of INTEGER to INTEGER exponentiation, because the input condition for (I**J), where I and J are of type INTEGER, requires that J be nonnegative.

We next introduce the usual collection of relations on the integers (e.g. "less than," etc.). There is a mild problem caused by our use of the shell principle to introduce the negatives: (MINUS 0) is an object different from 0. Consequently, we cannot use the usual equality predicate as the "meaning" of the FORTRAN relation .EQ. on INTEGERs. Instead, we must define an equality relation on the ZNUMBERPs, called ZEQP, under which (MINUS 0) and 0 are equal. We therefore define (ZNORMALIZE X) to return 0 if X is (MINUS 0) and X if X is any other ZNUMBERP. Our definition of ZEQP ZNORMALIZEs both arguments and then checks equality.

Definition.

    (ZNORMALIZE X)

    =

    (IF (NEGATIVEP X)

       (IF (EQUAL (NEGATIVE.GUTS X) 0) 0 X)

       (FIX X))

Definition.

    (ZEQP X Y)

    =

    (EQUAL (ZNORMALIZE X) (ZNORMALIZE Y))

Definition.

    (ZNEQP X Y)

    =

    (NOT (ZEQP X Y))

Definition.

    (ZLESSP X Y)

    =

    (IF (NEGATIVEP X)

       (IF (NEGATIVEP Y)

          (LESSP (NEGATIVE.GUTS Y)

              (NEGATIVE.GUTS X))

          (NOT (AND (EQUAL (NEGATIVE.GUTS X) 0)

                 (ZEROP Y))))

       (IF (NEGATIVEP Y) F (LESSP X Y)))

Definition.

    (ZLESSEQP X Y)

    =

    (NOT (ZLESSP Y X))

Definition.

    (ZGREATERP X Y)

    =

    (ZLESSP Y X)

Definition.

    (ZGREATEREQP X Y)

    =

    (NOT (ZLESSP X Y))

Note. We now introduce two undefined constants that denote the upper and lower bounds of the machine's integer arithmetic. These bounds are used in the definition of the function EXPRESSIBLE.ZNUMBERP. Our verification condition generator produces formulas that guarantee that the INTEGER constants mentioned in the program text (except in DIMENSION statements) are EXPRESSIBLE.ZNUMBERPs. EXPRESSIBLE.ZNUMBERP is also used in the input condition formulas for the built-in FORTRAN INTEGER operations. For example, the value produced by the FORTRAN expression (X + Y) is a certain sum, as defined by ZPLUS, *provided* that sum is an EXPRESSIBLE.ZNUMBERP. (Since we guarantee that all constants are expressible and that all built-in operations produce expressible answers, we do not have to consider the possibility that the arguments to a function are inexpressible because there is no way to construct such an integer.)

To reduce the number of trivial verification conditions, such as (EX-PRESSIBLE.ZNUMBERP 4), we have added an axiom to the basic FOR-TRAN theory that is nowhere justified by the definition of FORTRAN, but which is quite reasonable: we assume that the integers between −200 and 200 are all expressible. We know of no FORTRAN processors for which this is false.

Since nothing else is assumed about the range of expressible integers, the reader may wonder how the expressibility conditions are proved (when the value in question is not between −200 and 200). The answer is that they are proved from the input assertions the user supplies on the subprograms being verified. The specifier must state explicitly the size constraints under which his program operates. For example, consider a straightforward "big number" multiplication subroutine for arrays representing digit sequences in an arbitrary base, B. The subroutine must be able to multiply two digits together and obtain their product, to which it must be able to add a "carry" that is less than the base. Thus, the subroutine does not work correctly if one tries to use a base B for which ((B − 1)*B) is inexpressible.

Undefined function.
(GREATEST.INEXPRESSIBLE.NEGATIVE.INTEGER)

Undefined function.
(LEAST.INEXPRESSIBLE.POSITIVE.INTEGER)

Axiom. INTEGER.SIZE:
(AND
(ZLESSP (GREATEST.INEXPRESSIBLE.NEGATIVE.INTEGER)
        −200)
(ZLESSP 200
        (LEAST.INEXPRESSIBLE.POSITIVE.INTEGER)))

Note. The above axiom is consistent, since there are no other axioms about these two constants and −201 and 201 are constants in the theory satisfying the two conjuncts.

Definition.
(EXPRESSIBLE.ZNUMBERP X)
=
(AND
 (ZLESSP (GREATEST.INEXPRESSIBLE.NEGATIVE.INTEGER)
     X)
 (ZLESSP X
     (LEAST.INEXPRESSIBLE.POSITIVE.INTEGER)))

Note. For each of the finite number of tokens we introduce a constant function of the same name. Each function is required to have an expressible positive integer value. (In particular, 0 must be LESSP the value, from which it can be proved that the value is a positive *integer*.)

For each token, token:

Undefined function.
(token)

Axiom. token.POSITIVE
(AND (LESSP 0 (token))
     (EXPRESSIBLE.ZNUMBERP (token)))

Note. We now define the mathematical functions computed by the FORTRAN intrinsic functions over type INTEGER.

Definition.
     (IABS I)
       =
     (IF (NEGATIVEP I)
       (NEGATIVE.GUTS I)
       (FIX I))

Definition.
     (MOD X Y)
       =
     (ZDIFFERENCE X
              (ZTIMES Y (ZQUOTIENT X Y)))

Definition.
     (MAX0 I J)
       =
     (IF (ZLESSP I J) J I)

Definition.

(MIN0 I J)

=

(IF (ZLESSP I J) I J)

Definition.

(ISIGN I J)

=

(IF (NEGATIVEP J)
   (ZTIMES −1 (IABS I))
   (IABS I))

Definition.

(IDIM I J)

=

(ZDIFFERENCE I (MIN0 I J))

Note. We now define DEFINEDP, which is the negation of UNDEFINED, which is the recognizer of a new shell class containing an infinite set of objects. DEFINEDP is used in the enforcement of the FORTRAN requirement that variables be defined before they are used in the primitive arithmetic operations. We introduce it via a shell recognizer rather than as an undefined function so the knowledge that an object satisfies ZNUMBERP (for example) establishes that it is DEFINEDP.

Shell definition.

Add the shell UNDEF of one argument with
recognizer UNDEFINED,
accessor UNDEF.GUTS,
and default value 0.

Definition.

(DEFINEDP X)

=

(NOT (UNDEFINED X))

Note. We introduce four undefined functions: the constant function START used to denote the arbitrary state at the beginning of the initial paths through a subprogram being verified, and the three functions ELT1, ELT2 and ELT3, used in the denotation of the elements of one-, two- and three-dimensional arrays.

Undefined function.

(START)

Undefined function.
(ELT1 A I)

Undefined function.
(ELT2 A I J)

Undefined function.
(ELT3 A I J K)

Note. We now define the function LEX. Suppose L1 is the list containing the $k + 1$ natural numbers $\langle n_0 \ldots n_k \rangle$ and L2 is the list containing the $k + 1$ natural numbers $\langle m_0 \ldots m_k \rangle$. Then (LEX L1 L2) is (TRUE) if and only if the ordinal $\omega^k * n_0 + \omega^{k-1} * n_1 + \ldots + \omega^0 * n_k$ is less than the ordinal $\omega^k * m_0 + \omega^{k-1} * m_1 + \ldots + \omega^0 * m_k$. That is, for each natural number k, LEX is the well-founded relation on $(k + 1)$-tuples of natural numbers induced by the less than relation on ω^{k+1}.

Definition.

        (LEX L1 L2)

        =

        (IF (OR (NLISTP L1) (NLISTP L2))

        F

        (OR (LESSP (CAR L1) (CAR L2))

            (AND (EQUAL (CAR L1) (CAR L2))

                (LEX (CDR L1) (CDR L2)))))

This completes the specification of the integer fragment of the basic FORTRAN theory.

To construct the basic FORTRAN theory, we extend the integer fragment of the basic FORTRAN theory. The first step is to add notational conventions suitable for admitting noninteger FORTRAN arithmetic constants (e.g. 1.23E45 and $(-1.2, 3.4)$) as terms. We do not specify those conventions in this document. The second step is the addition of the following functions and axioms concerning the mathematical counterparts of types REAL, DOUBLE and COMPLEX.

We introduce the monadic Boolean functions RNUMBERP, DNUMBERP and CNUMBERP to recognize the objects of type REAL, DOUBLE and COMPLEX, respectively. Thus (RNUMBERP 0.0E-999) is a theorem.

We introduce the constant functions (RZERO), (DZERO) and (CZERO) to be the zero elements of type REAL, DOUBLE and COMPLEX, respectively.

We introduce the monadic Boolean functions EXPRESSIBLE.RNUMBERP, EXPRESSIBLE.DNUMBERP and EXPRESSIBLE.CNUMBERP to play the roles for types REAL, DOUBLE and COMPLEX (respectively) that EXPRESSIBLE.ZNUMBERP plays for type INTEGER. For example, if a program mentions the REAL 0.2E-999, then one of the verification conditions will include the proposition:

(EXPRESSIBLE.RNUMBERP 0.2E-999).

Thus, whoever specifies the operations on the REALs need not include (in the input condition formulas for those operations) the requirement that each REAL input is expressible provided he guarantees that no such operation can generate an inexpressible REAL result.

We introduce the dyadic function symbols RPLUS, RTIMES, RDIF-FERENCE, RQUOTIENT, RLESSP, RLESSEQP, REQP, RNEQP, RGREATEREQP and RGREATERP.

We introduce the dyadic function symbols DPLUS, DTIMES, DDIF-FERENCE, DQUOTIENT, DLESSP, DLESSEQP, DEQP, DNEQP, DGREATEREQP and DGREATERP.

We introduce the dyadic function symbols CPLUS, CTIMES, CDIF-FERENCE, CQUOTIENT, CEQP and CNEQP.

We introduce the dyadic function symbols REXPTZ, DEXPTZ, CEXPTZ, REXPTR, REXPTD, DEXPTR and DEXPTD. (ZEXPTZ, the INTEGER to INTEGER exponentiation function was handled in the integer fragment.)

For each intrinsic function pattern with name fn and n arguments (except those intrinsic functions already introduced in the integer fragment, IABS, MOD, MAX0, MIN0, ISIGN and IDIM), we introduce the n-ary function symbol fn, eventually to be defined to represent the mathematical function specified in the FORTRAN definition for the intrinsic function named fn.

Note. We do not specify in this document what the properties of the REAL, DOUBLE or COMPLEX operations are. Intuitively, if the REAL variables X and Y have the values x and y at run time, then the value of the FORTRAN expression $(X + Y)$ is understood to be (RPLUS x y), provided x and y satisfy the input conditions specified for RPLUS.

APPENDIX B
INPUT CONDITION FORMULAS

The table below gives the "input condition formula" for each built-in INTEGER operation, relation and intrinsic function. The formula is used in the definition of the "input condition" for an expression. Eventually such formulas must be supplied for all the REAL, DOUBLE and COMPLEX routines as well. At the moment, the formula for these routines is (FALSE), which means that a program involving REAL, DOUBLE PRECISION or

COMPLEX arithmetic cannot be proved correct by our system since the input conditions could never be established.

Rather than give the input condition formula for the FORTRAN symbol that appears in an expression e, e.g. + or .LE., we give the formula for the function symbol of the term [e], e.g. ZPLUS or ZLESSEQP, since the types of the arguments determine the precise interpretation of the symbol.

Definition. input condition formula. The *input condition formulas* for certain function symbols in the basic FORTRAN theory are specified by the table below. The input condition formula for a name not in the left-hand column is (FALSE).

name	input condition formula
ZPLUS	(EXPRESSIBLE.ZNUMBERP (ZPLUS (I STATE) (J STATE)))
ZDIFFERENCE	(EXPRESSIBLE.ZNUMBERP (ZDIFFERENCE (I STATE) (J STATE)))
ZTIMES	(EXPRESSIBLE.ZNUMBERP (ZTIMES (I STATE) (J STATE)))
ZQUOTIENT	(AND (ZNEQP (J STATE) 0)) (EXPRESSIBLE.ZNUMBERP (ZQUOTIENT (I STATE) (J STATE))))
ZEXPTZ	(AND (NOT (AND (ZEQP (I STATE) 0) (ZEQP (J STATE) 0))) (ZLESSP −1 (J STATE)) (EXPRESSIBLE.ZNUMBERP (ZEXPTZ (I STATE) (J STATE))))
ZLESSP	(TRUE)
ZLESSPEQP	(TRUE)
ZEQP	(TRUE)
ZNEQP	(TRUE)
ZGREATEREQP	(TRUE)
ZGREATERP	(TRUE)
NOT	(TRUE)
AND	(TRUE)
OR	(TRUE)
IABS	(EXPRESSIBLE.ZNUMBERP (IABS (I STATE)))
MOD	(AND (ZNEQP (J STATE) 0) (EXPRESSIBLE.ZNUMBERP

	(MOD (I STATE) (J STATE))))
MAX0	(TRUE)
MIN0	(TRUE)
ISIGN	(AND (ZNEQP (J STATE) 0)
	(EXPRESSIBLE.ZNUMBERP
	(ISIGN (I STATE) (J STATE))))
IDIM	(EXPRESSIBLE.ZNUMBERP
	(IDIM (I STATE) (J STATE)))

REFERENCES

1. American National Standards Institute, Inc. (1978). *American National Standard Programming Language FORTRAN*, ANSI X3.9-1978, 1430 Broadway, New York.
2. R. B. Anderson (1979). "Proving Programs Correct". John Wiley & Sons, New York.
3. J. Backus (1978). "The History of FORTRAN I, II and III," SIGPLAN Notices, 13(8), pp. 165–180. Association for Computing Machinery, Inc., reprinted by permission.
4. R. S. Boyer and J S. Moore (1977). "A Fast String Searching Algorithm," *Commun. Assoc. Comput. Mach.* 20(10), 762–772.
5. R. S. Boyer and J S. Moore (1979). "A Computational Logic". Academic Press, New York.
6. R. S. Boyer and J S. Moore (1981). Metafunctions: proving them correct and using them efficiently as new proof procedures. *In* "The Correctness Problem in Computer Science" (R. S. Boyer and J S. Moore, eds.). Academic Press, London.
7. W. S. Brown (1977). A realistic model of floating-point computation. *In* "Mathematical Software III" (J. R. Rice, ed.), pp. 343–360. Academic Press, New York.
8. R. W. Floyd (1967). Assigning meanings to programs. "Mathematical Aspects of Computer Science, Proc. Symp. Appl. Math." ,Vol. XIX, pp. 19–32. American Mathematical Society, Providence, Rhode Island.
9. H. H. Goldstine and J. von Neumann (1961) Planning and coding problems for an electronic computing instrument, Part II, Vol. 1, 1947. Reproduced *In* "John von Neumann Collected Works", Vol. V, p. 113. Pergamon Press, Oxford.
10. J. C. King (1969). "A Program Verifier," Ph.D. Thesis, Department of Computer Science, Carnegie-Mellon University, Pennsylvania.
11. Z. Manna (1974). "Mathematical Theory of Computation". McGraw-Hill, New York.
12. United States of America Standards Institute (1966). *USA Standard FORTRAN*, USAS X3.9-1966, 10 East 40th Street, New York.

3. Metafunctions: proving them correct and using them efficiently as new proof procedures

R. S. BOYER and J STROTHER MOORE

ABSTRACT

We describe a sound method for permitting the user of a mechanical theorem-proving system to add executable code to the system, thereby implementing a new proof strategy and modifying the behavior of the system. The new code is mechanically derived from a function definition conceived by the user but proved correct by the system before the new code is added. We present a simple formal method for stating within the theory of the system the correctness of such functions. The method avoids the complexity of embedding the rules of inference of the logic in the logic. Instead, we define a meaning function that maps from objects denoting expressions to the values of those expressions under a given assignment. We demonstrate that if the statement of correctness for a given "metafunction" is proved, then the code derived from that function's definition can be used as a new proof procedure. We explain how we have implemented the technique so that the actual application of a metafunction is as efficient as hand-coded procedures in the implementation language. We prove the correctness of our implementation. We discuss a useful metafunction that our system has proved correct and now uses routinely. We discuss the main obstacle to the introduction of metafunctions: proving them correct by machine.

1. SUMMARY*

How can the user of an automatic theorem-prover respond to the failure of the system to prove a given theorem? We know of three conventional responses: (1) modify the theorem-proving program itself, (2) guide the machine to the proof by interacting with a proof-checker-like facility and

* The work reported here was supported in part by NSF Grant MCS-7904081 and ONR Contract N00014-75-C-0816.

(3) guide the machine to the proof by adding to its database of lemmas. Alternative (1) can be easy, but it may result in bugs in the theorem-prover and therefore requires extreme caution and expertise not to be expected of every user. Even if an error-free modification is made, it may amount to the assumption of what was supposed to be proved. Alternative (2) is safe and sound, but very tedious and it does not improve the theorem-prover for the next occasion on which a similar proof is required. Alternative (3) is also safe and sound if the theorem-prover proves the lemmas before accepting them. But this alternative, too, can be very tedious, or even hopeless, if the theorem-prover's heuristics fail to use the new lemmas in the ways intended by the user.

In this paper we describe and justify logically an implementation of a fourth alternative. We have improved the theorem-prover described in "A Computational Logic" [1] so that one of the alternatives now available to the user is to modify the theorem-prover by adding executable code. This code can cause the system to pursue new strategies and apply new proof techniques under arbitrary heuristic control. However, to ensure the soundness of the resulting theorem-prover, each purported proof technique must be proved correct by the theorem-prover before it is incorporated into the system.

To extend our theorem-prover by adding a new piece of code the user proceeds as follows.

(1) The user conceives some transformation from terms of the theory to terms of the theory that he wishes the theorem-prover would make.

(2) The user must understand a correspondence between terms of the theory and certain constants of the theory. This correspondence is simple and resembles the use of lists and atoms to represent the expressions of LISP.

(3) The user must define a new function in the logic of our system. While defining this function the user can think of himself as implementing the term transformation that he desires. He writes the function so that if his desired transformation takes a term t to a term t′, then his function maps the constant corresponding to t to the constant corresponding to t′. (Because our language is related to that of Pure LISP, it will often not be difficult for the user to define his function in our theory if he can define it in Pure LISP. In "A Computational Logic" [1], we present many examples of functions that perform simple list processing operations and we even present some functions that are actually simple theorem-provers.)

(4) The user presents the definition of his function to our theorem-prover. The theorem-prover attempts to check that the definition satisfies our principle of definition. If the theorem-prover is successful, then the definition is admitted and the user is assured that there does exist one and only one function satisfying his definition.

(5) If the definition is admitted, the user asks the system to prove a certain "correctness" theorem about the new function. The correctness theorem will be described informally in the next subsection.

(6) If the correctness theorem is proved, the system incorporates into its simplifier new compiled code, derived from the function definition, that operates on the very INTERLISP data structures used to represent terms in our theorem-proving program. If the new code is applied to an INTERLISP object that represents a term t, the result of the application will be an INTER-LISP object that represents the term into which the user wished to transform t.

Once all these steps have been completed, the future behavior of the theorem-prover will be altered as follows. At a certain place in our theorem-prover's simplification routine, the code for the user's function is applied to the representation of the term that the theorem-prover is currently working on. The theorem-prover uses the output of that application as the representation of the new current term, thereby fulfilling the user's desire to transform terms.

In this paper we describe (a) the correspondence between terms and constants, (b) the correctness theorem for metafunctions and (c) the translation from user definition to compiled code. We establish in this paper that the new compiled code is a correct simplifier. We illustrate all the ideas discussed with a metafunction that usefully extends our system and that has been proved correct. We also discuss the difficulty of proving useful metafunctions correct. Before presenting the details, we now sketch the entire paper and compare our work to that of others.

1.1. The correctness theorem

Suppose that the user has defined his function, fn, and that it has been accepted under our principle of definition. At this time, there are only a finite number of function symbols, say $f_1, \ldots, f_m$, about which any axioms (e.g. definitions) have been made.

Before formulating the correctness theorem for fn, we first introduce and axiomatize in our current theory, T, two functions, FORMP and MEANING, which take one and two arguments, respectively. We assume, without loss of generality, that the symbols FORMP and MEANING are not among the $f_1, \ldots, f_m$.

The precise axioms added to define these two functions are presented later. Intuitively, the axioms about FORMP are sufficient to derive for any constant c whose only function symbols are in $f_1, \ldots, f_m$ whether c corresponds to some term in the theory T. Intuitively, MEANING is axiomatized to take as its first argument a constant corresponding to some term in T and as its second argument an assignment of values to variables; MEANING returns the value of the term under the assignment.

For example, consider the term (PLUS XY). The constant corresponding to this term is

(CONS "PLUS" (CONS "X" (CONS "Y" "NIL"))).

MEANING is axiomatized so that when it is applied to this constant and to the assignment that assigns 5 to "X" and 6 to "Y", then MEANING returns 11. (As will be explained, "X" is an abbreviation for a certain constant in our theory, namely (PACK (CONS 88 0)). 88 happens to be the ASCII code for the character X.)

The correctness theorem for the metafunction fn is:

(IMPLIES (FORMP X)
        (AND (EQUAL (MEANING X A)
                    (MEANING (fn X) A))
            (FORMP (fn X))))).

That is, for all X, if X is a constant corresponding to some term, then for all assignments A, the MEANING of X under A is the same as the MEANING of (fn X) under A. Furthermore (fn X) also corresponds to some term.

Suppose that the theorem-prover can prove the correctness theorem for fn. "So what," the reader may say, "if random axioms are assumed, then anything can be proved. How do I know that the axioms about FORMP and MEANING have any sense? Furthermore, even if they are sound, why should I be interested in a theorem that is a consequence of those axioms? In particular, how does your correctness theorem let me use fn as a proof procedure?" We now answer these questions by demonstrating how fn can be used to simplify terms.

First, let us delete the axioms about FORMP and MEANING that we added to the theory T after the definition of fn. Suppose that sometime later, perhaps even after adding some new function definitions (or even some other kinds of axioms), the user wishes some term p to be replaced by its transform. Let $f_1, \ldots, f_p$ be the sequence of function symbols about which there are now axioms. Of course, all of the function symbols occurring in the term p will be among the $f_1, \ldots, f_p$. Let us now *define* the functions MEANING and FORMP in such a way that the axioms that were previously added will be true. In our definition of MEANING, we shall adopt an entirely arbitrary position about the meaning of constants that contain function symbols other than $f_1, \ldots, f_p$. We shall define FORMP so that it is false on constants not corresponding to terms of the current theory.

Because FORMP and MEANING are defined to satisfy the axioms we had previously added, there exists a proof of the correctness theorem for fn in our current theory.

Now suppose that c is the constant of the theory that corresponds to p. Since the definition of fn was accepted under our principle of definition, there exists a constant d such that

$$\text{(EQUAL (fn c) d)}$$

is a theorem. Since c corresponds to p, c satisfies FORMP. By the correctness theorem for fn, d will satisfy FORMP and will in fact be the constant corresponding to some term q. Furthermore, by the correctness theorem for fn, it will be a theorem that:

$$\text{(EQUAL (MEANING c A)}$$
$$\text{(MEANING d A)).}$$

Finally, it can be shown that there will exist a trivial assignment a such that

$$\text{(EQUAL (MEANING c a) p)}$$

and

$$\text{(EQUAL (MEANING d a) q))}$$

are both theorems. To see that there always exists such a trivial assignment a, consider this example: let p be the term (PLUS X Y) and let c be the corresponding constant

$$\text{(CONS "PLUS" (CONS "X" (CONS "Y" "NIL")));}$$

then for the assignment a

$$\text{(CONS (CONS "X" X)}$$
$$\text{(CONS (CONS "Y" Y)}$$
$$\text{"NIL"))}$$

it is the case that (EQUAL (MEANING c a) p).

Since the user's definition of fn transforms c into d, it is understood that the user wishes the theorem-prover to transform p into q. But we have proved that p = (MEANING c a) = (MEANING d a) = q. Hence, there is a proof that p is equal to q, and the theorem-prover is justified in replacing p with q.

1.2. The implementation

In the preceding section we demonstrated how the proof of the correctness theorem for a function fn could be used to justify the transformation of some term p into another term q. It is not necessary to repeat the proof that such transformations are legal every time we make such a transformation. However, to take advantage of the metatheorem, we want our theorem-prover to obtain q from p efficiently. Specifically, we would like to obtain q from p with approximately the same speed that we could obtain q from p if we had hand-coded an INTERLISP function analogous to fn instead of introducing fn into our theory. There were three steps in computing q from p. The first step was finding the constant c corresponding to p. The second step was finding the constant d such that (EQUAL (fn c) d). And the final step was finding the term q to which d corresponded.

In our implementation of metafunctions we have arranged for the first and third steps to be exceedingly efficient: in fact, they literally take no time at all. The trick we use is to arrange our INTERLISP representation of terms so that if obj is an INTERLISP object representing a term t, then the INTERLISP list of length two whose first member is the atom QUOTE and whose second member is obj represents the constant corresponding to t.

Thus, if obj is an INTERLISP object we use to represent the term (PLUS X Y), then the INTERLISP object constructed by consing QUOTE onto obj onto NIL (in INTERLISP) is an object representing

(CONS "PLUS" (CONS "X" (CONS "Y" "NIL"))).

Thus, should we have a representation of p and desire to represent c, we embed the representation of p in a QUOTE. On the other side, should we have a representation of d and desire to obtain a representation of q, we take the cadr (i.e. car of the cdr) of the representation of d. It will turn out that we never actually have to represent c and d in going from p to q, but it is the term representation above that makes it possible. We will prove that if obj represents the term t then the result of embedding obj in a QUOTE represents a term whose MEANING under an appropriate assignment is t. The proof is complicated mainly by the limitations and restrictions imposed by efficiency considerations and INTERLISP (or any other real implementation language).

Now suppose we have the above representation of c. How can we obtain d quickly? Recall that d is the constant equal to (fn c). When a function is accepted under our definition principle our system compiles an INTERLISP routine whose body is analogous to the definition. For example, when the function APPEND is introduced with the definition:

Definition.

           (APPEND X Y)

           =

           (IF (LISTP X)
               (CONS (CAR X) (APPEND (CDR X) Y))
               Y).

the system generates and compiles the INTERLISP routine .APPEND.:

(.APPEND. (LAMBDA (X Y)
  (COND ((AND (LISTP X) (NEQ (CAR X) .SQM.))
    (CONS (CAR X) (.APPEND. (CDR X) Y)))
  (T Y)))).

The relationship between the mathematical function APPEND and the INTERLISP routine .APPEND. is then as follows. If obj_1 and obj_2 are INTERLISP objects that, when embedded in QUOTEs, represent the constants c_1 and c_2 in the theory, then the INTERLISP object computed by (.APPEND. obj_1 obj_2), when embedded in a QUOTE, represents a constant term d such that (EQUAL (APPEND c_1 c_2) d) is a theorem.

Thus, if fn has been accepted by the principle of definition the INTERLISP routine .fn. has also been introduced. Suppose that after we have proved the correctness theorem for fn we desire to use fn to transform p to q. Suppose objc represents p. Let objc' be the result of embedding objc in a QUOTE. Then objc' represents c. Let objd' be the result of embedding in a QUOTE the result of executing .fn. on the cadr of objc'. Then objd' represents d. Let objd be the cadr of objd'. Then objd represents q. By the metatheorem, p and q are provably equal, so we may substitute objd for objc in the representation of the conjecture being proved. But if x' is the result of embedding x in a QUOTE, the cadr of x' is x. Thus, the above scenario is equivalent to applying .fn. to objc (the representation of p) to obtain objd (the representation of q).

1.3. A useful metafunction

We have used metafunctions to improve the power of the theorem-prover described in "A Computational Logic". That theorem-prover was powerful enough to prove its way from the Peano-like axioms for the natural numbers and sequences to the existence and uniqueness of prime factorizations without any built-in arithmetic procedures or heuristics. However, it could not cancel an addend occurring arbitrarily deeply on both sides of an equation. The reason was that it was not possible to state any useful lemma describing a schematic transformation. After implementing metatheoretic extensibility as described, we used it to add schematic cancellation.

The metafunction CANCEL was defined so that when given the symbolic expression representing the equation:

(EQUAL (PLUS B (PLUS C (PLUS I X)))
  (PLUS (PLUS A (PLUS I J)) (PLUS K X)))

CANCEL produces the symbolic expression for

(EQUAL (PLUS B C)
(PLUS A (PLUS J K)))).

CANCEL works by computing the fringe of the two PLUS-trees on each side of the symbolic equation, intersecting the fringes with the "bag" intersect function, subtracting the bag of common addends from each fringe, and then reconstituting the modified fringes into right-associated PLUS-trees in a new symbolic equation. However, to be correct CANCEL must take into account the typeless syntax of our theory. Thus, when given

(EQUAL A (PLUS A B))

it returns

(IF (NUMBERP A)
(EQUAL 0 (FIX B))
(FALSE)).

Furthermore, it does not bother to construct this expression if one side of the equation is not an element of the fringe of the other because it would be a heuristic mistake.

CANCEL is fairly complicated. In all, its definition (together with those of its subfunctions) requires 100 lines of "prettyprinted" text. In this paper we carefully describe the cancellation function and the proof of its correctness. The proof is constructed by our theorem-prover from the axioms of Peano integers, atoms and ordered pairs, without any built-in knowledge of arithmetic. We also explain the INTERLISP code generated for the function and explain how it is integrated into our automatic theorem-prover. The incorporation of this new proof procedure, which was mathematically defined and mechanically proved correct, increases the power of the system without noticeably affecting its speed.

1.4. Related research

We now compare our approach to extensibility with recent work by others on the same subject. The basic premise of all work on extensible theorem-provers is that it should be possible to add new proof techniques to a system without endangering the soundness of the system. It seems possible to divide current work into two broad camps. In the first camp are those systems that allow the introduction of arbitrary new procedures, coded in the implementation language, but require that each application of such a procedure produce a formal proof of the correctness of the transformation performed. In the second camp are those systems that contain a formal notion of what it means for a proof technique to be sound and require a machine-checked proof of the soundness of each new proof technique. Once proved, the new proof technique can be used without further justification. Our system is in the second camp.

The LCF system, described by Milner *et al.* [5], is an example of a system in the first camp. The LCF metalanguage is a programming language that provides the data type "theorem". "Theorems" can be produced only by the basic rules of inference, which are implemented as procedures. The user can define new rules of inference as procedures that produce theorems by calling lower-level procedures under the control of arbitrary heuristics. The new rules of inference are sound (when they do not cause run-time errors) since the result produced by any given application must in fact have been produced by a correct sequence of applications of the lowest-level rules of inference.

Brown [3], proposes another system in the first camp. He suggests that each new proof procedure be coded in some conventional implementation language (e.g. LISP or machine code) but have an auxiliary procedure capable of producing a formal justification of any given application. To illustrate the idea, he exhibits a LISP program to find and cancel a single common addend on each side of an equation. As one example justification he suggests the proof procedure that derives the output from the input using only the associative, commutative and cancellation laws for PLUS*.

In essence systems from the first camp are extensible because they provide a facility whereby the user can define succinct abbreviations that may be mechanically translated into long sequences of proof steps. The advantage such systems have over those of the second camp is that new proof procedures can be used without having to prove them correct. The primary disadvantage we see is one of efficiency: no matter how elaborate one's new rules of inference are, the system must plod through proofs at the lowest level.

Weyhrauch's work on FOL [7] exemplifies the second camp. He has implemented in FOL a system in which the formulas of one theory are the objects in another. In the upper theory he formalizes the syntax and rules of inference of the lower theory. To prove that a function in the upper theory is a sound simplifier for the lower theory one must prove in the upper theory that there exists a proof in the lower theory of the equality of the input and output. To apply such a metafunction to a formula during a proof at the lower level, Weyhrauch "reflects" the formula into a constant at the upper level, symbolically applies the metafunction to that constant, and then reflects the result back down. To make the process more efficient, Weyhrauch

---

* As a second justification Brown uses a meaning function, virtually identical to ours and described earlier by Brown [2], to express the schematic cancellation law. However, he does not express the law in a way that permits its mechanical application. In fact, he says that all of his mathematical justification procedures are sufficiently inefficient that they should be run to obtain a formal proof only when a step of the informal proof is "challenged".

provides the perilous act of "semantic attachment" by which the user can associate programming entities (data structures and procedures) with logical entities (formulas and functions). Of course, perilous acts, while perfectly legitimate in the hands of a careful implementor, are to be considered illegal in the hands of careless users. Using semantic attachment, Weyhrauch arranges for the programming objects that represent formulas at one level to represent objects at the other. He can also arrange for certain built-in meta-functions (namely, those corresponding to the proof procedures in his system) to be executed very efficiently (as calls to the appropriate procedures).

Another example of the second camp was proposed by Davis and Schwartz [4]. Like Weyhrauch they propose to embed formally the rules of inference of their logic in the logic. Unlike Weyhrauch they do not introduce a new "metatheory" but rather embed the rules of inference in a decidable sub-theory. Like us, they then provide a MEANING-like function to map from formulas in the logic to constants. They propose to prove the correctness of "metafunctions" by proving that there exists a constant that is a "proof" of the equivalence of the input and output of the function.

Of course, while the second camp has only in the last few years begun to attract the attention of researchers in automatic theorem-proving, Gödel lit the campfire in 1931 when he showed that one can define functions that are proof-checkers for the theory containing them.

We can thus summarize the relationship between our work and that of others as follows. Our work is different from that of Milner *et al.* [5] and Brown [3] primarily because we are in the second camp. Our theoretical approach is different from Weyhrauch's [7] and Davis and Schwartz's [4] because we avoid the complexity of embedding the rules of inference of our logic in our logic and (unlike Weyhrauch) do not have to formalize the notion that one theory is the metatheory of another.* Our implementation is different from any reported implementation of metatheoretic extensibility because we show how the user can achieve efficiency comparable to hand-coded pro-cedures in the implementation language without availing himself of perilous acts.

1.5. The key problem: theorem-proving

Once the theoretical justification and practical implementation of meta-theoretic extensibility is completed, the researcher must confront the funda-mental problem for those in the second camp: proving the correctness of new

---

* In defense of Weyhrauch's logical machinery it must be observed that his goal is the study of formal theories of reasoning—in which metatheoretic reasoning plays a crucial role—while ours is the much less ambitious one of getting permission to apply user-supplied proof procedures.

metafunctions with a mechanical theorem-prover. If it is not practical to prove the correctness of new procedures with the tools provided, then—depending on whether users can add new axioms—the extensibility is either unusable or unsafe because users will add axioms stating the correctness of new procedures. The latter is little better than the ad hoc approach of alternative (1), i.e. the arbitrary hand-recoding of the theorem-prover.

We did not begin to consider seriously the incorporation of metafunctions until we had some evidence that our system could prove the correctness of metafunctions that would actually improve the system. The evidence came in September, 1978, when we had the system prove that CANCEL preserved MEANING (even though at that time the system could not employ that result metatheoretically).

The proof of the correctness theorem for the cancellation function did provide an interesting exercise for our theorem-prover. However, the number and difficulty of the intermediate lemmas that we formulated and the theorem-prover proved on the way to the main correctness theorem were less than the number and difficulty of the lemmas used in our proof of the correctness of a tautology-checker in Chapter IV of "A Computational Logic". To formulate the lemmas and get the theorem-prover to prove the correctness theorem took one of the authors less than a day from the time the exercise was conceived. The earliest proof attempt found a bug in CANCEL: it cancelled multiple occurrences of an addend on one side against one occurrence on the other, due to the use of "list difference" rather than "bag difference". Because of the small amount of user effort necessary to introduce a correct cancellation procedure we are optimistic that our approach to extensibility may be feasible.

However, we conclude with three observations:

(1) No implementation of metatheoretic extensibility will be feasible unless the mechanical theorem-prover can prove theorems about inductively defined concepts such as terms, formulas, and their meanings.

(2) It is interesting to ask whether a sound and practical approach to metatheoretic extensibility can be based on a simpler theorem-prover than ours. We suspect that it might take weeks to prove the correctness of a useful metafunction, such as our cancellation function, if one used a simple proof-checker.

(3) Some theorem-prover researchers who, like us, are in the business of building theorem-provers to be used by a large community of users, may regard the provision for user extensibility (via either camp) to be an adequate response to the constant appeals from users to improve the power of the system. After all, extensibility gives the user the ability to tailor the system to his needs. But we do not see extensibility as a panacea for the current lack of theorem-proving power. It is a solution to a relatively simple problem: how to obtain insurance against unsoundness. The truly hard intellectual problem

remains: the discovery of harmoniously cooperating heuristics for marshalling a very large number of facts and constructing difficult proofs.

1.6. Organization of this paper

The structure of our presentation is as follows. In Section 2 we illustrate the introduction and use of a metafunction after briefly reviewing our formal logic as it was presented in [1]. In Section 3 we describe certain minor revisions made to the logic described in [1] to undertake the meta-approach conveniently, and we present some formal nomeclature used in the proof of the Metatheorem. In Section 4 we state and prove the Metatheorem, which establishes that metafunctions can be applied. In Section 5 we outline our INTERLISP implementation of metafunctions in our theorem-proving program. In Section 6 we describe the representation of terms in our theorem-proving program and in Section 7 we prove some lemmas used in the demonstration that we have correctly implemented the Metatheorem. In Section 8 we explain how we translate user-defined functions into efficient INTERLISP procedures. In Section 9 we describe the mechanical proof of the correctness of the example metafunction described in Section 2 and we comment on the difficulty of such proofs. In Section 10 we describe details of the implementation of metafunctions and give some output generated by our theorem-prover while using a metafunction.

2. AN EXAMPLE

In this section we illustrate the use of metafunctions by writing in our logic a recursive function for cancelling all common addends on opposite sides of an equation. Our example is similar to but more elaborate than the one used by Brown [3].

2.1. A sketch of our formal theory*

A *term* is either a variable symbol (which we define precisely in Section 3), or else it is a sequence consisting of a function symbol of n arguments, followed by n terms. We use the prefix syntax of Church to write down terms. For example, if PLUS is a function symbol of two arguments, we write (PLUS X Y) where others might write PLUS (X, Y) or X + Y.

Our theory is obtained by starting with the axioms and rules of inference of propositional calculus with equality and function symbols (including the rule of inference that any instance of a theorem is a theorem) and adding (a)

---

* Our formal theory is described in detail in Chapter III of "A Computational Logic".

axioms for certain basic function symbols, (b) a rule of inference permitting proof by induction, (c) a principle of definition permitting the introduction of total recursive functions, and (d) the "shell principle", permitting the introduction of axioms specifying "new" types of inductively defined objects.

The basic function symbols are TRUE, FALSE, IF and EQUAL. The first two are function symbols of no arguments and may be thought of as distinct truth values. IF is a function symbol of three arguments and is axiomatized so that (IF X Y Z) = Z if X = (FALSE) and (IF X Y Z) = Y if X $\neq$ (FALSE). EQUAL is a function symbol of two arguments and axiomatized so that if X = Y, (EQUAL X Y) = (TRUE), and if X $\neq$ Y, (EQUAL X Y) = (FALSE). (The "=" sign used here is the usual equality predicate.)

In our logic, terms also play a role similar to the one that formulas play in predicate calculus. For example, by an abuse of the word "theorem" (which is usually only applied to formulas), when we say (EQUAL X X) is a theorem we mean (EQUAL X X) $\neq$ (FALSE) is a theorem. Using IF we define the function NOT, of one argument, that returns (TRUE) if its argument is (FALSE) and returns (FALSE) otherwise. We similarly define the dyadic functions AND, OR and IMPLIES.

Our principle of induction is based on the notion of well-founded relations (i.e. relations for which there exists no infinite sequence of successively smaller objects). Suppose r is a well-founded relation and that the measure m of (d X) is r-smaller than m of X when X has property q. Then the induction principle permits one to prove (p X Y) by proving two other conjectures. The first, called the "base case", is that (p X Y) is true when X does not have property q. The second, called the "induction step", is that (p X Y) is true when X has property q and (p (d X) a) is true.

Our principle of definition provides the ability to introduce new recursive function definitions, provided certain theorems can be proved beforehand. The theorems require the exhibition of a measure and well-founded relation under which the arguments of recursive calls are getting smaller. Such theorems, together with some trivial syntactic requirements, are sufficient to guarantee the existence and uniqueness of a function satisfying the defining equation.

Finally, the "shell principle" provides a means for introducing "new" types of inductively defined objects that may be thought of as typed n-tuples with type restrictions on the components. The shell principle allows the user of the theorem-prover to characterize the desired objects by specifying n, the type restrictions, and (new) names for the primitive functions on the new type. Provided certain trivial syntactic requirements are met, the shell principle adds to the theory a set of axioms describing the new type. Using the shell principle we introduce three sets of objects into the initial version of the theory. These initial shells are:

The Peano integers, with recognizer NUMBERP, bottom object (ZERO), constructor ADD1 of one argument which must be a NUMBERP or else defaults to (ZERO), accessor SUB1 and well-founded relation SUB1P.

The "literal atoms," with recognizer LITATOM, bottom object (NIL), constructor function PACK of one argument of arbitrary type, accessor UNPACK (which returns (ZERO) on non-LITATOMs), and well-founded relation UNPACKP.

The "ordered pairs" or "lists," with recognizer LISTP, no bottom object, constructor function CONS of two arguments of arbitrary type, accessors CAR and CDR (which default to (NIL) on non-LISTPs) and well-founded relation CAR/CDRP.

The "recognizer" function is axiomatized to return (TRUE) or (FALSE) according to whether its argument is a member of the new type. The optional "bottom object" function of no arguments represents an "empty" object of the new type. The "constructor" function takes n arguments and has as its value an n-tuple of the new type. If the ith argument position has a "type restriction" that is not satisfied by the ith argument, the argument is "coerced" into the right type by being replaced by a "default value". The "type restriction" either requires that the argument be of one of a finite number of types or requires that the argument not be of one of a finite number of types. The ith "accessor" function is axiomatized so that when applied to an n-tuple of the new type it returns the ith component. When applied to an object other than a tuple of the new type, the ith accessor returns the ith default value. Finally, the "well-founded relation" is axiomatized so that the components of an n-tuple are smaller than the tuple.

We complete the initial development of the theory by introducing the well-founded relation and the measure function that are most commonly used in our theory: the "less than" relation on the Peano integers and the "size" of a shell object. The "less than" relation is introduced as the recursively defined function LESSP, which returns (TRUE) if its first argument is less than its second, and (FALSE) otherwise. LESSP treats any nonnumeric argument as though it were (ZERO).

The "size" of an object is computed by the function COUNT, which is defined to be (ZERO) on bottom objects and nonshells and one plus the sum of the sizes of the components on n-tuples.

The function PLUS is defined to compute the sum of its two arguments. Our theory does not provide a "typed" syntax. Thus terms such as (PLUS (TRUE) (TRUE)) are well formed. Our definition of PLUS "coerces" non-integers to (ZERO). In particular, we define PLUS with the equation:

Definition.

$$(PLUS\ X\ Y)$$
$$=$$
$$(IF\ (ZEROP\ X)$$
$$(FIX\ Y)$$
$$(ADD1\ (PLUS\ (SUB1\ X)\ Y))),$$

where (ZEROP X) is defined to be (TRUE) when X is (ZERO) or not a number, and (FALSE) when X is a non-(ZERO) number; (FIX Y) is defined to be Y if Y is a number and (ZERO) otherwise.

That completes our brief sketch of the theory.

2.2. Abbreviations

It is convenient to be able to write down certain terms succinctly. In [1] we introduce certain abbreviations, such as using (AND P Q R) as an abbreviation of (AND P (AND Q R)), using 3 as an abbreviation of (ADD1 (ADD1 (ADD1 (ZERO)))), and using (CADDR X) as an abbreviation of (CAR (CDR (CDR X))).

In this paper we modify one of our conventions and introduce two new ones.

We modify the convention in [1] under which expressions such as "X" and "PLUS" were abbreviations for certain LITATOM constants. We continue to use quotation marks to abbreviate LITATOMs, but we change the encoding. That is, we here adopt a new convention under which "X" is an abbreviation for a LITATOM, but for a different LITATOM than specified in [1]. Our new encoding (which makes it easier to implement metafunctions efficiently) is as follows. Suppose wrd is a sequence of ASCII characters $c_1, \ldots, c_n$ satisfying the definition of a "symbol" (see Section 3). Suppose the ASCII character codes for $c_1, \ldots, c_n$ are the integers $i_1, \ldots, i_n$. Then "wrd" is an abbreviation of

$$(PACK\ (CONS\ i_1\ (CONS\ i_2 \ldots (CONS\ i_n\ 0) \ldots))).$$

Thus, "NIL" is an abbreviation of

$$(PACK\ (CONS\ 78\ (CONS\ 73\ (CONS\ 76\ 0)))),$$

and "QUOTE" is an abbreviation of

$$(PACK\ (CONS\ 81\ (CONS\ 85\ (CONS\ 79\ (CONS\ 84\ (CONS\ 69\ 0)))))).$$

One of the axioms for the PACK shell is that (EQUAL (PACK X) (PACK Y)) is true if and only if (EQUAL X Y) is true. Thus, "NIL" is not "QUOTE" because, using the similar axioms about the CONS and ADD1 shells, (CONS

78 ...) is not equal to (CONS 81 ...). In general, two abbreviated literal atoms are EQUAL if and only if the abbreviations are identical.

We introduce the following two new abbreviation conventions.

First, following LISP, we use (LIST t_1 ... t_n) as an abbreviation of

$$\text{(CONS } t_1 \text{ (CONS } t_2 \text{ ... (CONS } t_n \text{ ``NIL''))).}$$

Thus (LIST A B C), is an abbreviation of (CONS A (CONS B (CONS C "NIL"))).

Second, in Section 3 we will introduce a shell representing the negative integers and we shall there adopt a convention for abbreviating negative constants.

2.3. A hypothetical problem

We will now describe a realistic scenario in which the user of an automatic theorem-prover is confronted with the inadequacy of the system and is forced to consider the various alternative means of overcoming the problem.

Suppose we have a mechanical theorem-prover for the logic just described and that the theorem-prover can use equations as rewrite rules. Further suppose that we had instructed our theorem-prover to prove and then use the following equation as a rewrite rule:

$$\text{(EQUAL (EQUAL (PLUS X Y) (PLUS X Z))}$$
$$\text{(EQUAL (FIX Y) (FIX Z))).}$$

This theorem is the cancellation law for addition. Roughly speaking, it says that if X is an addend on both sides of an equation it can be "cancelled". FIX is used because PLUS coerces its arguments to integers.

Applying this lemma as a rewrite rule from left to right allows the system to rewrite the equation:

$$\text{(EQUAL (PLUS I (PLUS X Y))}$$
$$\text{(PLUS I (PLUS J K)))}$$

to the equation

$$\text{(EQUAL (PLUS X Y)}$$
$$\text{(PLUS J K))}$$

(since (FIX (PLUS x y)) reduces to (PLUS x y) because PLUS is always numeric). So, apparently, our rewrite-driven system now "knows" how to cancel common addends.

But consider the following equation:

$$\text{(EQUAL (PLUS (PLUS A I) (PLUS B K))}$$
$$\text{(PLUS J (PLUS K (PLUS I X)))).}$$

The cancellation law cannot be applied here, because the law requires that the common addend be the first argument of the outermost PLUS-expression. Here we want to cancel the second and fourth addends on one side against the third and second on the other.

How might the user of our system respond to this failure of the system to carry out such a step in the proof? We consider the three alternatives sketched in the introduction and then the meta-approach.*

2.4. An example of alternative 1

Alternative (1) is to recode the theorem-prover. One suitable modification would be to build in an associative-commutative unification routine that "knows" PLUS is such a function and thus allows the cancellation law, in the form in which it was stated, to apply. A more direct solution would be to write a special-purpose routine for cancellation of PLUS. Roughly speaking, the code for such a modification would be as follows. If the expression in question is of the form (EQUAL t_1 t_2), regard t_1 and t_2 as trees of addends and compute their fringes. The intersection of the two fringes is the list of common addends. The result of cancelling all common addends is then obtained by removing each common addend from each fringe, reconstituting two PLUS expressions from the altered fringes and constructing the equation of those two expressions.

Such a program would correctly transform:

$$\text{(EQUAL (PLUS (PLUS A I) (PLUS B K))}$$
$$\text{(PLUS J (PLUS K (PLUS I X))))}$$

to

$$\text{(EQUAL (PLUS A B)}$$
$$\text{(PLUS J X)).}$$

However, one must be careful. For example if the intersect and delete operations do not respect duplications, one is liable to incorrectly simplify:

$$\text{(EQUAL (PLUS A (PLUS A (PLUS B C)))}$$
$$\text{(PLUS A (PLUS X Y)))}$$

to

---

* Lest the reader think that a mechanical theorem-prover without built-in cancellation is a straw man designed to show off the use of metafunctions, it should be observed that our theorem-prover, as described in [1], has no built-in arithmetic of any sort and yet can prove its way from the Peano axioms through the prime factorization theorem. Nevertheless, the addition of a cancellation mechanism improves the power and performance of the system.

$$\text{(EQUAL (PLUS B C)}$$
$$\text{(PLUS X Y)),}$$

cancelling two occurrences of A on the left against only one on the right. In addition, one must remember that PLUS coerces its arguments. For example, the simplification of:

$$\text{(EQUAL (PLUS A B) (PLUS A (PLUS C D)))}$$

to

$$\text{(EQUAL B (PLUS C D))}$$

is invalid, because the former might be true for a nonnumeric B while the latter would be false.

Thus, the implementor of the theorem-prover must consider these issues carefully before modifying the system. A less expert user of the system should not be allowed to make such a change.

2.5. An example of alternative 2

Alternative (2) is to carry out the cancellation by directing a proof-checker-like facility. This assumes the system has been well enough engineered to allow the user to intervene at this step in the proof without disabling all the desirable aspects of the automatic theorem-prover. But suppose we can so intervene. Recall the equation we wish to simplify

$$\text{(EQUAL (PLUS (PLUS A I) (PLUS B K))}$$
$$\text{(PLUS J (PLUS K (PLUS I X)))).}$$

To describe the proof steps we must refer to individual PLUS-expressions in the formula. We number the PLUS-expressions consecutively from 1 to 6, in the left-to-right order in which they appear. Each time we change the equation, we renumber the PLUS terms with the same algorithm. Here is one of many possible sequences for simplifying the formula above, assuming we have proved that PLUS is associative and commutative:

Commute 2
Reassociate 1
Commute 5
Reassociate 5
Commute 4
Reassociate 4
Cancel
Commute 2
Commute 1

Reassociate 1
Commute 4
Reassociate 3
Cancel

The result is

(EQUAL (PLUS B A)
(PLUS X J)).

This alternative does not solve the general problem of enabling the automatic theorem-prover to carry out arbitrary cancellations. Consequently, the user of the system must still be prepared to intervene when opportunities for cancellation arise in the future.

To solve the general problem with this technique we would have to write a program that detects the presence of common addends and generates a sequence of proof steps for cancelling them. This is just the approach of the first "camp" described in Section 1. The program could use the fringe-intersection technique described above to identify the common addends. Then, for each common addend, t, the program could generate a sequence of commute and associate instructions intended to move t into the first argument of the outermost PLUS on each side, and then generate a cancel instruction. Finally, the entire sequence of instructions would be given to the proof-checker and actually carried out. Of course, we do not have to worry about a mistake in our program rendering our theorem-prover unsound, but the process of generating the proof steps and then carrying them out is far more tedious than the ad hoc approach of the first alternative.

2.6. An example of alternative 3

Alternative (3) is to prove sufficient lemmas to let the theorem-prover carry out the necessary proof steps. In this case, it is sufficient to prove the ugly lemma:

(EQUAL (EQUAL (PLUS (PLUS A I) (PLUS B K))
(PLUS J (PLUS K (PLUS I X))))
(EQUAL (PLUS A B)
(PLUS J X))).

This lemma is merely an ugly version of the PLUS-cancellation law.

Once again we see that the solution to the specific problem does not solve the general one of enabling the rewrite rules to carry out an arbitrary cancellation. For example, each of the equations below requires different versions of the cancellation law.

(EQUAL (PLUS X Y)
       (PLUS X Z))

(EQUAL (PLUS A1 (PLUS X Y))
       (PLUS B1 (PLUS X Z))

(EQUAL (PLUS A1 (PLUS A2 (PLUS X Y)))
       (PLUS B1 (PLUS B2 (PLUS X Z))))

...,

not to mention the "skewed" versions such as:

(EQUAL (PLUS A1 (PLUS A2 (PLUS X Y)))
       (PLUS X Z))

(EQUAL (PLUS A1 (PLUS A2 (PLUS X Y)))
       (PLUS B1 (PLUS X Z)))

....

It should be clear that no finite set of such rewrite rules will suffice to carry all cancellations (unless we opt for alternative (1) and first build in some facts about the equivalence classes of PLUS expressions under associativity and commutativity).

2.7. The meta-approach

So much for the conventional alternatives. The meta-approach proposed in this paper is to encode the cancellation algorithm as a function in the logic itself and to prove it correct. We first describe how we represent symbolic expressions as objects in our theory, then we derive a definition of the cancellation function, and the statement of its correctness. Finally, we show how the statement of correctness, once proved, enables us to perform arbitrary cancellations from within the theory.

(a) Symbolic expressions

Since we want to write recursive functions on symbolic expressions we have to represent such expressions in terms of the objects of our theory, e.g. LITATOMs and LISTPs. Our symbolic expressions will be either variable symbols or the applications of function symbols to argument expressions. We represent function and variable symbols by LITATOMs. We represent the application of a function symbol to some arguments by the LISTP object whose CAR is the function symbol and whose CDR is a list of the appropriate number of argument expressions. Thus, the LITATOM (PACK (CONS 65 0)), abbreviated as "A", is a symbolic expression that can be thought of as representing a variable symbol. The LISTP object

(CONS "PLUS" (CONS "A" (CONS "I" "NIL")))

which may be abbreviated as

(LIST "PLUS" "A" "I")

is a symbolic expression representing the application of the function symbol "PLUS" to two variable expressions, "A" and "I".

Intuitively, the symbolic expression above corresponds to (PLUS A I), the application of the function PLUS to two arguments. Eventually we will formally assign meanings to symbolic expressions, making clear the connection between the LITATOM "PLUS" and the function PLUS. But at the moment, the reader is advised to ignore that aspect of the problem, forget that we are in a mathematical logic, and just pretend we are writing a program to manipulate such expressions according to the intuitive notion of their semantics.

(b) The cancellation algorithm

We want a function, which we will call CANCEL, that when applied to a symbolic expression representing an equation such as

(EQUAL (PLUS (PLUS A I) (PLUS B K))
(PLUS J (PLUS K (PLUS I X))))

yields the symbolic expression representing the cancelled equation,

(EQUAL (PLUS A B)
(PLUS J X)).

Here is how our function works. We first ask whether the expression is an equality with PLUS-expressions in both arguments. If so, we compute the fringe of the two PLUS-trees and intersect them (with a "bag intersection" function which respects duplications) to obtain a list of common addends. We subtract the common addends from each fringe (with "bag difference" which also respects duplications). Finally, we construct two new PLUS-trees from the two resulting bags of addends and embed them in an EQUAL expression.

We thus need functions for recognizing symbolic equations and PLUS-expressions, a function for computing the fringe of a tree of PLUS-expressions, the bag intersection and difference functions, and the function for constructing a tree of PLUS-expressions given the list of addends.

The function PLUS.TREE?, defined below, returns (TRUE) or (FALSE)

according to whether its argument is a symbolic expression representing the application of the function symbol "PLUS":

Definition.

$$(\text{PLUS.TREE? } X)$$
$$=$$
$$(\text{AND (LISTP } X)$$
$$(\text{EQUAL (CAR } X) \text{ "PLUS"})).$$

If (PLUS.TREE? X) is (TRUE) we call X a "PLUS-tree". We could have defined PLUS.TREE? to check that (CDR X) is a list of two elements, but we will always be able to derive that if X is known to be well-formed. If X is a PLUS-tree then (CADR X) is the first argument expression and (CADDR X) is the second. The function EQUALITY? is similarly defined but recognizes symbolic equations.

We define the "fringe" of an expression with the function FRINGE. If its argument is a PLUS-tree, FRINGE recursively determines the fringe of the two arguments and concatenates them using the function APPEND. If its argument is not a PLUS-tree, FRINGE returns the singleton list containing that argument.

Definition.

$$(\text{FRINGE } X)$$
$$=$$
$$(\text{IF (PLUS.TREE? } X)$$
$$(\text{APPEND (FRINGE (CADR } X))$$
$$(\text{FRINGE (CADDR } X)))$$
$$(\text{CONS } X \text{ "NIL"})).$$

Before the equation above is admitted into the theory, the definitional principle requires the exhibition of a measure under which the argument is getting smaller according to some well-founded relation. The measure COUNT and relation LESSP are sufficient—in particular both (CADR X) and (CADDR X) have smaller COUNT than X when X is a LISTP even if X is not a well-formed PLUS-expression. Thus, the equation above is satisfied by one and only one function (as proved in [1]).

If X is

$$(\text{LIST "PLUS"}$$
$$(\text{LIST "PLUS" "A" "I"})$$
$$(\text{LIST "PLUS" "B" "K"}))$$

then (FRINGE X) is

$$(\text{LIST "A" "I" "B" "K"}).$$

To operate on fringes we need the bag intersection and difference functions. Since the definitions are similar, we consider only the bag intersection function. The usual *list* intersection function asks of each element, e, in its first argument whether e is in the second. If so, e is put into the answer list, and if not, e is not put into the answer list. If e occurs m times in the first argument and at least once in the second, it is put into the answer m times. This will not do for our purposes, since it would lead us to believe we could cancel m occurrences of e. We must pay special attention to duplications. In particular, if e occurs in the first argument m times and in the second n times, then it must occur in the answer min (m, n) times. This can be arranged by deleting an occurrence of e from the second argument as soon as it has been used against an occurrence in the first argument. Here is the definition of the bag intersection function:

Definition.
      (BAGINT X Y)
      =
      (IF (LISTP X)
         (IF (MEMBER (CAR X) Y)
           (CONS (CAR X)
              (BAGINT (CDR X)
                   (DELETE (CAR X) Y)))
           (BAGINT (CDR X) Y))
         "NIL").

For example,
      (BAGINT (LIST "B" "C" "C" "D" "D")
            (LIST "A" "C" "C" "D" "E" "F"))

is equal to (LIST "C" "C" "D").* The bag difference function, BAGDIFF, is similarly defined.

Finally, we must define the function PLUS.TREE that converts a list of addends into a tree of PLUS-expressions. Recall that PLUS.TREE is used to "reconstitute" a PLUS-expression from its fringe minus any common addends. There are several special cases. If the new fringe is empty, it means all the elements of the old fringe were cancelled. Thus, PLUS.TREE should return the term representing 0. If the new fringe contains only one addend, x,

---

* The reader may be uncomfortable with the claim that BAGINT is the bag intersection function. How do we know we have thought of all the cases? The fact is that it does not matter. Since our functions are introduced under the principle of definition we are certain they *are* functions. Our bag intersection function might not be the same function the reader is thinking of, but it does exist and is uniquely defined. The proof of the correctness of CANCEL will establish that it has the necessary properties.

then PLUS.TREE should return a symbolic term that "coerces" x to a number since that is what the original PLUS expression would have done. A suitable expression is (FIX x). Otherwise, PLUS.TREE builds a right-associated PLUS-tree from the list.

Definition.

```
(PLUS.TREE L)
=
(IF (NOT (LISTP L))
    (LIST "ZERO")
    (IF (NOT (LISTP (CDR L)))
        (LIST "FIX" (CAR L))
        (IF (NOT (LISTP (CDDR L)))
            (LIST "PLUS" (CAR L) (CADR L))
            (LIST "PLUS"
                  (CAR L)
                  (PLUS.TREE (CDR L)))))))).
```

For example, when PLUS.TREE is given the list containing the symbolic expressions for the variables A, B and C, it returns the symbolic expression for

(PLUS A (PLUS B C)),

that is, (PLUS.TREE (LIST "A" "B" "C")) is

```
(LIST "PLUS"
      "A"
      (LIST "PLUS" "B" "C")).
```

We are now prepared to write a preliminary definition of CANCEL:

Definition.

```
(CANCEL X)
=
(IF (AND (EQUALITY? X)
         (PLUS.TREE? (CADR X))
         (PLUS.TREE? (CADDR X)))
    (LIST "EQUAL"
          (PLUS.TREE
            (BAGDIFF (FRINGE (CADR X))
                     (BAGINT (FRINGE (CADR X))
                             (FRINGE (CADDR X)))))
          (PLUS.TREE
            (BAGDIFF (FRINGE (CADDR X))
```

$$
\text{(BAGINT (FRINGE (CADR X))}
$$
$$
\text{(FRINGE (CADDR X))))))}
$$
X).

But this definition of CANCEL does not handle the cancellation suggested by (EQUAL (PLUS A (PLUS B C)) A) because the second argument to the EQUAL is not a PLUS-tree. This situation will be handled specially. It is incorrect to follow the paradigm above and produce (EQUAL (PLUS B C) 0), because if A is nonnumeric, the former equation is (FALSE) while the latter might be (TRUE). A correct way to cancel (EQUAL (PLUS A (PLUS B C)) A) is to produce:

```
(IF (NUMBERP A)
    (EQUAL (PLUS B C) 0)
    (FALSE)).
```

We therefore add two more cases to the definition of CANCEL, one to handle the possibility that the second argument to the equation is not a PLUS-tree but is a member of the fringe of the first, and the other to handle the symmetric case.

Here is the final definition of CANCEL.

Definition.
```
(CANCEL X)
   =
(IF (AND (EQUALITY? X)
         (PLUS.TREE? (CADR X))
         (PLUS.TREE? (CADDR X)))
    (LIST "EQUAL"
        (PLUS.TREE
          (BAGDIFF (FRINGE (CADR X))
                   (BAGINT (FRINGE (CADR X))
                           (FRINGE (CADDR X)))))
        (PLUS.TREE
          (BAGDIFF (FRINGE (CADDR X))
                   (BAGINT (FRINGE (CADR X))
                           (FRINGE (CADDR X))))))
    (IF (AND (EQUALITY? X)
             (PLUS.TREE? (CADR X))
             (MEMBER (CADDR X) (FRINGE (CADR X))))
        (LIST "IF"
            (LIST "NUMBERP"
                (CADDR X))
            (LIST "EQUAL"
```

```
                              (PLUS.TREE
                               (DELETE (CADDR X)
                                       (FRINGE (CADR X))))
                              (LIST "ZERO"))
                     (LIST "FALSE"))
         (IF (AND (EQUALITY? X)
                  (PLUS.TREE? (CADDR X))
                  (MEMBER (CADR X)
                          (FRINGE (CADDR))))
             (LIST "IF"
                   (LIST "NUMBERP"
                         (CADR X))
                   (LIST "EQUAL"
                         (LIST "ZERO")
                         (PLUS.TREE
                          (DELETE (CADR X)
                                  (FRINGE (CADDR X)))))
                   (LIST "FALSE"))
             X)))
```

The table below illustrates CANCEL's input-output behavior. If c is a symbolic expression corresponding to the equation in some row of the "input" column, then the equation corresponding to (CANCEL c) is given in the same row of the "output" column.

Input	Output
(EQUAL (PLUS (PLUS A I) (PLUS B K)) (PLUS J (PLUS I (PLUS K X))))	(EQUAL (PLUS A B) (PLUS J X))
(EQUAL (PLUS A X) (PLUS A (PLUS B X)))	(EQUAL (ZERO) (FIX B))
(EQUAL A (PLUS A B))	(IF (NUMBERP A) (EQUAL (ZERO) (FIX B)) (FALSE))

The reader may be discouraged by the complicated nature of the cancellation algorithm. However, the algorithm is no more complicated than the logic requires and raises the very issues we would have to face were we to build a general-purpose cancellation algorithm into the theorem-prover by any of the alternatives sketched. Furthermore, in stark contrast to alternative 1, we will here have our fears of lurking bugs eradicated by the system's proof of the correctness of the algorithm.

(c) Correctness of CANCEL

What does it mean to say that CANCEL is correct? Intuitively, we would like to require that the output equation have the same truth value under all assignments as the input equation. To express this exactly, we introduce the notion of the "value" or "meaning" of an expression under an assignment to the variables in it.

For example, the meaning of (LIST "PLUS" "A" "I") under a given assignment is the sum of the meanings of "A" and "I" under the assignment. Suppose the only function symbols in which we were interested were FALSE, ZERO, FIX, NUMBERP, PLUS, TIMES, EQUAL and IF. Then we can define the function MEANING of two arguments, an expression and a list of pairs associating variables (in the CAR of each pair) with values (in the CDR). Given an atomic symbol, MEANING looks up and returns its value under the list of pairs using the function LOOKUP.*

Given an expression representing the application of one of the function symbols above, MEANING returns the result of applying the corresponding function to the recursively obtained MEANINGs of the arguments. Given any other object, MEANING returns the arbitrarily chosen value (TRUE).

Definition.

    (MEANING X A)

    =

    (IF (NOT (LISTP X))
    (LOOKUP X A)

    (IF (EQUAL (CAR X) "FALSE")
    (FALSE)

    (IF (EQUAL (CAR X) "ZERO")
    (ZERO)

    (IF (EQUAL (CAR X) "FIX")
    (FIX (MEANING (CADR X) A))

    (IF (EQUAL (CAR X) "NUMBERP")
    (NUMBERP (MEANING (CADR X) A))

    (IF (EQUAL (CAR X) "PLUS")
    (PLUS (MEANING (CADR X) A)
    (MEANING (CADDR X) A))

    (IF (EQUAL (CAR X) "TIMES")
    (TIMES (MEANING (CADR X) A)
    (MEANING (CADDR X) A))

---

* LOOKUP is defined in Section 3.

(IF (EQUAL (CAR X) "EQUAL")
    (EQUAL (MEANING (CADR X) A)
           (MEANING (CADDR X) A))
(IF (EQUAL (CAR X) "IF")
    (IF (MEANING (CADR X) A)
        (MEANING (CADDR X) A)
        (MEANING (CADDDR X) A))
    (TRUE)))))))))))

There is nothing magic or "meta" about this function.* The equation defines a unique function and is accepted under the principle of definition because in each recursive call the COUNT (i.e. size) of the first argument gets smaller according to the well-founded relation LESSP. We happen to use the function PLUS to compute the value of a form beginning with the LITATOM "PLUS", but this association between the two is only an artifact of our definition of MEANING.

The intuitive statement that CANCEL is correct is that under any assignment the MEANINGs of the input and output of CANCEL are identical.

Theorem. CANCEL.PRESERVES.MEANING
(EQUAL (MEANING X A)
       (MEANING (CANCEL X) A)).

This conjecture can be proved by our theorem-prover; the proof is discussed later in this paper. For the moment, suppose we have proved CANCEL.PRE-SERVES.MEANING.

(d) Using CANCEL to cancel

We now have a recursive function, CANCEL, that manipulates LISTP objects as though they were equations, and we can prove that the function is correct with respect to a particular definition of MEANING. But how can we use CANCEL to prove theorems?

Let us consider our example again. Suppose we are proving some conjecture and would like to cancel the common addends in the following equation, which we will call p:

(EQUAL (PLUS (PLUS A I) (PLUS B K))
       (PLUS J (PLUS I (PLUS K X)))).

---

* The prefix "meta" suggests something arcane, such as metaphysics. In fact, "meta" is Greek for "after". Metaphysics is so named not because it is subtly related to physics but because in the received order of Aristotle's works, the treatment of being, substance, cause, etc. comes *after* the treatises on physical matters.

That is, we would like to replace p by its cancelled form, which we will call q:

$$(EQUAL\ (PLUS\ A\ B)$$
$$(PLUS\ J\ X)).$$

How can we use CANCEL, which operates on symbolic expressions, to derive the equation q from p and how do we know that q and p are provably equal?

Let c stand for the following term

```
(CONS "EQUAL"
 (CONS (CONS "PLUS"
             (CONS (CONS "PLUS"
                         (CONS "A" (CONS "I" "NIL")))
                   (CONS (CONS "PLUS"
                               (CONS "B" (CONS "K" "NIL")))
                         "NIL")))
       (CONS (CONS "PLUS"
                   (CONS "J"
                         (CONS (CONS "PLUS"
                                     (CONS "I"
                                           (CONS (CONS "PLUS"
                                                       (CONS "K"
                                                             (CONS "X" "NIL")))
                                                 "NIL")))
                               "NIL")))
             "NIL"))),
```

which may be abbreviated as

```
(LIST "EQUAL"
      (LIST "PLUS"
            (LIST "PLUS" "A" "I")
            (LIST "PLUS" "B" "K"))
      (LIST "PLUS"
            "J"
            (LIST "PLUS"
                  "I"
                  (LIST "PLUS" "K" "X")))).
```

Let alist stand for the term:

```
(LIST (CONS "A" A) (CONS "I" I) (CONS "B" B)
      (CONS "K" K) (CONS "J" J) (CONS "X" X)).
```

Then it is straightforward to confirm that the MEANING of c under alist is in fact p, the formula we wish to simplify. That is, the following is a theorem that may be proved by tediously expanding the definition of MEANING:

*1   (EQUAL p (MEANING c alist)).

But by CANCEL.PRESERVES.MEANING we have the theorem:

*2   (EQUAL (MEANING c alist)
        (MEANING (CANCEL c) alist)).

By expanding the definition of CANCEL we see that (CANCEL c) is equal
to:

$$(\text{LIST ``EQUAL''}$$
$$(\text{LIST ``PLUS'' ``A'' ``B''})$$
$$(\text{LIST ``PLUS'' ``J'' ``X''})),$$

which we will call d. Thus, we have the theorem:

*3   (EQUAL (MEANING (CANCEL c) alist)
        (MEANING d alist)).

But, by expanding the definition of (MEANING d alist) we have

*4   (EQUAL (MEANING d alist)
        (EQUAL (PLUS A B) (PLUS J X))),

or, equivalently

        (EQUAL (MEANING d alist) q)

since the right-hand side of *4 is the equation we named q.

Thus, we can indeed use MEANING, CANCEL.PRESERVES.MEAN-
ING and CANCEL to derive q from p; furthermore, the chain of equalities
*1–*4 is a proof, within the theory, that p is equal to q, so we may replace
p by q.

The paradigm for using CANCEL as a formula simplifier is to "lift" the
formula to a symbolic expression with MEANING, "compute" CANCEL
on that symbolic expression, and then use MEANING again to "drop"
the symbolic expression back down to a formula. Of course, using the words
"lift" and "drop" suggests that we are "ascending" to and "descending"
from the metatheory, when in fact we are just translating the problem from
one form to another.

It should be clear that we can use MEANING and CANCEL in this way
to carry out an arbitrary cancellation, provided we can "lift" the formula
into symbolic form and "drop" the output of CANCEL.

However, were we to implement the mechanical application of "metafunctions" along the lines just described, the implementation would sink
into a swamp of PLUS-trees. Note for example that in lifting p we had to

create a very large term, c. How do we even know such a term exists? Can we obtain it without a lot of work? Can we be sure that its MEANING is equal to p without the tedious expansion of MEANING required to justify *1? How can we quickly simplify (CANCEL c) to some new symbolic expression? Once that expression is obtained, do we know we can drop it back down to a formula—that is, a formula not involving MEANING?

The remainder of this paper answers these and other questions. In particular, we carefully develop the logic behind the introduction and use of metafunctions, we describe an INTERLISP implementation that is very efficient, and we prove the correctness of our implementation.

3. FORMALITIES

Here we lay some groundwork for the proof of the Metatheorem.

3.1. Alterations to "A Computational Logic"

The basic logic for which we prove the Metatheorem is the one described in Chapter III of "A Computational Logic". To implement our approach to metafunctions, we found it desirable to make the following superficial changes to that logic.

(a) Syntax

Here we alter the syntax of our language by increasing the set of characters that can be used in symbols.

A *symbol* is a nonempty sequence of characters $c_1, \ldots, c_n$ such that (a) for each i greater than 0 and less than $n + 1$, c_i is one of the following printing ASCII characters:

A B C D E F G H I J K L M N O P Q R S T U V W X Y Z
a b c d e f g h i j k l m n o p q r s t u v w x y z
0 1 2 3 4 5 6 7 8 9
! ≠ $ & + , − . / : ; ⟨ = ⟩ ? @ \ ↑ _ ~

and (b) c_1 is not a digit, the plus sign, the minus sign, or period.

We assume that associated with each symbol is a nonnegative integer called the *arity* of the symbol.

Intuitively, the arity of a symbol is the number of arguments the symbol takes when used as a function symbol. For example, the arities of TRUE, NOT, PLUS and IF are, respectively 0, 1, 2 and 3. The arity of other symbols will become clear as time goes by.

A *term* is either a symbol or a finite sequence of length n + 1 whose first member is a symbol of arity n, and whose remaining members are terms.

Although we now formally permit lower case letters in our terms, in this document we adhere to our convention of using lower case words to denote "metavariables" standing for terms. When we say that a term p *has the form* q, we mean that p can be obtained by replacing the lower case symbols in q by symbols or terms. For example, (LESSP (D X) X) has the form (r (D x) x) since it may be obtained by replacing r by LESSP and x by X. (CONS A (CONS B "NIL")) has the form (CONS x y) and also the form (LIST a b), since (LIST a b) is an abbreviation for (CONS a (CONS b "NIL")). Finally (CONS A B), does not have the form (CONS X y).

When we enclose a lower case symbol in quotation marks it should be understood to denote the same thing denoted by enclosing in quotation marks the denotation of the symbol. For example, if wrd is understood to denote ABC, then "wrd" is understood to denote "ABC".

(b) Literal atoms

The shell definition for LITATOMs is modified: there is no bottom object.

We abandon the conventions in [1] specifying the interpretation of symbols in quotation marks (including the convention that "NIL" was an abbreviation of the (now absent) bottom object). We define our new abbreviation conventions below.

(c) Ordered pairs

The default values for the CONS shell are 0 and 0 (instead of "NIL" and "NIL").

(d) Negative integers

Shell definition.

Add the shell MINUS of one argument
with recognizer NEGATIVEP,
accessor NEGATIVE.GUTS,
type restriction (NUMBERP X1),
default value 0, and
well-founded relation NEGATIVE.GUTSP.

(e) Abbreviations

We continue to use the abbreviation conventions introduced in [1], except that we modify the conventions concerning the abbreviation of LITATOMs: if wrd is a symbol, and the ASCII character codes for the characters in wrd are, in order, $i_1, \ldots, i_n$, the n"wrd" is an abbreviation of the term (PACK (CONS i_1 (CONS $i_2 \ldots$ (CONS i_n 0) $\ldots$))).

In addition, we add two new abbreviations.

If n is a positive integer and $t_1, t_2, \ldots, t_n$ are terms, then (LIST $t_1 \ldots t_n$) is an abbreviation of (CONS t_1 (LIST $t_2 \ldots t_n$)). (LIST) is an abbreviation of "NIL".

If n is a positive integer, then $-n$ is an abbreviation of (MINUS n).

(f) SYMBOLP

In preparation for defining FORMP, we add definitions for the functions LEGAL.CHAR.CODES, ILLEGAL.FIRST.CHAR.CODES, LEGAL.-CHAR.CODE.SEQ, SYMBOLP and LOOKUP to our basic theory. (LEGAL.CHAR.CODES) has as its value the list of ASCII codes of those characters we permit to occur in symbol names (A–Z, a–z, 0–9, and a certain set of signs). (ILLEGAL.FIRST.CHAR.CODES) has as its value the list of those characters we do not permit as the first character of a symbol name (0–9, +, −, and .):

Definitions.
(LEGAL.CHAR.CODES)
=
(LIST 65 66 67 ... 88 89 90
     97 98 99 ... 120 121 122
     48 49 50 ... 55 56 57
     33 35 36 38 43 44 45 46 47 58
     59 60 61 62 63 64 92 94 95 126),

(ILLEGAL.FIRST.CHAR.CODES)
=
(LIST 48 49 50 ... 55 56 57 43 45 46),

(LEGAL.CHAR.CODE.SEQ L)
=
(AND (LISTP L)
    (SUBSETP L (LEGAL.CHAR.CODES))
    (NOT (MEMBER (CAR L) (ILLEGAL.FIRST.CHAR.CODES)))
    (EQUAL (CDR (LAST L)) 0)),

(SYMBOLP X)
=
(AND (LITATOM X)
    (LEGAL.CHAR.CODE.SEQ (UNPACK X))),

(LOOKUP X ALIST)
=
(IF (NLISTP ALIST)
    "NIL"
    (IF (AND (LISTP (CAR ALIST))
             (EQUAL X (CAAR ALIST)))
        (CDAR ALIST)
        (LOOKUP X (CDR ALIST))))).

Functions used but not defined in this paper (e.g. NLISTP, LAST, MEM-
BER and SUBSTEP) are defined in [1] and are to be considered part of the
basic theory. Informally, (NLISTP X) is (NOT (LISTP X)), (LAST X) is the
last CONS in the CDR chain of X, (MEMBER X L) is (TRUE) or (FALSE)
according to whether X is a member of the list L, and (SUBSET L1 L2) is
(TRUE) or (FALSE) according to whether every member of L1 is a member
of L2.

(g) Miscellaneous

We prohibit the introduction of QUOTE and NIL as function symbols
in axioms (including definitions and invocations of the shell principle).

3.2. Histories and theories

The *basic axioms* are the axioms and definitions of Chapter III of "A
Computational Logic", as amended above.

t *can be proved directly from* a set of axioms A if and only if t may be derived
from the axioms in A and the basic axioms by applying the following rules
of inference:

the propositional calculus with equality and function symbols;

the rule of inference that any instance of a theorem is a theorem;

our principle of induction.

There are three kinds of *axiomatic acts:* (a) an application of the shell
principle, (b) an application of the principle of definition and (c) the arbitrary
addition of an axiom. Each such act adds one or (in the case of the shell
principle) more axioms.

A *history* is a finite sequence of axiomatic acts such that for each application of the principle of definition in the sequence, the theorems required by
the principle of definition can be proved directly from the axioms added by
the previous acts in the history.

If for some m, T_1 is the sequence of axiomatic acts $a_1, \ldots, a_m$ and for some n, T_2 is the sequence of axiomatic acts $a_1, \ldots, a_m, \ldots, a_n$, where n is greater than or equal to m, then T_2 is an *extension* of T_1.

If a history T_2 may be obtained from a history T_1 merely by adding definition acts to the end of T_1, then T_2 is a *definitional extension* of T_1.

A conjecture t *can be proved* in a history T if and only if t can be proved directly from the axioms of some definitional extension of T. (For example, even though the proof of the correctness of the tautology-checker presented in [1] involves the introduction of the new, auxiliary concept of "IF-normal form," we say that the correctness theorem "can be proved" in the history before the addition of the definition of IF-normal form.)

A history is *constructive* if it contains no arbitrary axioms.

A history is *ordinary* if there are no axioms of the history that mention APPLY, MEANING, MEANING.LST, ARITY, FORM.LSTP or FORMP as function symbols.

t is a *term of* T if and only if t is a term, T is a history, and every symbol mentioned as a function symbol in t is used as a function symbol in some axiom of T.

3.3. Assumption of consistency

We assume that if T is a constructive history, then T is consistent, i.e. (EQUAL (FALSE) (TRUE)) cannot be proved in T. This assumption plays an interesting role in the proof and implementation of the Methatheorem; we comment further upon that role in Section 6.

If any constructive history is inconsistent, then elementary number theory, at least, is inconsistent, since the constructive history can be embedded in elementary number theory.

While we might offer a "proof" that every constructive history is consistent, the only proof that we imagine requires at least the power of elementary number theory. We find it difficult to imagine a *proof* of the consistency of a constructive history within a mathematical theory that was less powerful than a constructive history because all logical theories of which we are aware require the power of inductive definition merely to *define* the language of any other logical theory.

3.4. Explicit value terms

In "A Computational Logic" we define the notion of an "explicit value term". We make extensive use of the properties of such terms in this paper, so we here summarize their properties.

Suppose T is a history.

A term in T is said to be an *explicit value term* with respect to T provided (i) it contains no variables, (ii) every function symbol in it is either TRUE, FALSE, or the bottom object or constructor function symbol of some shell class in T, and (iii) for each subterm of t of the form (const $t_1 \ldots t_n$), where const is the constructor function symbol of some shell class in T, each t_i satisfies the type restriction on the ith argument position of const.

Examples of explicit value terms are (ZERO), (ADD1 (ADD1 (ADD1 (ZERO)))), and (CONS (ADD1 (ZERO)) (ZERO)). (ADD1 (TRUE)) is not an explicit value because (TRUE) violates the numeric type restriction for ADD1.

Theorem. If t_1 and t_2 are two distinct explicit value terms with respect to T, then (NOT (EQUAL t_1 t_2)) is a theorem.

Proof. We induct on the structure of t_1 and t_2.

Base case. If either t_1 or t_2 is a variable, then the theorem is vacuously true because variables are not explicit values.

Induction step. If t_1 and t_2 are both function applications, say (f $s_1 \ldots s_m$) and (g $r_1 \ldots r_n$), then either f and g are the same function symbol or not. If f is not g, then the theorem follows, without appeal to the inductive hypotheses, merely by considering the shell axioms and the axiom that (TRUE) is not equal to (FALSE). If f and g are the same function symbol, then m is n and there is some i such that s_i is not the same term as r_i. By inductive hypothesis we can prove that (NOT (EQUAL s_i r_i)), and the desired conclusion follows from the shell axiom for f that (EQUAL (f $x_1 \ldots x_n$) (f $x_1' \ldots x_n'$)) is equivalent to the conjunction of (EQUAL x_1 x_1') ... and (EQUAL x_n x_n'), provided each x_i and x_i' satisfies the ith type restriction on const. Q.E.D.

A function symbol f_n is *explicit value preserving* with respect to T if it is TRUE, FALSE, IF, EQUAL, a function symbol axiomatized in T with an application of the shell principle, or a function symbol defined in T such that (a) every other function symbol used in the body of the definition is explicit value preserving with respect to T and (b) the theorems that must be proved under the pirinciple of definition before fn is admitted can be proved directly from the shell axioms of T and the definitions of explicit value preserving functions with respect to T defined before fn.

For example, APPEND, as defined as follows:

Definition.

(APPEND X Y)

=

(IF (LISTP X)

(CONS (CAR X) (APPEND (CDR X) Y))
Y)

is explicit value preserving.

The name "explicit value preserving" is derived from the observation that if some term t is the application of such a function to explicit values then it is possible to use the shell axioms and function definitions to derive an explicit value v such that (EQUAL t v) is a theorem. For example, using shell axioms and the definition of APPEND it is easy to reduce (APPEND (CONS 1 (CONS 2 "NIL")) (CONS 3 "NIL")) to the equivalent explicit value (CONS 1 (CONS 2 (CONS 3 "NIL"))). We now make this observation more formal.

A term t is *reducible* with respect to T if and only if t mentions no variable and every function symbol mentioned in t is explicit value preserving with respect to T.

We define recursively the *reduction* of a reducible term t of T. If t is an explicit value, then the reduction of t is t. If t is not an explicit value, then let s be the leftmost nonexplicit value subterm of t, (fn t_1 ... t_n), such that either each t_i is an explicit value or fn is IF and t_1 is an explicit value. The reduction of t is the reduction of the term that results from replacing the leftmost occurrence of s in t with the term ans defined as follows:

(1) If fn is EQUAL, ans is (TRUE) or (FALSE) according to whether t_1 is identical to t_2.

(2) If fn is IF, ans is t_3 or t_2 according to whether t_1 is (FALSE) or not.

(3) If fn is a recognizer for a shell class with constructor function symbol c (and optionally, bottom object (btm)), then if the function symbol of t_1 is c (or btm) then ans is (TRUE), and otherwise ans is (FALSE).

(4) If fn is the constructor function symbol for a shell class of T, ans is the result of replacing in s each argument t_i that does not satisfy the type restriction of the ith argument of fn with the ith default value.

(5) If fn is the ith accessor for some shell class of T with constructor function symbol c, then if t_1 has the form (c v_1 ... v_n) for some v_1, ..., v_n, then ans is v_i and otherwise ans is the ith default value for c.

(6) If fn is a defined function in T, ans is the result of substituting each t_i for the corresponding formal parameter of the definition of fn in the body of fn.

That "the reduction of a reducible term" is well defined can be proved by induction because the definition of every defined function satisfies our principle of definition. That the reduction of a reducible term t is an explicit value that is provably equal to t follows from the fact that each step in the computation is justified by an axiom.

Theorem. If c is an explicit value with respect to T, then the reduction of (SYMBOLP c) in T is (TRUE) if and only if for some symbol w, c is "w".

For example, let c be the explicit value (PACK (CONS 65 0)). Note that (SYMBOLP c) reduces to (TRUE). Then the theorem says there is a symbol, w, such that "w" is c. The appropriate choice for w here is the symbol A since "A" is (PACK (CONS 65 0)).

Proof. Suppose (SYMBOLP c) reduces to (TRUE). Then, by definition, the reduction of (AND (LITATOM c) (LEGAL.CHAR.CODE.SEQ (UNPACK c))) is (TRUE). Thus (LITATOM c) reduces to (TRUE) and c must have the form (PACK 1st) and (UNPACK c) reduces to 1st. Continuing the argument through LEGAL.CHAR.CODE.SEQ we finally conclude that c must have the form (PACK (CONS t_1 (CONS t_2 ... (CONS t_n 0) ...))), where t_1, ..., t_n are MEMBERs of (LEGAL.CHAR.CODES) and t_1 is not a MEMBER of (ILLEGAL.FIRST.CHAR.CODES). Thus, t_1, ..., t_n are NUMBERPs that may be abbreviated with the integers i_1, ..., i_n. Furthermore, by the definitions of LEGAL.CHAR.CODES and ILLEGAL.FIRST.CHAR. CODES, i_1, ..., i_n are ASCII codes satisfying the restrictions we place on symbols. Let w be the symbol obtained by concatenating the ASCII characters for i_1, ..., i_n. It is easy to confirm that c is "w". The proof in the other direction is similar. Q.E.D.

3.5. Quotations

We now define the "correspondence" between terms.

Suppose that T is any history.

c is a *quotation* of t with respect to T if and only if c and t are terms and either (i) t is a symbol and c is "t" or (ii) t has the form (fn a_1 ... a_n) and either (a) t is an explicit value with respect to T and c is (LIST "QUOTE" t) or (b) for some q_1, ..., q_n that are quotations, respectively, of a_1, ..., a_n with respect to T, c is (LIST "fn" q_1 ... q_n). If c is a quotation of t with respect to T, then we say t is the *dequotation* of c with respect to T.

Thus, a quotation of the variable symbol X is (PACK (CONS 88 0)), which may be abbreviated "X". A quotation of (ADD1 (ZERO)), which is the explicit value we abbreviate as 1, is (LIST "QUOTE" 1). But another quotation of 1 is (LIST "ADD1" (LIST "ZERO")). A quotation of (NOT X) is (LIST "NOT" "X"). Readers who feel uneasy about the use of such expressions as "QUOTE" and "ADD1" in terms should recall that they are mere abbreviations:

"QUOTE" (PACK (CONS 81 (CONS 85 (CONS 79 (CONS 84 (CONS 69 0))))))

"ADD1" (PACK (CONS 65 (CONS 68 (CONS 68 (CONS 49 0)))))

"ZERO" (PACK (CONS 90 (CONS 69 (CONS 82 (CONS 79 0)))))

"NOT"   (PACK (CONS 78 (CONS 79 (CONS 84 0)))))

"X"   (PACK (CONS 88 0))

Theorem. If c is a quotation of t with respect to T, then c is an explicit value term.

Proof. We induct on t. If t is a variable, c is "t", which is an explicit value. Otherwise, t has the form (fn $a_1 \ldots a_n$). If c has the form (LIST "QUOTE" d) then, since QUOTE is not a function symbol, d is an explicit value and, thus, so is c. Otherwise, c has the form (LIST "fn" $q_1 \ldots q_n$), where each q_i is a quotation of the corresponding a_i. By induction hypothesis, each q_i is an explicit value. Thus c is an explicit value. Q.E.D.

Theorem. If c is a quotation of both t_1 and t_2 with respect to T, then t_1 is the same term as t_2.

Proof. We induct on the structure of c.

Base case 1. If the top function symbol of c is not CONS, then c is not the quotation of any term except a symbol. c cannot be a quotation of two distinct symbols.

Base case 2. If c has the form (LIST "QUOTE" d), then since QUOTE is not a function symbol, c is a quotation only of the explicit value d.

Induction step. If the top function symbol of c is CONS but c does not have the form (LIST "QUOTE" d), then for some fn, $q_1, \ldots, q_n$, c has the form (LIST "fn" $q_1 \ldots q_n$) where, by inductive hypothesis, each q_i is a quotation of some unique t_i. But then c can only be a quotation of the term (fn $t_1 \ldots t_n$). Q.E.D.

4. THE METATHEOREM

4.1. The metaaxioms and metadefinitions

When we are trying to prove the correctness of a metafunction, we have some axioms about MEANING, FORMP, and some auxiliary functions. These axioms, called the "metaaxioms", specify the values of MEANING and FORMP on symbolic expressions corresponding to terms in the current theory. The axioms do not specify the values of MEANING and FORMP on objects that "look like" symbolic expressions but that have unrecognized function symbols.

Once a metafunction has been proved correct, we may apply it as a new proof procedure—even if new function symbols have been added to the theory. Formally speaking, its application involves the introduction of *definitions* of MEANING, FORMP, and some auxiliary functions. These definitions are called the "metadefinitions". The definitions not only specify the values of MEANING and FORMP on symbolic expressions corresponding to terms in the new theory, but on all explicit values. For example, FORMP is (FALSE) on any object that "looks like" a symbolic expression but has an unrecognized function symbol. But because the metaaxioms are easy consequences of the metadefinitions, we can prove the correctness of the metafunction—and use it—in the new theory.

By not completely specifying MEANING and FORMP during the correctness proof for a metafunction, we permit the application of the metafunction in extensions containing new function symbols. By introducing MEANING and FORMP under the principle of definition when the metafunction is used in the proof of a new conjecture, the proof of the conjecture does not depend upon nondefinitional axioms about MEANING and FORMP.

Assume we have a standard ordering of all symbols and that TRUE, NOT, IF and PLUS come first, in that order.

Suppose that (a) T is a history, (b) TRUE, NOT, IF, PLUS, f_5, . . . , f_m is the sequence of symbols mentioned as function symbols in axioms of T in the standard order, and (c) 0, 1, 3, 2, a_5, . . . , a_m is the sequence of the arities of the symbols TRUE, NOT, IF, PLUS, f_5, . . . , f_m.

(a) The metaaxioms

The *metaaxioms* for T are as follows:

(MEANING.LST X A)
=
(IF (NLISTP X)
    "NIL"
    (CONS (MEANING (CAR X) A)
          (MEANING.LST (CDR X) A))),

(IMPLIES (NLISTP X)
         (EQUAL (MEANING X A) (LOOKUP X A))),

(EQUAL (MEANING (LIST "QUOTE" X) A)
       X),

(IMPLIES (NOT (EQUAL FN "QUOTE"))
         (EQUAL (MEANING (CONS FN X) A)
                (APPLY FN (MEANING.LST X A)))),

(EQUAL (APPLY "TRUE" X)
       (TRUE)),

```
(EQUAL (APPLY "NOT" X)
       (NOT (CAR X))),

(EQUAL (APPLY "IF" X)
       (IF (CAR X) (CADR X) (CADDR X))),

(EQUAL (APPLY "PLUS" X)
       (PLUS (CAR X) (CADR X))),
```

... and so on for all of the functions $f_5, \ldots, f_m$,

```
(EQUAL (ARITY "TRUE") 0),

(EQUAL (ARITY "NOT") 1),

(EQUAL (ARITY "IF") 3),

(EQUAL (ARITY "PLUS") 2),
```

... and so on for all of the symbols "f_5", ..., "f_m",

```
(FORM.LSTP X)
=
(IF (NLISTP X)
    (EQUAL X "NIL")
    (AND (FORMP (CAR X))
         (FORM.LSTP (CDR X)))),

(FORMP X)
=
(IF (NLISTP X)
    (SYMBOLP X)
    (IF (EQUAL (CAR X) "QUOTE")
        (AND (LISTP (CDR X))
             (EQUAL (CDDR X) "NIL"))
        (AND (EQUAL (ARITY (CAR X)) (LENGTH (CDR X)))
             (FORM.LSTP (CDR X))))).
```

Note that the value of (ARITY X) is unspecified if X is not one of the LITATOMS "TRUE", "NOT", "IF", "PLUS", "f_5", ..., "f_m". Further, (FORMP X) is unspecified if X is a LISTP and (ARITY (CAR X)) is unspecified.

Note also that FORMP is more elaborate than we sketched it in the discussion of CANCEL. In particular, we require that function and variable symbols be SYMBOLPs and that objects used as function symbols have numeric arity and be provided with the proper number of arguments; in addition, we allow the symbolic expression whose CAR is the LITATOM

"QUOTE" and whose MEANING is defined to be the CADR of the expression. Note that we are not elevating QUOTE to a "function symbol" even at the meta level of FORMP. We are merely axiomatizing the recursive functions FORMP and MEANING to behave in a certain way when they encounter a LISTP object whose CAR is (PACK (CONS 81 (CONS 85 (CONS 79 (CONS 84 (CONS 69 0)))))).

(b) The metadefinitions

The *metadefinitions* for T are as follows:

(APPLY X L)
=
(IF (EQUAL X "TRUE")
    (TRUE)
(IF (EQUAL X "NOT")
    (NOT (CAR L))
(IF (EQUAL X "IF")
    (IF (CAR L) (CADR L) (CADDR L))
(IF (EQUAL X "PLUS")
    (PLUS (CAR L) (CADR L))
(IF (EQUAL X "f$_5$")
    (f$_5$ (CAR L) ... (CAD ... R L))
...

(IF (EQUAL X "f$_m$")
    (f$_m$ (CAR L) ... (CAD ... R L))
    (TRUE)))))))),

(MEANING.LST X A)
=
(IF (NLISTP X)
    "NIL"
    (CONS (IF (NLISTP (CAR X))
              (LOOKUP (CAR X) A)
              (IF (EQUAL (CAAR X) "QUOTE")
                  (CADR (CAR X))
                  (APPLY (CAAR X)
                         (MEANING.LST (CDAR X) A))))
          (MEANING.LST (CDR X) A))),

(MEANING X A)
=

(CAR (MEANING.LST (LIST X) A)),

(ARITY X)
=
(IF (EQUAL X "TRUE")
0
(IF (EQUAL X "NOT")
1
(IF (EQUAL X "IF")
3
(IF (EQUAL X "PLUS")
2
(IF (EQUAL X "f_5")
a_5
. . .

(IF (EQUAL X "f_m")
a_m
"NIL")))))),

(FORM.LSTP X)
=
(IF (NLISTP X)
(EQUAL X "NIL")
(AND (IF (NLISTP (CAR X))
(SYMBOLP (CAR X))
(IF (EQUAL (CAAR X) "QUOTE")
(AND (LISTP (CDAR X))
(EQUAL (CDDR (CAR X)) "NIL"))
(AND (EQUAL (ARITY (CAAR X))
(LENGTH (CDAR X)))
(FORM.LSTP (CDAR X)))))
(FORM.LSTP (CDR X))))),

(FORMP X)
=
(FORM.LSTP (LIST X)).

If T is an ordinary history, let $MA[T]$ be the history that results from adding the mextaaxioms for T to T as arbitrary axioms and let $MD[T]$ be the history that results from adding the metadefinitions for T to T, in order, as (explicit value preserving) definitions.

4.2. Statement and proof of the metatheorem

For the remainder of this section, let us make the following suppositions.

(1) T_1 is a constructive, ordinary history,

(2) simp is an explicit value preserving function defined in T_1 with arity 1,

(3) in MA[T_1] we can prove the formula

```
*META
(IMPLIES (FORMP X)
         (AND (EQUAL (MEANING X ALIST)
                     (MEANING (simp X) ALIST))
              (FORMP (simp X)))), and
```

(4) T_2 is an ordinary extension of T_1.

It is our objective to show that if p is a term of T_2, c is a quotation of p with respect to T_2, and d is the reduction of (simp c), then d is a quotation of some term q of T_2 with respect to T_2 and (EQUAL p q) is a theorem of T_2. Thus, while proving theorems in T_2, we may at any time replace a term p of T_2 with the dequotation of the reduction of the application of simp to a quotation of p. First we note a few lemmas.

Let $T_{1.5}$ be the extension of T_1 that results from adding (a) the applications of the shell principle made while extending T_1 to T_2 and (b) the metadefinitions for T_2 as definitions.

We now make a few trivial observations about $T_{1.5}$:

(1) In $T_{1.5}$, APPLY may mention functions that are undefined. Nevertheless, $T_{1.5}$ is constructive since T_1 is constructive and in producing the extension we added no arbitrary axioms.

(2) In $T_{1.5}$, ARITY, FORM.LSTP and FORMP are explicit value preserving.

(3) The explicit values of T_2 are just the explicit values of $T_{1.5}$.

(4) If t is reducible with respect to $T_{1.5}$, then t is reducible with respect to MD[T_2] and the reduction of t in $T_{1.5}$ is the reduction of t in MD[T_2].

(5) Finally, c is a quotation of t with respect to T_2 if and only if c is a quotation of t with respect to $T_{1.5}$.

We are interested in $T_{1.5}$ because, being constructive, it is consistent and yet has the property proved below. Our interest in consistency is explained in Section 6, after we have proved the metatheorem and discussed its use.

Theorem A. If c is an explicit value with respect to $T_{1.5}$, then the reduction of (FORMP c) in $T_{1.5}$ is (TRUE) if and only if for some term t of T_2, c is a quotation of t with respect to $T_{1.5}$.

The proof is by induction on the structure of c.

Base case 1. If the top function symbol of c is not CONS, then the reduction of (FORMP c) is the reduction of (SYMBOLP c). But the reduction of (SYMBOLP c) is (TRUE) if and only if for some symbol w, c is "w". But "w" is a quotation of w.

Base case 2. If c is a term of the form (LIST "QUOTE" d), then the reduction of (FORMP c) is (TRUE), d is an explicit value, and c is a quotation of d.

Induction step. Suppose the function symbol of c is CONS but c does not have the form (LIST "QUOTE" d). Suppose that the reduction of (FORMP c) is (TRUE). Then for some symbol fn and for some explicit values $c_1, \ldots,$ c_n, c has the form (LIST "fn" $c_1 \ldots c_n$), the reduction of (ARITY "fn") is n, and the reduction of each (FORMP c_i) is (TRUE). By inductive hypothesis, there exist terms $t_1, \ldots, t_n$ of T_2 such that c_i is a quotation of t_i with respect to $T_{1.5}$. By the construction of the definition of ARITY, the arity of fn is n and c is a quotation of the term (fn $t_1 \ldots t_n$). On the other hand, suppose that for some term t, c is a quotation of t. t must have the form (fn $t_1 \ldots t_n$) and c must have the form (LIST "fn" $a_1 \ldots a_n$) for some quotations $a_1, \ldots,$ a_n of $t_1, \ldots, t_n$. Hence the reduction of (FORMP c) is (TRUE). Q.E.D.

If $v_1, \ldots, v_n$ is a sequence of symbols, then the *standard alist* for $v_1, \ldots, v_n$ is the term:

$$(\text{LIST (CONS "}v_1\text{" } v_1) \ldots (\text{CONS "}v_n\text{" } v_n)).$$

Theorem B. If c is a quotation of t with respect to T_2, t is a term of T_2, and a is the standard alist for any sequence of variables that contains all of the symbols that are used as variables in t, then the following can be proved in $\text{MD}[T_2]$:

$$(\text{EQUAL (MEANING c a)}$$
$$\text{t)}.$$

Proof. We prove this theorem by induction on the structure of the term t.

Base case. If t is a symbol, then c is "t" and (MEANING "t" a) is (LOOKUP "t" a) which is (CDR (CONS "t" t)) which is t.

Induction step. Suppose t has the form (fn $t_1 \ldots t_n$). If t is an explicit value and c is (LIST "QUOTE" t), then by the definition of MEANING, (MEANING c a) is t. If c does not have the form (LIST "QUOTE" d), then c has the form (LIST "fn" $q_1 \ldots q_n$), where each q_i is a quotation of t_i. Since every variable of any t_i is a variable of t, we have, by inductive hypothesis that for each i, (EQUAL (MEANING q_i a) t_i). Because fn is a function symbol used in an axiom of T_2 and is not QUOTE, we have by the definition of MEANING that

$$(\text{EQUAL (MEANING (LIST "fn" } q_1 \ldots q_n) \text{ a)}$$
$$(\text{fn (MEANING } q_1 \text{ a}) \ldots (\text{MEANING } q_n \text{ a}))).$$

Thus we derive

$$\text{(EQUAL (MEANING (LIST "fn" } q_1 \ldots q_n) \text{ a)}$$
$$\text{(fn } t_1 \ldots t_n))\text{.}$$

Q.E.D.

The metatheorem.

Suppose that:
(1) p is a term of T_2,
(2) c is a quotation of p with respect to T_2, and
(3) d is the reduction of (simp c) in T_2.
Then, the reduction of (FORMP d) in T_2 is (TRUE), d is the quotation of some term q of T_2, and in T_2 we can prove

$$\text{(EQUAL p q)}\text{.}$$

Proof. Since c is a quotation with respect to T_2 of a term of T_2, (FORMP c) reduces to (TRUE) in $T_{1.5}$ by Theorem A. Because we can prove *META in MA[T_1] and because the metaaxioms of T_1 are each theorems of $T_{1.5}$, we can prove *META in $T_{1.5}$. Detaching the hypothesis of *META, we can prove in $T_{1.5}$ that (FORMP d). The reduction of (FORMP d) in $T_{1.5}$ is either (TRUE) or (FALSE). If it is (FALSE), then $T_{1.5}$ is inconsistent. But we have assumed that $T_{1.5}$ is consistent since it is constructive. Thus the reduction of (FORMP d) in $T_{1.5}$ is (TRUE) and its reduction in T_2 is (TRUE) also.

By Theorem A there exists a term q of T_2 such that d is a quotation of q. Let q be the dequotation of d. Let a be the standard alist for a sequence containing all of the variables in p and q. Since every axiom (including the definitions) of MA[T_1] can be proved in MD[T_2], both *META and (FORMP c) can be proved in MD[T_2]. Detaching the hypothesis of *META in MD[T_2], we derive that (EQUAL (MEANING c a) (MEANING d a)). But since (EQUAL p (MEANING c a)) and (EQUAL q (MEANING d a)) by Theorem B we obtain (EQUAL p q) in MD[T_2]. Since MD[T_2] is a definitional extension of T_2, we can prove (EQUAL p q) in T_2. Q.E.D.

5. OUR IMPLEMENTATION OF METAFUNCTIONS

In the next three sections of this paper we describe our efficient implementation of metafunctions in INTERLISP [6]. Here are the steps in our description and the proof of the implementation's correctness:
(1) We describe in Section 6 how in our theorem-proving program we

represent the terms of our theories with INTERLISP objects.

(2) Let (list 'QUOTE obj) denote an INTERLISP list of length two with the INTERLISP atom QUOTE as its first element and the INTERLISP object obj as its second. In Section 7, Lemma 18, we demonstrate, under the suppositions and hypothesis of the Metatheorem, that if (list 'QUOTE obj) represents some explicit value w of T_2, (FORMP w) reduces to (TRUE) in MD[T_2] (or, equivalently, in $T_{1.5}$), and the INTERLISP machine state corresponds to the history T_2, then obj represents a term of T_2.

(3) We then demonstrate in Section 7, Lemma 19, that if the INTERLISP machine state corresponds to any history T and in that state obj is an INTER-LISP object that represents a term p of T, then (list 'QUOTE obj) represents a term in T that is a quotation of p with respect to T.

(4) Finally, in Section 8 we describe how we have arranged so that if the INTERLISP machine state corresponds to any theory T and fn is an explicit value preserving function with respect to T, then stored in the definition cell of the INTERLISP literal atom .fn. is a routine such that if $c_1, \ldots, c_n$ are explicit values of T represented by the INTERLISP objects (list 'QUOTE obj_1), $\ldots$, (list 'QUOTE obj_n), and val is the INTERLISP object computed by applying .fn. to $obj_1, \ldots, obj_n$, then (list 'QUOTE val) represents the reduction of (fn $c_1 \ldots c_n$).

We are then free to utilize the Metatheorem in the following way. Suppose that during a proof in T_2 we have in hand an INTERLISP object objc representing some term p of T_2. By Lemma 19, (list 'QUOTE objc) represents some term c that is a quotation of p. Let objd be the result of applying .simp. to objc. By our implementation of .functions., (list 'QUOTE objd) represents the term d that is the reduction of (simp c). From the Metatheorem, we know that (FORMP d) reduces to (TRUE). From Lemma 18, we learn, then, that objd represents some term q of T_2. From Lemma 19, again, we learn that d is a quotation of q. Finally, from the Metatheorem, we learn that (EQUAL p q) is a theorem of T_2. Consequently, we may engage in the typical theorem-prover activities justified by "substitution of equals", replacing objc with objd.

The place in our theorem-prover where metafunctions are thus utilized is described in Section 10.

6. INTERLISP REPRESENTATION OF TERMS

In this section, we explain how we represent terms in our theorem-prover.

6.1. The role of consistency

Before describing our representation, let us first anticipate some problems we face and explain why we are interested in consistency.

Recall how we use the metafunction simp to simplify a term represented by the INTERLISP object objc: the theorem-prover executes the routine .simp. on objc, obtains some INTERLISP object objd as a result, and uses objd in place of objc.

We find the fact that objd represents a term to be remarkable in light of all the invariants a data object must satisfy to represent a term in an efficiently implemented theorem-prover. To appreciate the subtlety of the situation, consider what might happen when the compiled INTERLISP code for the theorem-prover begins to operate on objd. If objd is an INTERLISP list cell, our theorem-proving code will assume that the car of objd, x, is an INTER-LISP literal atom representing a function symbol and may fetch x's property list (the left half-word of the location addressed by x) where information about the function is stored. But what would happen if x were not a literal atom—for example, what would happen if it were an INTERLISP number? Then the machine instruction used to obtain the property list might return an illegal object whose use could lead the theorem-prover to random, unpredictable behavior.

For efficiency, we do not check that objd actually satisfies all the properties the theorem-prover requires of an object representing a term; so what ensures us that it does? The answer is that we know that the INTERLISP object obtained by embedding objd in a QUOTE represents a term, d, and that (FORMP d) reduces to (TRUE). We will *prove*, in Lemma 18, that objd must therefore represent a term.

How do we know that (FORMP d) reduces to (TRUE)? One's first reaction is: d is (simp c), (FORMP c) is (TRUE) and *META establishes (IMPLIES (FORMP c) (FORMP (simp c))). But wait. That argument only implies that (FORMP d) is provably (TRUE). But our Lemma 18 requires that it *reduce* to (TRUE). However, as we argued in the proof of the Metatheorem, (FORMP d) must reduce to (TRUE) or (FALSE) and were it to reduce to (FALSE) a constructive theory (namely $T_{1.6}$) would be inconsistent.

Let us consider the role of consistency from another point of view. Recall that we require that *META be proved in a constructive (consistent) theory, T_1. Suppose we weakened that and permitted it to be proved in any theory. What would happen if the theory were inconsistent? One consequence of an inconsistency in T_1 is that one admits a proof procedure that might prove falsehoods. But nothing is wrong with that state of affairs, for if T_1 is inconsistent, one may indeed prove anything in it. However, something worse happens. Suppose the inconsistency permits (FORMP (simp c)) to be proved when in fact it reduces to (FALSE). Then objd will not in fact be an object satisfying the theorem-prover's restrictions on terms. Consequently, the application of simp may cause totally unpredictable behavior by the theorem-prover (e.g. the smashing of disk files, illegal memory fetches, loss of the day's work, and so on).

Such catastrophic behavior is a far cry from the expectation that an inconsistent T_1 leads to well-behaved proofs of falsehoods. Some readers may feel that the user of an inconsistent theory deserves even catastrophic failures. This is an ill-considered position. Mechanical theorem-provers often deal with inconsistent theories because a standard proof strategy is to assume the negation of what one desires to prove and then seek to prove (FALSE). The theory T_2 in which one may apply simp may be such a theory and cause no catastrophic effects. The moral however is that one should not prove the soundness of one's new proof procedures while in an inconsistent theory.

Finally, we should observe that we could have stated *META so that (FORMP (simp c)) did not have to be proved in T_1 and then could have implemented a run-time check that objd indeed represents a term. We then could have permitted T_1 to be inconsistent without catastrophic consequences. We did not adopt this approach because in most cases the proof of the FORMP part of *META is straightforward (see Section 9) and buys efficiency at the mere expense of complicating this paper.

6.2. Our subset of INTERLISP

Our objective in this section is to describe how we represent terms in our theorem-prover in a way that permits the efficient implementation of the Metatheorem without sacrificing efficiency in more routine activities. We describe our representation by exhibiting two INTERLISP programs. The first determines whether its argument represents a term. The second returns a conventional representation of the term represented. We chose to describe our representation with such programs because INTERLISP provides a very succinct way to describe complicated INTERLISP data structures.

The INTERLISP definitions we present in this paper and our proofs about those definitions are made in a vastly simplified version of INTERLISP akin to Pure Lisp. We do not specify the subset precisely. However, the subset does have the following properties.

We make no use of "destructive" operations such as SETQ, SET and RPLACA.

We restrict our attention to INTERLISP structures that are not "circular".

In establishing the correctness of our mapping between terms in the theory and INTERLISP objects, we assume we have an INTERLISP machine with unlimited resources.

The third assumption permits us to ignore such problems as running out of list space or exhausting the machine's stack while proving, for example, that we can represent every explicit value. Of course, we did not make this assumption while designing the representation, since the economical representation of terms is one of our objectives, and our theorem-prover actually causes errors and aborts the proof attempt when resources are exhausted. But at the moment we are engaged in the mathematical exercise of establishing the correctness of a mapping between terms in our theory and INTERLISP objects and we are using INTERLISP as a mathematical language to describe those objects.

We assume the reader is familiar with the standard, primitive LISP routines such as cond, cons, car, cdr and listp. (MACLISP users: read "consp" for "listp".)

6.3. Conventions for mixing INTERLISP and the theory

The syntax of INTERLISP expressions is very similar to that of our theory. Because we will often be referring to functions in our theory and to INTER-LISP functions (henceforth called "routines") in close proximity, we adopt the following three conventions to demark clearly the boundary between the two.

First, despite the fact that most INTERLISP routines are spelled in upper case, we spell them in lower case here. We will use upper case words to denote functions in our theory. Thus (LENGTH X) is a term in our theory, while (length x) refers to the value of the INTERLISP routine length applied to the value of the variable x.

Second, we shall adopt the syntactic convention of writing 'w for (QUOTE w) when w is an INTERLISP literal atom. Thus, the INTERLISP form that might be written as:

$$\text{(COND ((EQ I 0) (LIST (QUOTE ZERO)))}$$
$$\text{(T (LIST (QUOTE ADD1) (FN (SUB1 I)))))}$$

will here be displayed as

$$\text{(cond ((eq i 0) (list 'ZERO))}$$
$$\text{(T (list 'ADD1 (fn (sub1 i)))))}.$$

Third, it is often necessary in this paper to refer to characters obtained by printing certain INTERLISP objects. To indicate the result of printing the value of an INTERLISP form, we surround the form with vertical bars. Such an expression is to be understood as denoting the sequence of characters obtained by printing the value of the enclosed INTERLISP form (with prin4, using the original read table and decimal radix). Thus, if we say "We can prove (EQUAL |(cons 'ZERO NIL)| (REMAINDER X X))", then we mean "We can prove (EQUAL (ZERO) (REMAINDER X X))". Of course, to use the vertical bar notation in a context where a term is expected, we will have to establish that the result of printing the value of the form denotes a term.

6.4. Basic INTERLISP routines

Our representation of terms will involve the following defined auxiliary INTERLISP routines:

The routine legal.char.codes takes no arguments and returns a list, in ascending numerical order, of the integers mentioned in the definition of LEGAL.CHAR.CODES in Section 3, which are the ASCII codes for the characters that we permit in symbols.

The routine illegal.first.char.codes takes no arguments and returns a list, in ascending numerical order, of the integers mentioned in the definition of ILLEGAL.FIRST.CHAR.CODES in Section 3, which are the ASCII codes for the characters that may appear in symbols, but not first.

The routine legal.char.code.seq returns T or NIL according to whether its argument x has or does not have all of the following properties: (i) (listp x), (ii) for every c, if (member c x), then (member c (legal.char.codes)), (iii) it is not the case that (car x) is a member of (illegal.first.char.codes), and (iv) the cdr of the last list cell in x is 0.

The routine unpack0, when given a literal atom x, returns a list of the ASCII codes of the characters in the "print name" of x, in the order in which the characters occur in the print name, and terminating in a 0 instead of a NIL. (The "print name" of a literal atom is the sequence of characters produced when the atom is printed. Thus, (unpack0 'ABC) is a list that prints as (65 66 67 . 0).)

The routine pack0, when given an object x satisfying (legal.char.code.seq x), returns the unique INTERLISP literal atom atm such that (unpack0 atm) is x.

The routine symbolp returns T or NIL according to whether its argument represents a symbol in our logic. The definition of symbolp is:

```
(symbolp (lambda (x)
          (and (litatom x)
               (legal.char.code.seq
                 (unpack0 x)))))).
```

Note that if (symbolp x) holds, then x is a literal atom and its print name is a legal.char.code.seq. If (symbolp x) holds, (pack0 (unpack0 x)) is x. Furthermore, if (legal.char.code.seq seq) holds then (unpack0 (pack0 seq)) is equal to seq and (symbolp (pack0 seq)) holds. These are the basic properties required of symbolp, pack0, unpack0, and legal.char.code.seq. INTERLISP contains literal atoms for which pack0 and unpack0 are inverses but which we do not use as symbols. For example, there is one whose print name is 1A2. We could have defined legal.char.code.seq to check for precisely the syntax of those objects for which pack0 and unpack0 are inverses, but that would have made its definition far more complicated, for while 1A2 is such an object, 1E2 is not (it is $1.0 \times 10^2 = 100.0$).

As the user of our theorem-prover adds definitions, shells and other kinds of axioms, our theorem-prover naturally changes the state of the INTERLISP machine.

The routine arity, of one argument x, is defined so that if x is a symbol which is used as a function symbol in some axiom of the history represented by the current state of INTERLISP, then arity returns an INTERLISP integer representing the number of arguments that x takes. Otherwise, (arity x) is NIL.

The routine shell.state, of no arguments, returns an alist which incapsulates information about the uses of the shell principle in the construction of the history represented by the current state of INTERLISP. Each member of the list has a shell constructor function symbol or a bottom object function symbol as its car. The cdr is a list whose length is the number of arguments of the function symbol. Each element of the cdr encodes the type restrictions placed on the corresponding argument to the constructor function. Recall that each type restriction for a shell can be expressed as a requirement that the corresponding argument either be recognized by one of a finite collection of shell recognizers or else be recognized by none of a finite number of shell recognizers. Thus, it would be sufficient if each element of the cdr were either of the form (ONE.OF . r) or (NONE.OF . r), where r was a list of recognizers. However, for convenience we define r to be the list of all constructor and bottom object function symbols recognized by the recognizers in question.

The routine add1.nest takes a nonnegative integer x as its argument and it returns an object that prints as (ZERO) for 0, (ADD1 (ZERO)) for 1, (ADD1 (ADD1 (ZERO))) for 2, and so on. Its definition is

```
(add1.nest
(lambda (i)
(cond ((equal i 0) (list 'ZERO))
(T (list 'ADD1 (add1.nest (sub1 i)))))))).
```

The routine bminus, if given an argument representing an integer x, returns an INTERLISP representation of the negative of x.

The routine badd1, if given an argument representing an integer x, returns an INTERLISP representation of $x + 1$.

The routine plistp returns T or NIL according to whether or not its argument is a (possibly empty) list whose final cdr is NIL. Its definition is

```
(plistp (lambda (x)
        (cond ((nlistp x) (eq x NIL))
              (T (plistp (cdr x)))))).
```

6.5. Global variables

For our representation of terms, we have assigned distinct values to three INTERLISP global variables .t., .f. and .sqm.. Each value is an INTERLISP literal atom, and none of the values represents a symbol in the logic (i.e. (symbolp .t.), (symbolp .f.) and (symbolp .sqm.) are all NIL). The role of these variables is explained below. By choosing names that begin with periods we are guaranteed that these INTERLISP variables never have the same names as variables in our logic. This plays a minor role in the efficient compilation of explicit value preserving functions.

6.6. The definition of terms

Roughly speaking we shall represent variables as symbolps and function applications as lists in which the car is the function symbol and the cdr is the list of the appropriate number of argument terms. However, we wish to encode explicit value terms efficiently. For example, we prefer to represent the explicit value term

```
(CONS (PACK (CONS 78 (CONS 79 (CONS 84 0))))
      (CONS (PACK (CONS 80 0))
            (PACK (CONS 78 (CONS 73 (CONS 76 0)))))),
```

which may be abbreviated by:

$$(\text{LIST ``NOT'' ``P''})$$

with the INTERLISP list constant that prints as (QUOTE (NOT P)). There are two reasons: we consume much less space, and if constants in the theory are represented efficiently by INTERLISP constants then we can choose to represent terms in our program by INTERLISP constants which simultaneously represent constants in our theory and facilitate the efficient application of metafunctions to formulas.

For example, we can represent some NUMBERPs and NEGATIVEPs by INTERLISP integers, some LITATOMs by INTERLISP literal atoms, and some LISTPs by INTERLISP lists. Of course, we cannot use the INTERLISP literal atom 'P to represent both the variable P and the explicit value (PACK

(CONS 80 0)). So we use 'P to represent the variable P and the value of (list 'QUOTE 'P) to represent (PACK (CONS 80 0)).

Similarly, if the value of (list 'QUOTE obj_1) represents some explicit value term t_1 and the value of (list 'QUOTE obj_2) represents some explicit value term t_2, then the value of (list 'QUOTE (cons obj_1 obj_2)) represents the explicit value term (CONS t_1 t_2). To obtain the CAR of (CONS t_1 t_2) from its representation, we apply car to (cons obj_1 obj_2). To obtain the UNPACK of (PACK (CONS 80 0)) from its representation, we apply unpack0 to 'P. However, we must address three problems.

The first problem concerns the precise choice of our representation of LITATOMs. The reason LITATOMs must be represented efficiently is that they are used by FORMP to stand for function and variable symbols. Thus, the internal representation of a LITATOM satisfying SYMBOLP must be an INTERLISP object the theorem-prover can use as a function or variable symbol. But to implement a theorem-prover efficiently one's function and variable symbols should be distinguishable by eq (in one machine instruction) and have property lists. The obvious candidates are literal atoms. So certain LITATOMs are represented by INTERLISP literal atoms. But for theoretical simplicity we allow a LITATOM to be constructed from any object (e.g. (PACK 1200) is a LITATOM in the theory), while INTERLISP requires that literal atoms be constructed only from lists of ASCII codes so that they are "printable". To represent the theory's "unprintable" LITATOMs we will use the structures described below for user-defined shells. Thus, there are two distinct ways LITATOMs are represented, but any given LITATOM will be represented in only one of the ways, depending on whether it is a SYMBOLP.

The second problem is that while certain shell constants in the theory (e.g. some NUMBERPs, LITATOMs and LISTPs) have obvious INTER-LISP representatives, others (e.g. (TRUE), (FALSE) and user-defined shells such as stacks or triples) do not. We could use the INTERLISP "user data type" facility to declare a new INTERLISP type for each of these unusual types in the theory. But this is unacceptable because (a) every user data type is initially allocated 512 words of storage, regardless of how many items of that type are required, (b) having additional data types in use slows down garbage collections, (c) the efficiently compiled and widely used INTERLISP routine equal does not work on user data types and (d) INTERLISP user data types do not print out or read in conveniently.

We shall therefore encode user-defined shell constants as INTERLISP list structures containing the name of the constructor (or bottom object) and the n-tuple of objects representing the explicit value arguments. But such a list structure could be confused with the representation of a LISTP containing n + 1 objects. To avoid ambiguity, we cons the value of .sqm.

(which stands for "shell quote mark") onto the front of the structure. This marking scheme avoids ambiguity because .sqm. is not the internal representation of any explicit value—in particular it does not satisfy symbolp and so does not represent a LITATOM—so a list with .sqm. as its car could not possibly represent a LISTP whose CAR was represented by .sqm.. For example, if TRIPLE is a user-defined shell constructor, then the explicit value (TRIPLE 1 (PACK (CONS 80 0)) 2) is represented by the value of (list .sqm. 'TRIPLE 1 'P 2), embedded in a QUOTE form.

We could represent (TRUE) and (FALSE) similarly—for example, (TRUE) could be represented by the value of (list .sqm. 'TRUE), embedded in a QUOTE form—but that would be very inefficient because (TRUE) and (FALSE) are constantly tested against in tight loops in the theorem-prover. Instead, we represent (TRUE) and (FALSE) with (the values of) the variables .t. and .f., embedded in QUOTE forms. These values cannot be mistaken as representing LITATOMs in the theory even though they are literal atoms in INTERLISP.

The third problem is the finite limitations imposed by INTERLISP (and all programming languages). For example, no INTERLISP literal atom can have more than 125 characters, nor can any integer require more than 36 bits to represent it. In this paper we pretend INTERLISP imposed no such limits. To ensure the correctness of our program, we have designed it to cause errors (which result in the abortion of any proof attempt) when the finite limitations of INTERLISP are reached. Thus, for example, we use our own badd1 routine for adding one to an integer—and causing an error if the result is unrepresentable—rather than use the built-in routine add1 which returns an inaccurate answer on overflow.

We now make the foregoing sketch precise. An INTERLISP object obj is called an *INTERLISP term* if (termp obj) is non-NIL. Below we define termp and its subroutine evg (for "explicit value guts") which recognizes the INTERLISP objects that may be embedded in QUOTEs to represent explicit value terms.

```
(termp
 (lambda (x)
  (cond
   ((nlistp x)
    (symbolp x))
   ((eq (car x)
        'QUOTE)
    (and (listp (cdr x))
         (null (cddr x))
         (evg (cadr x))))
```

```
(T (and (plistp (cdr x))
        (equal (length (cdr x))
               (arity (car x)))
        (for z in (cdr x) always (termp z)))))))).
```

We define (evg y) so that if y is an INTERLISP object that, when embedded in a QUOTE, represents some explicit value term v, then (evg y) is the top-level function symbol of v. Otherwise, (evg y) is NIL.

```
(evg
 (lambda (y)
  (cond ((nlistp y)
         (cond ((fixp y)
                (cond ((lessp y 0) (quote MINUS))
                      ((equal y 0) (quote ZERO))
                      (T (quote ADD1))))
               ((eq y .t.)
                (quote TRUE))
               ((eq y .f.)
                (quote FALSE))
               ((symbolp y)
                (quote PACK))
               (T NIL)))
        ((eq (car y) .sqm.)
         (cond
          ((and (listp (cdr y))
                (plistp (cdr y))
                (equal (length (cddr y))
                       (arity (cadr y)))
                (assoc (cadr y)
                       (shell.state))
                (for z in (cddr y) always (evg z))
                (for restriction in (cdr (assoc (cadr y)
                                                (shell.state)))
                     as arg in (cddr y) always
                     (cond ((eq (car restriction) 'ONE.OF)
                            (member (evg arg)
                                    (cdr restriction)))
                           (T (not (member (evg arg)
                                           (cdr restriction))))))
           (cond
            ((eq (cadr y) (quote PACK))
             (not (legal.char.code.seq (caddr y))))
```

```
                    ((eq (cadr y) (quote MINUS))
                    (equal (caddr y) 0))
                    (T (not (member (cadr y)
                              (quote (ADD1 ZERO CONS)))))))))
          (cadr y))
          (T NIL)))
        ((and (evg (car y))
              (evg (cdr y)))
          (quote CONS))
        (T NIL))))
```

The puzzled reader should be reminded that termp and evg are only used to say precisely how we represent terms. The theorem-prover only calls termp once when a term is submitted to it by the user. Internal subroutines know what terms look like—indeed, it is to make these internal subroutines efficient that termp is so complicated. As for the correctness of metafunctions, all we have to prove is that when given FORMPs they return FORMPs. The careful reader will note that FORMP is considerably simpler than termp—in particular there is nothing corresponding to the ghastly evg. The fact that a QUOTEd evg can be proved to be a FORMP if and only if the evg itself is a termp is what we have to prove once and for all as Lemma 18.

6.7. Solidification

We now specify what term in the theory is represented by a given INTER-LISP term. Given an INTERLISP term x, the routine s (for "solidify") returns an INTERLISP object that when printed is the term represented by x, displayed without any abbreviations. The subroutine sevg ("solidify explicit value guts") computes the explicit value term represented by an evg object. These two routines are never used by the theorem-prover. They are defined only to make precise the map from INTERLISP terms to terms in the theory.

```
       (s
        (lambda (x)
        (cond
        ((nlistp x)
        x)
        ((eq (car x) 'QUOTE)
        (sevg (cadr x)))
        (T (cons (car x)
                  (for z in (cdr x) collect (s z)))))))
```

```
(sevg
  (lambda (y)
    (cond
      ((nlistp y)
       (cond
         ((litatom y)
          (cond
            ((eq y .t.)
             (quote (TRUE)))
            ((eq y .f.)
             (quote (FALSE)))
            (T (list (quote PACK)
                     (sevg (unpack0 y))))))
         ((lessp y 0)
          (list (quote MINUS)
                (add1.nest (bminus y))))
         (T (add1.nest y))))
      ((eq (car y)
           .sqm.)
       (cons (cadr y)
             (for z in (cddr y) collect (sevg z))))
      (T (list (quote CONS)
               (sevg (car y))
               (sevg (cdr y)))))))
```

6.8. Some example INTERLISP terms and solidifications

Suppose that the value of .sqm. is the INTERLISP literal atom .sqm.
(which could not represent a symbol because it has a period as its first
character). Below we exhibit, in the left-hand column, some sample INTER-
LISP objects (as printed by prin4) and, in the right-hand column, the corresponding term in our theory. In the table we have printed some of the ADD1-
nests as integers even though |(s x)| never actually contains integers.

x	|(s x)|
(PLUS (QUOTE 1) X)	(PLUS (ADD1 (ZERO)) X)
(FN (QUOTE (A . B)))	(FN (CONS (PACK (CONS 65 0)) (PACK (CONS 66 0))))
(QUOTE (.sqm. PACK 2))	(PACK (ADD1 (ADD1 (ZERO))))
(QUOTE 0)	(ZERO)

(QUOTE (QUOTE 0))	(CONS (PACK (CONS 81 (CONS 85 (CONS 79 (CONS 84 (CONS 69 0)))))) (CONS (ZERO) (PACK (CONS 78 (CONS 73 (CONS 76 0))))))
(ZERO)	(ZERO)
(QUOTE (ZERO))	(CONS (PACK (CONS 90 (CONS 69 (CONS 82 (CONS 79 0))))) (PACK (CONS 78 (CONS 73 (CONS 76 0)))))

Displayed with some abbreviations, the last four entries in the table are:

x	|(s x)|
(QUOTE 0)	(ZERO)
(QUOTE (QUOTE 0))	(LIST "QUOTE" (ZERO))
(ZERO)	(ZERO)
(QUOTE (ZERO))	(LIST "ZERO")

These examples are included to encourage the reader to think about our claim that if obj represents the term t, then the result of embedding obj in a QUOTE represents a term whose MEANING, under the standard alist for the variables in t, is t. Note that (QUOTE 0) represents the term (ZERO); the result of embedding (QUOTE 0) in a QUOTE is (QUOTE (QUOTE 0)), which represents the term (LIST "QUOTE" (ZERO)). As claimed, the MEANING of (LIST "QUOTE" (ZERO)) is (ZERO). But the INTERLISP list that prints as (ZERO) is also a termp that represents (ZERO). The result of embedding (ZERO) in a QUOTE is (QUOTE (ZERO)), which represents the term (LIST "ZERO"). (LIST "ZERO") and (LIST "QUOTE" (ZERO)) are two distinct explicit values and are thus not EQUAL. Nevertheless, the MEANING of (LIST "ZERO") is (ZERO).

7. PROOFS OF THE LEMMAS

7.1. Lemmas 1 to 7

The first important lemma is Lemma 4, which establishes that every INTERLISP term actually represents a term in the logic. Lemma 4 guarantees that |(s obj)| is a term in our theory when (termp obj) is non-NIL. Lemma 5 states that if obj is an INTERLISP term, then (list 'QUOTE obj) is an INTERLISP term.

We will first state and prove a very simple lemma as a warm-up exercise.

Lemma 1 ("addl.nest of an integer is a term"). If i is a nonnegative INTERLISP integer, then |(addl.nest i)| is a term.

First consider an example. If i is the INTERLISP integer 3 then |(addl. nest i)| is the explicit value term (ADD1 (ADD1 (ADD1 (ZERO)))).

Proof. We prove Lemma 1 by induction on i.

Base case. If i is 0, (addl.nest i) returns the value of (list 'ZERO), which prints as (ZERO).

Induction step. If i is an integer greater than 0, we may inductively assume that |(addl.nest (subl i))| is a term. Then |(addl.nest i)| is |(list 'ADD1 (addl.nest (subl i)))| which is (ADD1|(addl.nest (subl i))|), which is a well-formed term since ADD1 is a function symbol of one argument and the argument, |(addl.nest (subl i))|, is a term by inductive hypothesis. Q.E.D.

Lemma 2 ("sevg of a list of integers is a term"). If obj is an INTERLISP list of nonnegative integers whose final cdr is 0, then |(sevg obj)| is a term.

Consider another example. If obj is an INTERLISP list which prints as

$$(1\ 2\ .\ 0),$$

then |(sevg obj)| is the term

$$(\text{CONS (ADD1 (ZERO)) (CONS (ADD1 (ADD1 (ZERO))) (ZERO)))},$$

or more succinctly, using the abbreviations of the theory,

$$(\text{CONS 1 (CONS 2 0)}).$$

Proof. The proof is by induction on the size of obj.

Base case. If obj is not a cons, then it must be 0. But |(sevg 0)| is |(addl.nest 0)|, which is a term by Lemma 1 ("addl.nest of an integer is a term").

Induction step. If obj is a cons, then (car obj) is a nonnegative integer and |(sevg (cdr obj))| is a term, by inductive hypothesis. Since (car obj) is not .sqm. (because .sqm. is not an integer),

$$|(\text{sevg obj})| = |(\text{list 'CONS (sevg (car obj)) (sevg (cdr obj)))}|$$

$$= |(\text{list 'CONS (add1.nest (car obj))}$$
$$(\text{sevg (cdr obj)))}|$$

$$= (\text{CONS } |(\text{add1.nest (car obj))}|$$
$$|(\text{sevg (cdr obj))}|),$$

which is a term since CONS is a function symbol of two arguments and both arguments in the CONS-expression above are themselves terms by Lemma 1 ("add1.nest of an integer is a term") and our induction hypothesis. Q.E.D.

Lemma 3 ("*sevg of an evg is a term*"). If (evg obj) is non-NIL, then |(sevg obj)| is a term. (In fact, |(sevg obj)| in this case is an explicit value term, but we will prove that later.)

Proof. We induct on the size of obj.

Base case. Suppose that obj is not a cons. By the definition of evg, obj must therefore be an integer (i.e. recognized by fixp), .t., .f., or a symbolp. (a) If obj is an integer, |(sevg obj)| is either |(add1.nest obj)| or (MINUS |(add1.nest (bminus obj))|), both of which are terms by Lemma 1 ("add1.nest of an integer is a term"). (b) If obj is .t. or .f., then |(sevg obj)| is (TRUE) or (FALSE), both of which are terms. (c) If (symbolp obj) then we also have (litatom obj) and thus |(sevg obj)| is (PACK |(sevg (unpack0 obj))|). But since (unpack0 obj) is an INTERLISP list of nonnegative integers whose final cdr is 0, Lemma 2 ("sevg of a list of integers is a term") tells us |(sevg (unpack0 obj))| is a term. Hence (PACK |(sevg (unpack0 obj))|) is a term.

Induction step. Suppose obj is a cons. We inductively assume that |(sevg obj')| is a term whenever obj' is an INTERLISP object such that (evg obj') holds and obj' is smaller than obj (as measured by the INTERLISP routine count). (a) if the car of obj is .sqm., then, by our (evg obj) hypothesis, obj must have the form (.sqm. fn arg_1 ... arg_n), where fn is a constructor function symbol or bottom object function symbol and n is the arity of fn and (evg arg_i) holds for each arg_i. |(sevg obj)| is (fn |(sevg arg_1)| ... |(sevg arg_n)|), which is a term by the induction hypothesis. (b) If car of obj is not .sqm., then we have (evg (car obj)) and (evg (cdr obj)) and therefore, by our induction hypotheses, |(sevg (car obj))| and |(sevg (cdr obj))| are terms. But |(sevg obj)| is (CONS |(sevg (car obj))| |(sevg (cdr obj))|), which is also a term. Q.E.D.

Lemma 4 ("*s of a termp is a term*"). If (termp obj), then |(s obj)| is a term.

Proof. We induct on the size of obj.

Base case. Given that obj is not a cons and (termp obj) is non-NIL, we know (symbolp obj). Thus, |obj| (i.e., the print name of obj) is a character sequence satisfying the restrictions on variable symbols in our logic. But |(s obj)| is |obj| and thus a term (in particular, a variable).

Induction step. Suppose obj is a cons. (a) If (car obj) is 'QUOTE, then (termp obj) implies that obj must have the form (QUOTE obj') where (evg obj'). |(s obj)| is then |(sevg obj')|, which is a term by Lemma 3 ("sevg of an evg is a term"). (b) If (car obj) is not 'QUOTE, then obj has the form (fn arg$_1$ ... arg$_n$) where n is the nonnegative arity of the function symbol fn and (termp arg$_i$) for each i. |(s obj)| is (fn |(s arg$_1$)| ... |(s arg$_n$)|), which is a term since each |(s arg$_i$)| is inductively a term. Q.E.D.

Lemma 5 ("*QUOTEd term is a term*"). If (termp obj), then (termp (list 'QUOTE obj)).

Proof. By the definition of termp, (termp (list 'QUOTE obj)) is equivalent to (evg obj). Thus it suffices to show that (termp obj) implies (evg obj).

The proof is by induction on the size of obj.

Base case. Suppose obj is not a cons. Then from (termp obj), we have (symbolp obj), which guarantees (evg obj).

Induction step. Suppose obj is a cons.

(a) If (car obj) is 'QUOTE, then, by (termp obj), we have (listp (cdr obj)), (evg (cadr obj)) and that (cddr obj) is NIL. Since (car obj) is not .sqm., (evg obj) is equivalent to the conjunction of (evg (car obj)) and (evg (cdr obj)). The first is immediate. The second is equivalent to the conjunction of (evg (cadr obj)) and (evg (cddr obj)) (both of which are also immediate) provided (cadr obj) is not .sqm.. But (cadr obj) cannot be .sqm. because (evg (cadr obj)) is non-NIL, while (evg .sqm.) is NIL (because .sqm. is a literal atom, distinct from .t. and .f., and not a symbolp).

(b) If (car obj) is not 'QUOTE, then obj has the form (fn arg$_1$ ... arg$_n$), where n is the length of (cdr obj), (arity fn) is n, and (termp arg$_i$) for each i. Provided neither fn nor any arg$_i$ is .sqm., (evg obj) is equivalent to the conjunction of (evg fn), (evg arg$_1$), ..., (evg arg$_n$), and (evg NIL). But (evg fn) follows from the fact that (arity fn) is (length (cdr obj)), which is a nonnegative integer, and (arity fn) is a nonnegative integer only if (symbolp fn). Each (evg arg$_i$) follows from our inductive hypotheses and (termp arg$_i$). (evg NIL) is immediate. Thus, we must show that neither fn nor any arg$_i$ is .sqm.. But since (evg .sqm.) is NIL, this must be the case. Q.E.D.

Lemma 6 ("*unique representation of explicit values*"). For each explicit value term t, there exists (modulo INTERLISP equality) exactly one INTER-LISP object v such that (evg v) is non-NIL and |(sevg v)| is t.

We do not prove this lemma here. The proof, by induction on the structure of explicit values, is tedious but straightforward. We indicate how the proof goes by considering the case for an explicit value of the form (CONS t_1 t_2). By induction hypothesis, the explicit values t_1 and t_2 are uniquely represented, say by v_1 and v_2. The existence part of the proof is easy. The evg (cons v_1 v_2) represents (CONS t_1 t_2): since v_1 is an evg, it is not .sqm. and so |(sevg (cons v_1 v_2))| is (CONS |(sevg v_1)| |(sevg v_2)|) which is (CONS t_1 t_2). The uniqueness argument is more tedious. Suppose that for some evg v not equal to (cons v_1 v_2), |(sevg v)| is (CONS t_1 t_2). Consider the structure of v. Suppose v is not a list. Then the function symbol of |(sevg v)| is either TRUE, FALSE, PACK, MINUS, ADD1 or ZERO, contradicting the assumption that it is CONS. Suppose v is a list whose car is .sqm.. Then the cadr of v must be CONS since the function symbol of |(sevg v)| is CONS. But (evg v) requires that the cadr of such a v not be CONS, so such a v is not an evg. Thus, v must be a list whose car is not .sqm.. But then its car must be an evg representing t_1 and its cdr an evg representing t_2. v_1 and v_2 are the only evgs with that property. Thus, v is equal to (cons v_1 v_2).

In general, the key to the uniqueness argument is that evg checks that .sqm. is not used to "counterfeit" terms that have more efficient representations. Thus, (list .sqm. 'CONS v_1 v_2), the counterfeit representation of (CONS t_1 t_2), fails to be an evg. Similarly, evg checks that .sqm. is not used to represent ADD1 terms, (ZERO), PACK terms of LEGAL.CHAR.CODE. SEQs, or MINUS terms other than (MINUS 0).

We next prove a result similar to but stronger than Lemma 3 ("sevg of an evg is a term").

Lemma 7 ("*sevg of an evg is an explicit value*"). If (evg v) then |(sevg v)| is an explicit value term.

Proof. By Lemma 3 we know |(sevg v)| is a term. To prove that it is an explicit value term we must prove that (i) there are no variables in it, (ii) there are no function symbols other than TRUE, FALSE and shell constructor and bottom object function symbols, and (iii) if the term t occurs as the ith argument to some constructor function const in |(sevg v)|, then the function symbol of t must be one of those recognized (or, depending on the type restriction, not recognized) by the finite set of recognizers specified for the ith component of const.

The proof of each of these facts is by induction on the size of v. Proving that |(sevg v)| contains no variables is immediate from inspection of sevg and one's inductive hypotheses. Proving that all the function symbols are as specified by (ii) is immediate from inspection of sevg and induction except for the case where v is a list whose car is .sqm.. In this case (sevg v) is (cons (cadr v) ...) and so might appear to have an arbitrary function symbol when printed. But (evg v) ensures us that (cadr v) is a shell constructor or bottom object, since it must be found on (shell.state). As for (iii), there are three interesting cases: |(sevg v)| is an (ADD1 ...), a (MINUS ...), or a user-defined shell constructor term. No other primitive shells have type restrictions on their components. A trivial case analysis shows that add1.nest produces only terms satisfying NUMBERP, so the first two cases are immediate. When the third case obtains, the car of v is .sqm. and we must prove that the function symbol of each of the arguments satisfies the corresponding type restriction. But (evg v) checks precisely that by insuring that the function symbol of each argument is a member of (or, depending on the type restriction, not a member of) the finite set specified by (shell.state). Q.E.D.

7.2. Lemmas 8 to 18

We now prove a series of lemmas that let us move from reductions in a history to computations in INTERLISP. Our main goal in this section is Lemma 18.

Lemma 8 ("*LISTP iff listp and not .sqm.*"). If (evg x), then the reduction of (LISTP |(sevg x)|) is (TRUE) if and only if (listp x) is non-NIL and (car x) is not .sqm..

Proof. If (listp x) is NIL or (car x) is .sqm., then the function symbol of |(sevg x)| is either TRUE, FALSE, a bottom object, or a shell constructor other than CONS. Thus, the reduction of (LISTP |(sevg x)|) is (FALSE). To prove the lemma in the other direction, suppose (listp x) is non-NIL and (car x) is not .sqm.. Then (LISTP |(sevg x)|) is (LISTP (CONS |(sevg (car x))| |(sevg (cdr x))|)), whose reduction is (TRUE). Q.E.D.

Lemma 9 ("*CDR is cdr when not .sqm.*"). If (evg x) and (listp x) and the car of x is not .sqm., then the reduction of (CDR |(sevg x)|) is |(sevg (cdr x))|.

Proof. The proof is trivial. Under the conditions given,

$$(CDR \ |(sevg \ x)|)$$

is

$$(CDR \ (CONS \ |(sevg \ (car \ x))| \ |(sevg \ (cdr \ x))|)),$$

whose reduction is |(sevg (cdr x))|. Q.E.D.

We state, without proof, the analogous lemma for CAR and car.

Lemma 10 ("*CAR is car when not .sqm.*"). If (evg x) and (listp x) and the car of x is not .sqm., then the reduction of (CAR |(sevg x)|) is |(sevg (car x))|.

Lemma 11 ("EQUAL iff identical"). If (evg x) and (evg y) then the reduction of (EQUAL |(sevg x)| |(sevg y)|) is (TRUE) if and only if x and y are equal.

Proof. Recall that the reduction of the equation of two explicit values is (TRUE) if and only if the two terms are identical. In addition, by Lemma 7 ("sevg of an evg is an explicit value"), |(sevg x)| and |(sevg y)| are both explicit values.

Suppose the reduction of (EQUAL |(sevg x)| |(sevg y)|) is (TRUE). Then |(sevg x)| and |(sevg y)| are identical. So x and y are equal by Lemma 6 ("unique representation of explicit values"). In the other direction, the reduction is immediate. Q.E.D.

Lemma 12 ("LEGAL.CHAR.CODE.SEQ iff legal.char.code.seq"). If (evg v), then the reduction of (LEGAL.CHAR.CODE.SEQ |(sevg v)|) is (TRUE) if and only if (legal.char.code.seq v) is non-NIL.

Recall that LEGAL.CHAR.CODE.SEQ checks that its argument is a LISTP whose first member is not in (ILLEGAL.FIRST.CHAR.CODES), is a subset of (LEGAL.CHAR.CODES), and terminates in a 0. legal.char.code.seq checks the same things at the level of INTERLISP.

We do not prove this lemma here. However, we will indicate how the proof goes. Our proof involves the following two lemmas:

(1) If (evg c), (evg x), and every element of x is an evg, then the reduction of (MEMBER |(sevg c)| |(sevg x)|) is (TRUE) if and only if (member c x) is non-NIL.

(2) If (evg x), (evg y), and y is a list of evgs, then the reduction of

```
(AND (SUBSETP |(sevg x)| |(sevg y)|)
     (EQUAL (ZERO)
            (IF (LISTP |(sevg x)|)
                (CDR (LAST |(sevg x)|))
                |(sevg x)|))))
```

is (TRUE) if and only if

```
(and (for c in x always (member c y))
     (equal 0
            (cond ((listp x) (cdr (last x)))
                  (T x)))).
```

To use these two lemmas in the proof of Lemma 12 ("LEGAL.CHAR. CODE.SEQ iff legal.char.code.seq") it is only necessary to observe that (LEGAL.CHAR.CODES) and (ILLEGAL.FIRST.CHAR.CODES) reduce to |(sevg (legal.char.codes))| and |(sevg (illegal.char.codes))|. Furthermore, since both (legal.char.codes) and (illegal.first.char.codes) are lists of integers, they are also lists of evgs.

Lemma 13 (*"SYMBOLP iff symbolp"*). If (evg v) then the reduction of (SYMBOLP |(sevg v)|) is (TRUE) if and only if (symbolp v) is non-NIL.

Proof. If the reduction of the SYMBOLP expression is (TRUE), we know the reduction of (LITATOM |(sevg v)|) is (TRUE) and that the reduction of (LEGAL.CHAR.CODE.SEQ (UNPACK |(sevg v)|)) is (TRUE). But by sevg and evg, if the reduction of the LITATOM expression is (TRUE) then either v is a literal atom and (legal.char.code.seq (unpack0 v)) holds so (symbolp v) holds, or else v is a list whose car is .sqm., whose cadr is PACK, and whose caddr is rejected by legal.char.code.seq. We can prove the latter cannot happen, because for such a v (UNPACK |(sevg v)|) is |(sevg (caddr v))| and hence the reduction of (LEGAL.CHAR.CODE.SEQ |(sevg (caddr v))|) is (TRUE), and so Lemma 12 ("LEGAL.CHAR.CODE.SEQ iff legal.char. code.seq") assures us that (legal.char.code.seq (caddr v)) is non-NIL, contradicting the hypothesis that (caddr v) was rejected by legal.char.code.seq. The argument in the other direction is similar. Q.E.D.

Lemma 14 (*"if PLISTP, then plistp and list of evgs"*). If (evg x) and the reduction of (PLISTP |(sevg x)|) is (TRUE), then (plistp x) is non-NIL and every element of x is an evg.

The definition of the function PLISTP, from [1], is:

Definition.

(PLISTP L)

=

(IF (LISTP L)
    (PLISTP (CDR L))
    (EQUAL L "NIL")).

Observe that if c is reducible and (FORM.LSTP c) reduces to (TRUE), then so does (PLISTP c). We introduce PLISTP only to make it easier to establish later that if (FORM.LSTP |(sevg x)|) reduces to (TRUE) then x is a proper list of evgs. We now prove Lemma 14.

Proof. We induct on x.

Base case. If x is not a cons, then the reduction of (LISTP |(sevg x)|) is (FALSE) by Lemma 8 ("LISTP iff listp and not .sqm."). Since the reduction of (PLISTP |(sevg x)|) is (TRUE), (EQUAL "NIL" |(sevg x)|) must reduce to (TRUE), which implies x is NIL by Lemma 11 ("EQUAL iff identical"). But if x is NIL, then our conclusion holds.

Induction step. If x is a cons, inductively assume that if the reduction of (PLISTP |(sevg (cdr x))|) is (TRUE), then (plistp (cdr x)) is non-NIL and every element of (cdr x) is an evg. We must show (plistp x) and that every element of x is an evg. We first observe that (car x) cannot be .sqm., for if it were, (LISTP |(sevg x)|) would reduce to (FALSE) by Lemma 8 ("LISTP iff listp and not .sqm.") and so the reduction of (EQUAL "NIL" |(sevg x)|) would have to be (TRUE), but is not, by Lemma 11 ("EQUAL iff identical") and the observation that NIL is not identical to x. So, we have that the reduction of (LISTP |(sevg x)|) is (TRUE) and thus the reduction of (PLISTP (CDR |(sevg x)|)) is also. But then the reduction of (PLISTP |(sevg (cdr x))|) is (TRUE) by Lemma 9 ("CDR is cdr when not .sqm."), so we get, from our induction hypothesis, that (plistp (cdr x)) is non-NIL and every element of (cdr x) is an evg. The former guarantees that (plistp x) is non-NIL, and the latter guarantees that every element of x is an evg if we can establish that (car x) is an evg. But this follows from (evg x), given that (car x) is not .sqm.. Q.E.D.

Lemma 15 ("*LENGTH is length when list of evgs*"). If (evg x) and x is a list of evgs, then the reduction of (LENGTH |(sevg x)|) is |(sevg (length x))|.

The proof, by induction on x, is omitted because it is so similar to the proof of the preceding Lemma 14.

For the remainder of this section, let us assume that the state of the INTERLISP machine (in particular, the definitions of arity and shell.state) reflect the history T_2 of the Metatheorem.

Lemma 16 ("*ARITY is arity*"). If (symbolp x), then the reduction in both $T_{1.5}$ and MD[T_2] of (ARITY |(sevg x)|) is |(sevg (arity x))|.

Proof. The function symbols TRUE, NOT, IMPLIES, PLUS, f_5, ... , f_m are, by definition, the only functions mentioned in the axioms of T_2. If x is one of these symbols, the theorem holds by the definitions of arity and ARITY. If x is not one of these symbols, both are "NIL". Q.E.D.

Lemma 17 ("*if FORM.LSTP, then list of FORMPs*"). If x is a proper list of evgs and the reduction of (FORM.LSTP |(sevg x)|) in T_2 is (TRUE), then for each element arg in x, the reduction of (FORMP |(sevg arg)|) is (TRUE).

Proof. The proof is by induction on x.

Base case. If x is not a cons, then the reduction of (LISTP |(sevg x)|) is (FALSE) by Lemma 8 ("LISTP iff listp and not .sqm.") so by our FORM. LSTP hypothesis we know the reduction of (EQUAL |(sevg x)| "NIL") is (TRUE), so x must be NIL by Lemma 6 ("unique representation of explicit values") and our conclusion is vacuously true.

Induction step. If x is a cons, we can inductively assume that if (cdr x) is a proper list of evgs and the reduction of (FORM.LSTP |(sevg (cdr x))|) is (TRUE), then for every arg in (cdr x), the reduction of (FORMP |(sevg arg)|)

is (TRUE). We must prove that if x is a proper list of evgs and the reduction
of (FORM.LSTP |(sevg x)|) is (TRUE), then for each element arg of x,
the reduction of (FORMP |(sevg arg)|) is (TRUE). Observe that (car x) is not
.sqm., for if it were, (LISTP |(sevg x)|) would reduce to (FALSE) by Lemma
8 but the reduction of (EQUAL |(sevg x)| "NIL") is (FALSE) by a unique
representation of explicit values argument. So the reduction of (LISTP
|(sevg x)|) is (TRUE) and we infer that the reduction of both (FORMP
(CAR |(sevg x)|)) and (FORM.LSTP (CDR |(sevg x)|)) is (TRUE). Moving
the CAR and CDR inside, using Lemmas 9 and 10, we determine that the
reduction of both (FORMP |(sevg (car x))|) and (FORM.LSTP |(sevg
(cdr x))|) is (TRUE), and by using our induction hypothesis, we establish
that the reduction of (FORMP |(sevg arg)|) is (TRUE) when arg is (car x)
or an element of (cdr x), which is to say, for each element arg of x. Q.E.D.

   We now prove the first of the two lemmas used directly in the proof that
our implementation of the Metatheorem is correct. Lemma 18 establishes
that if (FORMP c) reduces to (TRUE) and c is represented by (list 'QUOTE
obj), then obj itself represents a term. In fact, the lemma holds in the other
direction too, but we do not need it or prove it in that direction.

   Lemma 18 (*"FORMP of a QUOTEd evg iff termp"*). If (termp (list 'QUOTE
obj)) and the reduction of (FORMP |(s (list 'QUOTE obj))|) in $T_{1.5}$ (equiv-
alently, MD[T_2]) is (TRUE), then (termp obj).

Proof. Observe that the first hypothesis is equivalent to (evg obj) and the
second hypothesis is equivalent to the supposition that the reduction of
(FORMP |(sevg obj)|) is (TRUE). The proof is by induction on the size of
obj.

Base case. If obj is not a cons, then by Lemma 8 ("LISTP iff listp and not
.sqm.") we know (LISTP |(sevg obj)|) reduces to (FALSE). Thus, by our
FORMP hypothesis, we know the reduction of (SYMBOLP |(sevg obj)|) is
(TRUE). Hence, by Lemma 13 ("SYMBOLP iff symbolp") we know (symbolp obj), which guarantees (termp obj).

Induction step. obj is a cons. Consider (car obj).
   (a) If (car obj) is 'QUOTE, then we must show (i) (listp (cdr obj)), (ii)
(null (cddr obj)), and (iii) (evg (cadr obj)). The reduction of (FORMP |(sevg
obj)|) is the reduction of (FORMP (CONS "QUOTE" |(sevg (cdr obj))|)|),
which means that the reduction of both (LISTP |(sevg (cdr obj))|) and
(EQUAL "NIL" (CDR |(sevg (cdr obj))|)) is (TRUE). Lemma 8 ("LISTP
iff listp and not .sqm.") is sufficient to ensure (i). In addition, Lemma 8 tells
us (cadr obj) is not .sqm.. Thus the reduction of (EQUAL "NIL" (CDR
|(sevg (cdr obj))|)) is the reduction of (EQUAL "NIL" |(sevg (cddr obj))|)

by Lemma 9 ("CDR is cdr when not .sqm."). But then (cddr obj) is NIL, by a unique representation of explicit values argument. So (ii) holds. As for (iii), note that since both obj and (cdr obj) are listps and neither (car obj) nor (cadr obj) is .sqm., (evg obj) establishes (evg (cdr obj)) which in turn gives us (evg (cadr obj)), which is (iii).

(b) If (car obj) is not 'QUOTE, then we need to show (i) (plistp (cdr obj)), (ii) (equal (length (cdr obj)) (arity (car obj))), and (iii) (for z in (cdr obj) always (termp z)). Our hypotheses are (evg obj) and that the reduction of (FORMP |(sevg obj)|) is (TRUE). First we establish that (car obj) is not .sqm.. Suppose it were. Then the reduction of (LISTP |(sevg obj)|) would be (FALSE) by Lemma 8 ("LISTP iff listp and not .sqm.") and thus the reduction of (FORMP |(sevg obj)|) would be (FALSE) since the reduction of (SYMBOLP |(sevg obj)|) is (FALSE) by Lemma 13 ("SYMBOLP iff symbolp"). Thus, (car obj) is not .sqm. and the reduction of (LISTP |(sevg obj)|) is (TRUE).

Thus, our hypothesis that the reduction of (FORMP |(sevg obj)|) is (TRUE) gives us that the reductions of both

$$\text{(EQUAL (ARITY (CAR |(sevg obj)|))}$$
$$\text{(LENGTH (CDR |(sevg obj)|))))}$$

and

$$\text{(FORM.LSTP (CDR |(sevg obj)|))}$$

are (TRUE). Hence the reduction of

$$\text{(PLISTP (CDR |(sevg obj)|))}$$

is (TRUE). By Lemmas 9 and 10 ("CDR is cdr when not .sqm." and "CAR is car when not .sqm."), and Lemma 16 ("ARITY is arity"), the reduction of each of the following is (TRUE):

$$\text{(EQUAL |(sevg (arity (car obj)))|}$$
$$\text{(LENGTH |(sevg (cdr obj))|)),}$$

$$\text{(FORM.LSTP |(sevg (cdr obj))|),}$$

and

$$\text{(PLISTP |(sevg (cdr obj))|).}$$

Thus, by Lemma 14 ("if PLISTP, then plistp and list of evgs") we know (plistp (cdr obj)) is non-NIL (which establishes (i)) and that every element of (cdr obj) is an evg. But now we can apply Lemma 15 ("LENGTH is length when list of evgs") and Lemma 17 ("if FORM.LSTP, then list of FORMPs") to get that the reduction of

$$(\text{EQUAL } |(\text{sevg (arity (car obj)))}|$$
$$|(\text{sevg (length (cdr obj)))}|)$$

is (TRUE) and that for every arg in (cdr obj), the reduction of (FORMP |(sevg arg)|) is (TRUE). The former is sufficient to guarantee (ii), by a unique representation of explicit values argument. The latter guarantees (iii) since, by induction hypothesis, when the reduction of (FORMP |(sevg arg)|) is (TRUE) for an arg whose count is smaller than obj, then (termp arg) is non-NIL. Q.E.D.

7.3. Lemma 19

We now prove the final lemma used in the argument that our implementation of the Metatheorem is correct. Lemma 19 establishes that if obj represents term t, then (list 'QUOTE obj) represents a quotation of t.

Lemma 19 ("*QUOTEd term is a quotation*"). If (termp obj), then |(s (list 'QUOTE obj))| is a quotation of |(s obj)|.

Proof. By the definition of s, (s (list 'QUOTE obj)) is (sevg obj).
The proof is by induction on the size of obj.

Base case. If obj is not a cons, then from (termp obj), we have that (symbolp obj). But |(sevg obj)| is then "obj" and |(s obj)| is obj.

Induction step. If obj is a cons, consider (car obj).
(a) Suppose the car of obj is 'QUOTE. |(s obj)| is |(sevg (cadr obj))|. From (termp obj), we infer (evg (cadr obj)). From Lemma 7 ("sevg of an evg is an explicit value"), we infer that |(sevg (cadr obj))| is an explicit value. Hence one quotation of |(sevg (cadr obj))| is (LIST "QUOTE" |(sevg (cadr obj))|), which we now show is in fact |(sevg obj)|. Since (termp obj) and the car of obj is 'QUOTE, (cadr obj) is a list, (cadr obj) is an evg (and thus not .sqm.) and (cddr obj) is NIL. Thus, |(sevg obj)| is (CONS "QUOTE" (CONS |(sevg (cadr obj))| "NIL")), which is (LIST "QUOTE" |(sevg (cadr obj))|).
(b) If (car obj) is not 'QUOTE, then obj has the form (fn arg_1 ... arg_n), where n is the length of (cdr obj), (arity fn) is n, and (termp arg_i) for each i. Hence |(sevg obj)| is (LIST "fn" |(sevg arg_1)| ... |(sevg arg_n)|) since no arg_i is .sqm.. By inductive hypothesis, each |(sevg arg_i)| is a quotation of arg_i. Q.E.D.

8. EFFICIENT COMPUTATION ON EXPLICIT VALUES

To use metafunctions efficiently we need a method for rapidly computing the object objd such that the term represented by (list 'QUOTE objd) is the reduction of (simp |(s (list 'QUOTE objc))|), when simp is an explicit value preserving function.

Every time an explicit value preserving function fn is defined in our theorem-proving system, we store in the definition cell of the INTERLISP literal atom .fn. a routine with the following property:

> If fn takes n arguments and $c_1, \ldots, c_n$ are explicit values represented by (list 'QUOTE obj_1), ..., (list 'QUOTE obj_n) respectively, then (list 'QUOTE (.fn. $obj_1 \ldots obj_n$)) represents the reduction of (fn $c_1 \ldots c_n$).

Below we show how we generate the INTERLISP routine for .fn.. We leave to the reader the proof that the program constructed has the desired property. In most cases the proof is straightforward, given the lemmas already proved. The statement of this lemma makes no claim about the efficiency of .fn. but we will discuss efficiency after indicating how the routines are generated.

Consider first those functions that are built in. A suitable definition of .true., the routine corresponding to TRUE, is (lambda () .t.). FALSE is similar. The routine for EQUAL is (lambda (x y) (cond ((equal x y) .t.) (T .f.)))—i.e., it returns .t. if the two evgs are equal INTERLISP objects and .f. otherwise. The routine for IF should return the value of its third argument if that of its first is .f. and otherwise return the value of its second argument. Thus, (.if. x y z) should be macro-expanded into (cond ((eq x .f.) z) (T y)). Any function definition of .if. must first evaluate x in the environment of the calling procedure and then selectively evaluate either y or z in the environment of the calling procedure. We explain why .if. must not evaluate all three arguments when we examine the case for recursive functions.

Before proceeding, recall the property that .functions. are supposed to have. Consider .equal.. It is supposed to be the case that if c_1 and c_2 are explicit values represented by (list 'QUOTE obj_1) and (list 'QUOTE obj_2), then the reduction of (EQUAL c_1 c_2) is represented by (list 'QUOTE (.equal. obj_1 obj_2)). But Lemma 11 ("EQUAL iff identical") establishes that (EQUAL c_1 c_2) reduces to (TRUE) if and only if (equal obj_1 obj_2) is non-NIL, and (list 'QUOTE (.equal. obj_1 obj_2)) represents (TRUE) or (FALSE) according to whether (equal obj_1 obj_2). So .equal. has the property claimed. The proofs of the other .functions. are similar.

The .functions. for the various primitive shell functions are defined similarly so we will only exhibit the definitions of .listp., .cons., .car., and .cdr..

```
(.listp. (lambda (x)
  (cond ((and (listp x)
              (not (eq (car x) .sqm.)))
         .t.)
        (T .f.))))
```

(.cons. (x y) (cons x y))

(.car. (lambda (x)
    (.if. (.listp. x) (car x) 0)))

(.cdr. (lambda (x)
    (.if. (.listp. x) (cdr x) 0)))

Observe how their correctness follows immediately from such lemmas as 8 ("LISTP iff listp and not .sqm.") and 9 ("CDR is cdr when not .sqm.").

Now we consider functions introduced by the user, either via the shell principle or the principle of definition. Suppose we have correctly obtained the INTERLISP routines for all the previously introduced explicit value preserving functions and are now considering some newly introduced function fn.

Suppose fn is introduced by the shell principle. If fn is a recognizer, .fn. is the INTERLISP function that returns .t. or .f. according to whether its argument is a listp whose car is .sqm. and whose cadr is the name of the shell constructor or bottom object of the class. If fn is a bottom object function, .fn. returns the list of length 2 with .sqm. as its car and the bottom object name as its cadr. If fn is a constructor function, .fn. returns a list of length n + 2, with .sqm. as its car, the constructor function name as its cadr, and n elements in the cddr. The ith element of the cddr is just the ith argument to .fn. if that argument satisfies the ith type restriction and otherwise is the evg representing the ith default value. Type restrictions are checked by calling the already obtained routines corresponding to the finite set of recognizers that must approve or disapprove of the argument. The evg for the default value is obtained by calling the already defined routine for it. Finally, if fn is the ith accessor function of a shell, .fn. returns the i + 2nd element of its argument if its argument satisfies the recognizer routine for its shell class (but is not the representation of the optional bottom object), and otherwise returns the evg for the ith default value.

If fn is none of the above, it must be a defined function. Its definition must be of the form (EQUAL (fn $x_1 \ldots x_n$) body), where every function symbol in body (other than fn) is explicit value preserving. Thus, for each such function symbol we have a routine. Let .body. be the INTERLISP expression obtained by replacing uses of fn in body as a function symbol by .fn. and uses of other function symbols in body by the name of the corresponding routine. Define the INTERLISP routine .fn. with (lambda ($x_1 \ldots x_n$) .body.). For example, given the definition of APPEND:

Definition.

(APPEND X Y)
=
(IF (LISTP X)
   (CONS (CAR X) (APPEND (CDR X) Y))
   Y),

the definition for .append. is:

(.append. (lambda (x y)
  (.if. (.listp. x)
    (.cons. (.car. x) (.append. (.cdr. x) y))
    y))).

.fn. always terminates and has the desired property. The key observation is that a certain measure of the arguments decreases on every recursive call (namely the measure that "lifts" the evgs back into the theory and measures them with the function used to justify the definition of fn). The proof relies upon the fact that (.if. x y z) only evaluates y when x evaluates to non-.f., and only evaluates z otherwise. The reason is that the measure justifying the admission of fn was proved to decrease in all recursive calls of fn in the true-branch of the IF provided the test was true, and was proved to decrease in the false-branch provided the test was false. Thus, the inductive hypothesis that the computation of y is correct and terminates can only be obtained in the case where x is known to have computed to non-.f..

This concludes the sketch of how we can generate routines for each explicit value preserving function in the theory.

For efficiency the theorem-prover actually includes built-in definitions of PLUS and LESSP and hand-coded versions of .plus. and .lessp. that take advantage of the hardware for operating on evgs representing Peano integers and avoid the necessity for recursion by SUB1. However, once one gets away from the hardware level the functions one defines can usually take advantage of the same algorithms an efficient procedure might.

While the code we generate for user-defined functions is equivalent to that sketched above, we actually compile it after optimizing it in four ways.

The first optimization technique is to expand certain built-in functions to avoid incurring an INTERLISP procedure call in cases where the compiled code represents only a few machine instructions. For example we expand references to such basic functions as IF and LISTP by expanding the definitions of the corresponding INTERLISP procedures "inline".

The second optimization technique eliminates the tension between INTERLISP's convention of testing against NIL and the theory's convention of testing against (FALSE). In general, the code for (LISTP X) tests (and (listp x) (neq (car x) .sqm.)) against NIL and branches to return .f. or .t. accordingly. According to the optimization presented in the previous paragraph, if (LISTP X) occurs in the test of an IF, we might merely expand (LISTP X) and then test the result against .f. and branch accordingly. But it is inefficient for the expansion of (LISTP X) to branch on NIL to return .t. or .f. only for IF to test the result against .f. and branch again. By keeping track of whether the results of built-in predicates such as LISTP, EQUAL and AND are only being tested in IFs, our expansion avoids the redundant returning of .t. and .f. and the testing against .f..

The third optimization technique eliminates much of the testing of listp and .sqm. that would otherwise be necessary in list processing. In general, the code for (CAR X) expands to

$$(cond ((and (listp x) (neq (car x) .sqm.))$$
$$(car x))$$
$$(T\ 0)).$$

However, if we can prove that the tests governing that occurrence of (CAR X) imply (LISTP X), then (CAR X) can be expanded into (car x)—which compiles into a single machine instruction. Similarly, in expanding (EQUAL X Y), which in general must test (equal x y), we actually test (eq x y)—which requires a single machine instruction—when we know that one of X or Y is a QUOTEd literal atom.

The three optimization techniques above produce the following code from the definition of APPEND:

$$(.append. (lambda (x y)$$
$$(cond ((and (listp x) (neq (car x) .sqm.))$$
$$(cons (car x) (.append. (cdr x) y)))$$
$$(T\ y)))).$$

The fourth optimization technique eliminates the expense of recomputing common subexpressions in the body of a definition during any evaluation of that body. To each common subexpression we allocate a temporary variable that is set to the value of the subexpression the first time it is evaluated. Because we do not put the code into "COND-normal form", thereby removing all conditionals from the tests of other conditionals, a given occurrence o of a subexpression s of a definition can have the property that during some evaluations of the body, a prior occurrence of s has been evaluated before the occurrence at o is reached, while on other evaluations of the body, no prior occurrence of s has been evaluated before the evaluation at o. We therefore initialize our temporary variables with the atom .X. (which is not an evg) and during the evaluation of a body test the temporary variables against .X. in those situations in which our optimizer could not determine that the variable had been previously set. We do not save the values of car/cdr nests since they are compiled efficiently.

The INTERLISP compiler compiles certain forms of recursion as iteration. Thus, the second call of BAGINT in the compiled version of that function is actually implemented as a PDP-10 jump instruction rather than a true recursion.

Here is the INTERLISP code that is compiled for the definition of CANCEL discussed in Section 2. Each setq requires one instruction. Each neq test requires one instruction.

```
(.cancel. (lambda (x)
 (prog ((.temp1. (quote .X.)) (.temp2. (quote .X.))
        (.temp3. (quote .X.)) (.temp4. (quote .X.))
        (.temp5. (quote .X.)) (.temp6. (quote .X.)))
 (return
  (cond
   ((and (setq .temp6. (neq (.equality?. x) .f.))
         (setq .temp5. (neq (.plus.tree?. (.car. (cdr x))) .f.))
         (neq (.plus.tree?. (setq .temp4. (.car. (cddr x)))) .f.))
    (list
     (quote EQUAL)
     (.plus.tree.
      (.bagdiff.
             (setq .temp3. (.fringe. (cadr x)))
             (setq .temp2.
                   (.bagint. .temp3.
                             (setq .temp1. (.fringe. (caddr x)))))))
     (.plus.tree. (.bagdiff. .temp1. .temp2.))))
   ((and .temp6.
         (cond ((neq .temp5. (quote .X.)) .temp5.)
               (T (neq (.plus.tree?. (.car. (cdr x))) .f.)))
         (neq (.member. (cond ((neq .temp4. (quote .X.)) .temp4.)
                              (T (setq .temp4. (.car. (cddr x))))))
              (setq .temp3. (.fringe. (cadr x))))
         .f.))
    (cons
     (quote IF)
     (cons
      (list (quote NUMBERP) .temp4.)
      (cons (cons (quote EQUAL)
                  (cons (.plus.tree. (.delete. .temp4. .temp3.))
                        (quote ((ZERO)))))
```

```
                    (quote ((FALSE)))))))
       ((and .temp6.
          (neq (.plus.tree?. (.car. (.cdr. (cdr x)))) .f.)
          (neq (.member. (cadr x) (setq .temp1. (.fringe. (caddr x))))
             .f.))
        (cons (quote IF)
           (cons (list (quote NUMBERP) (cadr x))
              (cons (list (quote EQUAL)
                    (quote (ZERO))
                    (.plus.tree. (.delete. (cadr x) .temp1.)))
                 (quote ((FALSE)))))))
        (T x))))))
```

For example, if obj is the INTERLISP list structure that prints as

```
(EQUAL (PLUS (PLUS A I) (PLUS B K))
       (PLUS J (PLUS K (PLUS I X))))),
```

then (.cancel. obj) is the INTERLISP list structure

```
(EQUAL (PLUS A B)
       (PLUS J X)).
```

If obj is the INTERLISP list structure (EQUAL A (PLUS A B)) then (.cancel. obj) is the INTERLISP list structure

```
(IF (NUMBERP A)
    (EQUAL (ZERO) (FIX B))
    (FALSE)).
```

By all of the foregoing, we know that if obj represents a term, then (.cancel. obj) represents a term that is provably equal to that represented by obj.

Note that .cancel. sometimes returns a term containing a subterm with ZERO as its function symbol. The theorem-prover will spend a small amount of time converting that term to its normal internal form, (QUOTE 0), upon encountering it in the course of routine simplification. We could have defined CANCEL to return (LIST "QUOTE" 0) instead of (LIST "ZERO"). Both terms have the same MEANING, so the proof of correctness is no more difficult, but the former term compiles to '(QUOTE 0), which is the internal normal form for (ZERO). We did not define CANCEL this way only because at the time CANCEL was first described in this paper we had not defined the MEANING of QUOTE. The use of FALSE in .cancel. can be similarly eliminated.

9. PROOF OF THE CORRECTNESS OF CANCEL

The theorem-prover compiles every explicit value preserving function as soon as it has been admitted into the theory. During subsequent proofs, the compiled code is executed whenever constant expressions, such as (APPEND (LIST 1 2 3) (LIST 4 5 6)), arise. But the theorem-prover cannot use .cancel. as a proof procedure until it has been proved correct.

This raises the question: how hard is it to prove the correctness of metafunctions mechanically? We can report that it was not particularly difficult to prove the correctness of CANCEL using our theorem-prover.

Recall that we have two things to prove: that CANCEL returns a FORMP when given one, and that CANCEL preserves the MEANING of input FORMPs.

Despite the complicated definition of SYMBOLP and its subfunction LEGAL.CHAR.CODE.SEQ, the proof of the FORMP property of CANCEL is almost trivial. The reason is that because CANCEL constructs no new variable symbols, SYMBOLP never becomes involved in the correctness proof: the FORMP hypothesis lets the theorem-prover establish FORMP for every subform of the output that is a subform of the input. So the only work in proving that CANCEL produces FORMPs when given FORMPs is proving that the function applications "created" by CANCEL and its subfunctions are well-formed in the sense of having a function name in the CAR and the right number of FORMPs in the CDR.

To get the theorem-prover to prove the FORMP property of CANCEL, we suggested that it prove the following easy lemmas: when given a FORMP, FRINGE returns a FORM.LSTP, the result of DELETEing something from a FORM.LSTP is a FORM.LSTP, (BAGDIFF X Y) is a FORM.LSTP when X is, and (PLUS.TREE X) is a FORMP if X is a FORM. LSTP. The theorem-prover proves these lemmas without user assistance beyond the statement of the lemmas and the implication that they are useful. The proofs require induction—sometimes on the structure of FORMPs, sometimes on the process of considering the elements of one bag against those of another, and sometimes on linear lists. Besides induction, the proofs require a good deal of simplification and the careful expansion of certain function definitions at the right moments. Once it has established these properties of the subfunctions of CANCEL, the system can easily employ the lemmas to prove that CANCEL produces a FORMP when given one. The entire sequence of FORMP proofs requires about 25 seconds of CPU time on a DEC KL-10.

The proof that CANCEL preserves the MEANING of its input and output is somewhat more interesting. Starting from the basic axioms of the theory and the definitions of the functions concerned, we first got the theorem-prover to prove some obvious facts about the theory of lists (e.g. that X is a MEMBER of (APPEND A B) iff it is a MEMBER of A or B), the theory of bags (e.g. that the bag intersection of two bags is a subbag of both), and the theory of numbers (e.g. that PLUS is associative, commutative, and allows cancellation of a common first argument on each side of an equation). Most of these classic theorems require induction to prove.

Once these facts are available, we instructed the system to prove the fundamental relationships induced by MEANING and PLUS.TREE between bags and numbers. There are three key lemmas: (a) If X is a subbag of Y, then the MEANING of the PLUS.TREE constructed from the bag difference of Y and X is equal to the Peano difference of the MEANINGs of the PLUS.TREEs constructed from Y and X. (b) If X is a subbag of Y then the MEANING of the PLUS.TREE constructed from Y is a number greater than or equal to that constructed from X. (c) The MEANING of (PLUS. TREE (FRINGE X)) is the MEANING of X, when (PLUS.TREE? X) is true. The lemmas are all proved by induction—sometimes on the structure of FORMPs and sometimes on that of bags. The first lemma is the hardest and we invite the reader to prove it as an exercise.

Once these and several similar lemmas have been proved, the fact that CANCEL preserves MEANING is fairly obvious. We will sketch the system's proof for the first branch of CANCEL. Suppose the expression to be CANCELed has the form (EQUAL u v), where u and v are PLUS-trees. By expanding the definition of MEANING, we must prove that the MEANING of the output of CANCEL is equal to:

*1   (EQUAL (MEANING u A) (MEANING v A)).

The output of CANCEL in this case is

        (LIST "EQUAL"
              (PLUS.TREE (BAG.DIFF (FRINGE u) int))
              (PLUS.TREE (BAG.DIFF (FRINGE v) int))),

where int is the bag intersection of the FRINGEs of u and v. The MEANING of the output is thus the equation of the MEANINGs of the two PLUS.TREE expressions:

*2 (EQUAL (MEANING (PLUS.TREE (BAG.DIFF (FRINGE u) int)) A)
           (MEANING (PLUS.TREE (BAG.DIFF (FRINGE v) int)) A)),

and we must show that *1 and *2 are equal. But the MEANING of (PLUS. TREE (BAG.DIFF Y X)) is equal to the MEANING of (PLUS.TREE Y) minus the MEANING of (PLUS.TREE X), provided X is a subbag of Y. Since int is a subbag of both (FRINGE u) and (FRINGE v)—by the fact that the bag intersection of two bags is a subbag of both—we can rewrite *2 to:

*3   (EQUAL (DIFFERENCE (MEANING (PLUS.TREE (FRINGE u)) A)
                     (MEANING (PLUS.TREE int) A))
          (DIFFERENCE (MEANING (PLUS.TREE (FRINGE v)) A)
                     (MEANING (PLUS.TREE int) A))).

Since the MEANING of (PLUS.TREE int) is less than or equal to the two minuends, and the two minuends are always numeric, lemmas from Peano arithmetic let us reduce the above equality to:

*4   (EQUAL (MEANING (PLUS.TREE (FRINGE u)) A)
              (MEANING (PLUS.TREE (FRINGE v)) A)).

But the MEANING of (PLUS.TREE (FRINGE X)) is the MEANING of X, when (PLUS.TREE? X) is true. Thus, we can simplify *4 to:

*5   (EQUAL (MEANING u A) (MEANING v A)),

which is *1. Q.E.D.

The total CPU time required for the MEANING part of the CANCEL proofs (not counting the proofs of the list, bag, and arithmetic lemmas which are part of the system's standard repertoire) is about seven minutes. Thus, the entire CANCEL exercise consumes about eight CPU minutes plus the user's time to formulate the necessary lemmas—a small price to pay for the assurance that the new procedure is sound.

The theorem-prover has proved the correctness of a much more difficult metafunction, namely, the totality, soundness, and completeness of a decision procedure for propositional calculus. The proof of that theorem is discussed in [1]. The theorem-prover required no modification to prove the correctness of CANCEL. In particular, the heuristics developed to prove "ordinary" theorems were just as effective when applied to "metatheorems" stated in terms of MEANING. The proof of the correctness of CANCEL involved much less user direction (in the form of lemmas) than many other mathematical results the system has proved (e.g. the prime factorization theorem derived from our shell axioms for numbers and lists). The proof is also easier than the correctness proofs for many programs (e.g. our fast string searching algorithm).

We are therefore optimistic about the prospects for adding useful new proof procedures to our theorem-prover via this approach.

10. USING METAFUNCTIONS EFFICIENTLY

Whenever the user commands the theorem-prover to prove a theorem, he provides the system with a list of tokens indicating how the theorem is to be stored for future use. In [1] we employed four such tokens: REWRITE, indicating that the theorem is to be used as a rewrite rule, ELIM, indicating that it is to be used to eliminate certain "undesirable" function symbols, GENERALIZE, indicating that the theorem suggests properties to keep in mind when generalizing subgoals, and INDUCTION, indicating the theorem is useful in the search for well-founded relations and measures explaining definitions and inductions. The system checks that the theorem is suitable for use in the ways indicated (e.g. that an INDUCTION lemma really does state a property about a known well-founded relation). The purpose of the tokens is to allow the user to inform the system that the theorem *should* be used in the ways indicated.

We have added the new token META, indicating that the lemma establishes that a certain function is a correct simplifier. A META lemma must have the form of *META in our Metatheorem. Once proved, the compiled code for the metafunction, e.g. .cancel., is stored so that it is executed on each occurrence of certain terms encountered during simplification. Whenever the term returned by the compiled metafunction is different from the input term, that occurrence of the input term is replaced by the output.

For efficiency we require that the user specify the function symbols of the terms to which the metafunction should be applied. For example, when CORRECTNESS.OF.CANCEL is proved the user supplies the META token and the hint to use it to simplify terms with function symbol EQUAL. Had CANCEL been defined to simplify inequalities too, the function symbol LESSP would have been included in the hint. The reader should observe that the hint is entirely heuristic—when CANCEL is proved correct the information that it will be applied only to EQUALities is not available. To be proved correct, CANCEL must be defined to operate correctly on all FORMPs. Thus, soundness is not imperiled should the user supply an "incorrect" hint (e.g. that CANCEL should be tried on terms with function symbol PLUS). This organization of metafunctions was chosen because of the way the theorem-prover's rewrite driven simplifier is structured. When the simplifier encounters a term beginning with the function symbol fn it fetches (from the property list of fn) the list of rewrite rules in which fn is the top-level function symbol on the left-hand side and tries to apply each rule in turn. The compiled code for metafunctions is stored on the list of rewrite rules for each function symbol specified and is tried in its turn.

CANCEL is now in standard use as a META-type proof procedure in our system. The actual definition of CANCEL in use differs slightly from the one presented in Section 2. The real definition uses (LIST "QUOTE" 0) and (LIST "QUOTE" (FALSE)) instead of (LIST "ZERO") and (LIST "FALSE"). In addition, its propositional structure is slightly different so that it is more efficient: LISTP and EQUAL tests are used in place of the functions EQUALITY? and PLUS.TREE?, and the outermost IF first tests whether the argument is an equality and exits immediately when it is not, while the definition presented here tests for equality three times. Both versions of CANCEL have been proved correct and the proofs are virtually identical. The use of CANCEL as a META-type proof procedure slows down our system by roughly one half of one percent on a sample of several hundred theorems, most of which do not involve arithmetic.

To complete this description of our work on metafunctions, we give below our theorem-prover's output on a simple theorem, concocted to illustrate CANCEL at work. The proof is produced immediately after CANCEL has been proved correct and the numerically valued functions TIMES and EXPT have been introduced. The proof involves only equality reasoning and cancellation.

Theorem.

```
(IMPLIES (AND (NUMBERP A)
              (NUMBERP X)
              (NUMBERP B)
              (EQUAL (PLUS (PLUS A B) D)
                     (PLUS B (PLUS (TIMES I J) D)))
              (EQUAL (PLUS A X)
                     (PLUS B (TIMES I J))))
         (EQUAL (EXPT A X) (EXPT A B)))
```

This simplifies, applying the lemma CORRECTNESS.OF.CANCEL and expanding the definition FIX, to the new conjecture:

```
(IMPLIES (AND (NUMBERP A)
              (NUMBERP X)
              (NUMBERP B)
              (EQUAL A (TIMES I J))
              (EQUAL (PLUS A X)
                     (PLUS B (TIMES I J))))
         (EQUAL (EXPT A X) (EXPT A B))),
```

which again simplifies, rewriting with CORRECTNESS.OF.CANCEL and unfolding FIX, to the conjecture:

```
(IMPLIES (AND (NUMBERP X)
              (NUMBERP B)
              (EQUAL X B))
         (EQUAL (EXPT (TIMES I J) X)
                (EXPT (TIMES I J) B))),
```

which again simplifies, clearly, to:

```
                    (TRUE)
```

Q.E.D.

REFERENCES

1. R. S. Boyer and J S. Moore (1979). "A Computational Logic". Academic Press, New York.
2. F. M. Brown (1977). The theory of meaning, Department of Artificial Intelligence Research Report No. 35, University of Edinburgh.
3. F. M. Brown (1978). An investigation into the goals of research in automatic theorem proving as related to mathematical reasoning, Department of Artificial Intelligence Research Report No. 49, University of Edinburgh.
4. M. Davis and J. Schwartz (1977). Metamathematical extensibility for theorem verifiers and proof-checkers, Courant Computer Science Report No. 12, Courant Institute of Mathematical Sciences, New York.
5. M. Gordon, R. Milner, L. Morris, M. Newey and C. Wadsworth (1977). A metalanguage for interactive proof in LCF, Department of Computer Science Internal Report CSR-16-77, University of Edinburgh.
6. J S. Moore (1976). The INTERLISP virtual machine specification, CSL-76-5, Xerox Palo Alto Research Center, Palo Alto, California.
7. R. W. Weyhrauch (1980). Prolegomena to a theory of mechanized formal reasoning. "Artificial Intelligence", Vol. 13, No. 1, pp. 133–170.

4. An informal introduction to specifications using Clear

R. M. BURSTALL and J. A. GOGUEN

ABSTRACT

Precise and intelligible specifications are a prerequisite for any systematic development of programs, as well as being the starting point for correctness proofs. This paper describes "Clear", a language for giving modular and well-structured specifications; the informal presentation gives examples and sketches the algebraic background.

1. IMPORTANCE OF SPECIFICATIONS

If you want someone to build a house for you, it is wise to employ an architect to make sure that what gets built is what you want. The architect will prepare a detailed specification of the house which you can discuss and amend before anyone starts laying bricks. In the same way before anyone invests time and emotional energy in writing a program it is as well to have a specification to make sure that what is produced is what is required. Of course, this specification is usually an informal affair, a document written in technical English. Individual parts of the program also need to be specified and this is often done even more informally. When the house is to be electrically rewired, or the program is to be altered, the specification is consulted so that the original structure and intentions can be understood. In this maintenance phase, which in the case of programs accounts for much of the cost, a good specification is vital.

Specifications must be understandable, so we need informal specifications. They must be precise, so there is a strong case for formal specifications. We can go the whole way from English, to mathematical discourse, to formal logical language with a machine-checkable syntax.

185

The notion of program correctness presupposes a precise specification: a program is correct *relative to this specification*. Most work on correctness has had two aims:

(a) to find methods of attaching parts of the specification to the code (invariants, algorithmic or dynamic logic, weakest preconditions, intermittent assertions);

(b) to carry out proofs mechanically, showing that the program agrees with the specification.

We would like to argue here for paying attention to the specification itself, apart from any program. How can we conveniently but precisely say what we want done? In any realistic case saying what we want done will involve the definition of a large number of auxiliary concepts. We may hope that many of these will be well-known, such as "matrix", "graph" or "unification"; others will be peculiar to the project in hand.

So we should turn our attention to specification languages. Even if our correctness proof methods are too weak or laborious to use in practice, precise specifications and careful thought may enable us to write correct programs much of the time.

This paper is an informal account of one such specification language, Clear, touching briefly on the mathematical basis of the language and including some examples of specification.

1.1. State of the art, and motivation for Clear

The use of particular formalisms and languages for abstract program specifications is a relatively new endeavour. At first our approach was considerably influenced by the success of the algebraic approach to the specification of abstract data types, particularly the work of ADJ. In this tradition, a specification has two parts, one for syntactic declarations, and the other for axioms. The syntactic part is called a *signature* and consists of a set of *sort* names, one for each sort of data involved (such as nat and bool, for natural numbers and truthvalues, respectively), and a set of declarations for *operation* symbols (such as declaring + a binary infix operation on nat, or 'not' a unary operation on bool). The axioms in an algebraic specification are *equations*, that is, pairs of terms which are supposed to denote the same value in every valid interpretation. The "initial algebra" school takes such a specification to denote (an isomorphism class of) "prototypical" model(s) [12].

The area of software engineering (or program methodology) has a number of "specification languages" of a more or less informal character (see the JULY 1980 "SIGSOFT Notices" for information on many of these). Prominent among these is the SRI language SPECIAL, part of the HDM methodology [20]. While many of these languages have been used for the specification and verification of some fairly complex systems, none has been given a complete formal semantics (this is not, of course, a problem for those who are content to work within the limitations of some already established logical formalism, such as first order predicate logic).

A new generation of specification language is arising, based on experiences with the older work. These languages are more expressive than the formalisms used for abstract data types, and more precise than the languages of the programming methodologies. In general, they make use of strong typing and of parameterization. This paper is concerned with the Clear project, first described in [4]. Mention should also be made of the interesting and powerful Z language [1], which is based on axiomatic set theory, and the OBJ system [11], which can be seen as implementing an executable subset of Clear. Recent work, based like Clear on initial algebras, has been done by Reichel et al. [17]. An extension of these ideas using recursive definitions is proposed in [19]. Bjorner has done a number of specifications based on denotational semantic techniques [2], and Guttag and Horning have explored the combination of algebraic specifications with pre- and post-conditions [14].

General system theory has been another important influence on the development of Clear, in at least two different ways. The first, and rather technical influence, is to provide a mathematical foundation for the basic notion of "putting together", as discussed in Section 1.2 below.* The second and somewhat vaguer influence, was toward generality, in that we did not wish to be restricted to the use of only initial algebra semantics for equational axioms, but wanted to be able to use other kinds of axioms, such as first order sentences, if that seemed more appropriate to the problem at hand; this is discussed briefly in Section 1.4. In addition, we wanted to be able to use specifications for cases where *any* model satisfying the axioms would be acceptable; see Section 1.3.

The intention of Clear has been to provide a precise and flexible tool for the construction of program specifications. However, the primitive operations of Clear are very close to the underlying mathematical theory and they are not as powerful as one might desire for convenience of expression. Perhaps Clear could be thought of as analogous to an assembly language, though one with procedures and user definable types. We hope at some future time to provide higher level languages based on the same semantic ideas, which will be of greater practical value in software engineering.

Another important factor for the practical utilisation of abstract specification languages, is to build up a library of specifications which can then be used in putting together other larger specifications. Many of these library specifications will, of course, be parameterized. Without such a library,

---

* This foundation is the categorical notion of colimit, proposed for "putting together" arbitrary systems in [9].

every program specification effort will have to start from scratch, and there will be no significant progress. We believe that program specification should be a communal endeavour.

1.2. Putting theories together

Complex problems may have complex specifications. This means that the specifications will be hard to read, write, and modify, unless they are somehow broken down into pieces of understandable size. Because specification is a constructive process, this means providing a collection of operations on specifications which permit complex specifications to be put together from simple ones. Perhaps the most important such operation is the application of a parameterized specification to a suitable argument. Other operations will permit specifications to be enriched, or to have some of their parts hidden, or to be additively combined into a whole.

In all of this, we take the point of view that the essential purpose of a specification is to provide a *theory* of what some piece of program is supposed to do. Thus, a specification language should consist of *operations upon theories*, and Clear is in fact a language whose expressions denote theories. In particular, Clear takes the view that a parameterized specification is a *procedure* which takes theories as arguments and returns theories as values. An important aspect of this view is that these procedures impose *requirements* on their actual arguments, in the form of certain axioms required to be true before application is meaningful; these requirements are themselves theories.

A complication which must be taken into account in carrying out this program, is to insure that shared subtheories are properly treated. For example, we should expect that many particular theories will have the theories Bool of truthvalues and Nat of natural numbers, as subtheories, and we want to be certain that when such particular theories are combined, there remains at the end only one copy each of Bool and Nat. This leads to a concept of environments with sharing.

1.3. Data constraints

A theory used to specify a not entirely trivial piece of software generally has a number of interesting subtheories. Some of these subtheories specify particular data structures and operations, while others assert some axioms which may be satisfied by any of a variety of structures. For example, Bool specifies the particular (up to isomorphism) structure of truth values, while Poset can be satisfied by any partially ordered set. Note that Bool is a subtheory of Poset. We shall call *canonical* those theories which are intended to specify particular structures, and we shall call *loose* those which are used to specify any structure satisfying the axioms. A more complex situation is when we wish to specify some particular structure as canonical only once some other structure, satisfying a loose specification, has been fixed. For example, the parameterized specification List(X) specifies the data structure of lists of X's, once X has been given; but any interpretation of X is permitted, so long as it has at least one sort. We formalize all this with the notion of a *data constraint* which is an assertion that one theory shall be interpreted canonically relative to another (possibly empty) theory. Theories not so constrained are interpreted loosely. Canonical interpretations are defined mathematically by use of initial algebra semantics, using ideas originally due to Kaphengst and Reichel [18].

1.4. Generality

At this time, it is not entirely clear what underlying logic will be the most appropriate for writing the axioms to be used for program specification. Indeed, it may be that there is no single best choice, but that different logical systems will be more suitable for different applications. Clear has been defined in such a way that any underlying logical system can be used which satisfies certain conditions regarding the relationship between theories and models. We call such suitable logical systems *institutions*; they are discussed further in Section 10. Examples include equational logic, first order logic, temporal logic, and (putatively) error and continuous equational logic.

The last three are presumably useful for describing concurrent systems, error (or exception) handling, and non-terminating systems (such as operating systems), respectively.

2. THE CLEAR SPECIFICATION LANGUAGE

To specify some concepts in Clear we write them in the form of a theory. This theory will have *sorts*, *operations* and *equations* (we give examples mostly in equational logic). Further concepts are introduced by enriching this theory; we may add new sorts, operations and equations.

The sorts are different kinds of data, such as numbers, truthvalues or lists of these. They may also be "uninterpreted", as in considering some collection of elements with an ordering. We introduce the former using the word *data*. For example

> *const* Bool =
>> *theory data sorts* bool
>>> *opns* true, false: bool *endth*

This means that the sort bool can only be constructed by the operators true and false (constants count as nullary operations). Furthermore, since there are no equations given, true $\neq$ false. In general when *data* are used, terms using the operators are not equal unless their equality follows from the given equations. The theory of Boolean sequences could be done thus (note that . is an "infix" operation)

> *const* Bool-sequence =
>> *theory data sorts* bool,sequence
>>> *opns* true,false: bool
>>> empty: sequence
>>> unit: bool $\rightarrow$ sequence
>>> $-.-$: sequence,sequence $\rightarrow$ sequence
>>> *eqns* empty.s = s
>>> s.empty = s
>>> s.(t.u) = (s.t).u
>> *endth*

For example we may deduce from these equations that

$$\text{empty.(unit(true).empty)} = \text{unit(true).empty}$$

but

$$\text{unit(true).empty} \neq \text{unit(false).empty}$$

since the equality is not deducible. We will write this equality, or identity, as a boolean operation "$==$". We can then say "not (s $==$ t)", whereas we do not permit inequations such as s $\neq$ t.

We would like to add extra operations to Bool; this is an *enrichment*, say Bool1,

> *const* Bool1 =
>> Bool *enriched by*
>>> *opns* not: bool $\rightarrow$ bool
>>> $-$ and $-$: bool,bool $\rightarrow$ bool
>>> $-$ or $-$: bool,bool $\rightarrow$ bool
>>> *eqns* not(false) = true
>>> not(true) = false
>>> b and true = b
>>> b and false = false
>>> b or true = true
>>> b or false = b
>> *enden*

We could more elegantly have written Bool-sequence as an enrichment, thus

> *const* Bool-sequence =
> Bool *enriched by*
> > *data sorts* sequence
> > *opns* empty: sequence
> > > unit: bool $\to$ sequence
> > > $-.-$: sequence,sequence $\to$ sequence
> > > *eqns* empty.s = s
> > > s.empty = s
> > > s.(t.u) = (s.t).u
> > *enden*

But what if we want "not", "and", "or" as well as "."? We need to combine theories using "+", thus

$$\text{Bool1} + \text{Bool-sequence}$$

The part which is common to Bool1 and Bool-sequence, that is Bool, is not duplicated.

Strictly we should put a list of variables before each equation

$$\textit{forall } b: \text{bool. } b \text{ and true} = b$$

but we will allow ourselves to omit this.

So far we have introduced sorts which are intended to have one particular interpretation (to within isomorphism). But we can also introduce "loosely interpreted" sorts, which are intended to have a variety of interpretations. For example an automaton is a set of states, with a start state, a transition function and an accept predicate, say,

> Bool1 *enriched by*
> > *sorts* state
> > *opns* start: state
> > > transition: bool,state $\to$ state
> > > accept: state $\to$ bool
> > *enden*

We just omit the word *data* before the list of sorts.

The states of the automaton could be realized by many different (non-isomorphic) data types, for example, numbers, pairs of numbers or strings of characters; various interpretations could be given to the operations start, transition and accept. We will see later how state can be 'bound' to one of these particular data types. Such loosely interpreted sorts occur in theories used to state the requirement for a theory procedure, say one defining further concepts based on the notion of automaton. This procedure could then be applied to some particular automaton.

Other examples of theories with uninterpreted sorts would be concepts like "partially ordered set" and "monoid".

2.1. Models and inference

In the Boolean sequences example we wrote down three equations. Obviously we intend all the consequences of these equations to also hold, for example

$$\text{empty.unit(true)} = \text{unit(true)}$$
$$\text{s.}((\text{t.u}).\text{v}) = \text{s.}(\text{t.}(\text{u.v}))$$

Call a set of sorts and a set of operators with given argument and result sorts a *signature*. Thus the signature of a theory is the theory without the equations. An *algebra* for that signature is a structure which has a set associated with each sort and a function associated with each operator (a function from the sets associated with the argument sorts of the operator to the set associated with its result sort). See [5] or [12] for a more technical account of all this.

For example an algebra A for the Bool-sequence signature might have {0, 1} for bool, and the integers . . . − 1, 0, 1, 2, . . . for sequence. We could let true be 1, false be 0, empty be 0, unit be the identity function and concat be addition.

Now an algebra *satisfies* a theory (is a model of the theory) if it makes each equation in the theory true for any values of the variables. Just pick values for the variables in the sets associated with their sorts, evaluate the left and right-hand sides of the equation using functions for the operators and check that they are equal. In our example A does indeed satisfy Bool-sequence.

Suppose now that we have some set E of equations. Consider all the algebras which satisfy them. There may well be other equations which are also satisfied by all these algebras; these are called the *logical consequences* of the original set E. We call the union of E with its logical consequences the *closure* of E. Actually in Clear we just write a finite set of equations whose closure is the theory we wish to describe. To find whether an equation is in this closure we need inference rules and a theorem prover.

But something is not right with our algebra A as a model for Bool-sequence! We were trying to describe strings of truth values. There is no harm in using 0 and 1 instead of "TRUE" and "FALSE" since we are only interested in the mathematical properties of truth values and do not care whether they are represented by 0 and 1 or by Charlie Chaplin and Maggie Thatcher so long as negation, conjunction and disjunction do the right thing. But the integers with identity and addition really will not do for sequences. Consider unit(false) and empty; they would both be represented by 0. Also unit(true).unit(false) and unit(false).unit(true) would both stand for 1. There would be no way to denote −1.

We need algebras for which two extra conditions hold:

(1) Two expressions have the same value in the algebra if and only if the equations compel them to do so, that is if and only if they have the same value in every algebra which satisfies the equations.

(2) Every element in the algebra is the value of some expression.

It turns out that although there are many such algebras they are all "isomorphic", i.e. if the conditions hold for both A and B we can make a one to one correspondence between their elements which "respects" the sorts and operations. We can do an operation in A or on the corresponding elements of B and get corresponding results.

The slogans are:

(1) "no confusion"—expressions should not be equal unless they are forced to be so by the equations;

(2) "no junk"—the algebra should not have unnecessary elements.

We call such an algebra *initial.** The initial algebra satisfying Bool is easy: just take the domain to be {0, 1}, let true denote 1 and false denote 0.

What is an initial algebra for Bool-sequence? We can take bit-strings, with "empty" meaning the empty string and "." meaning concatenation of strings. This satisfies the equations but no two terms evaluate to the same value unless the equations compel them to do so; also each string is denoted by at least one term. Had we taken the integers as the denotation of sort "sequence" neither of these conditions would have held.

Consider now a "loose" theory "Poset" of partially ordered sets

> *const* Poset =
> Bool *enriched by*
> *sorts* element
> *opns* − ≤ −, == : element,element → bool
> *eqns* x ≤ x = true
> x ≤ y and y ≤ x => x == y = true
> x ≤ y and y ≤ z => x ≤ z = true
> *enden*

(Here "==" is the operation used for identity, whilst "=" is part of the notation for an equation. When a data sort is introduced it automatically gets an identity operation.)

Now consider a theory of sequences of partially ordered elements,

---

* There is a good (categorical) reason for this name but it does not concern us here.

const Poset-sequence =
  Poset *enriched by*
    data sorts sequence
      opns empty: sequence
            unit: bool → sequence
            −.− : sequence,sequence → sequence
      eqns empty.s = s
            s.empty = s
            s.(t.u) = (s.t).u
  enden

Which algebras satisfy Poset? Which satisfy Poset-sequence?

For Poset we must interpret the Bool part initially but we may take any set as the interpretation of sort element with any reflexive and transitive relation for ≤. (Indeed the initial algebra has the empty set as the interpretation of element; so it is dull.) However given an interpretation of element and ≤ there is only one way we wish to interpret Poset-sequence, as strings of such elements. Thus the enrichment in Poset-sequence denotes an algebra which is initial *relative to* a given Poset algebra A. We call this the *free* Poset-sequence algebra on A. It has the property that the two Poset-sequence terms only have the same value if they do so in all algebras which extend A and satisfy the equations of the enrichment, also that each value is denoted by at least one term.

Thus for an algebra to satisfy Poset-sequence not only must it obey all the equations but it must also interpet the data enrichments freely. This means that a Clear specification represents more than just a signature and some equations; we must also remember which parts are to be interpreted freely. We call the constraint that an enrichment is to be interpreted freely a *data constraint*, and call a theory together with a set of data constraints on parts of it a *data theory*. An algebra satisfies a data theory if it satisfies the theory and also satisfies the data constraints in the sense that the indicated parts have the free interpretation. The technical details, using the notion of theory morphism, are given in (5).

Since we have a notion of an algebra satisfying a data constraint we can treat constraints just as we do equations. We ask which algebras satisfy a set of equations and data constraints, and then what other equations are satisfied by the same set. These are the logical consequences. Thus we have defined logical consequence for data theories. A data constraint acts like an induction principle, for example it might be an enrichment introducing operations empty, unit and ".", in which case the associated induction principle says "prove it for empty, for unit(x) and assuming it for s and t prove it for s.t". Thus the data constraint has extra equations as its logical consequences, and even extra data constraints (derived induction principles).

The idea of data constraints on a theory is due to Kaphengst and Reichel [18]. It was developed in its present form by Reichel [22], and independently by us.* Reichel uses the term *canon* for essentially the same concept as our data theory. It seems an important notion and one which elegantly overcomes a number of difficulties encountered in defining the notion of parameterized theory and in permitting "loose" specifications which can be realised in more than one way.

2.2. Derive

We have seen how to enrich a theory by adding new sorts and operators, but we may sometimes wish to hide or to rename certain sorts and operators. Suppose for example that we wish to construct a theory of "characters" with a certain order relation "$\leq$", say $A \leq \ldots \leq Z \leq 0 \ldots \leq 9$. It may be convenient to use the existing theory of natural numbers with "$\leq$", but we do not require the operations of addition and multiplication on characters. We can accomplish this by giving the new sorts and operators (but not necessarily the equations they obey) and also giving a map from new sorts and operators to old ones.

> *const* Characters = *derive sorts* character
>   *opns* A, ..., Z, 0, ..., 9: character
> $- \leq -$: character,character $\rightarrow$ bool
>   *using* Bool
>   *from* Natleq
>   *by* character *is* nat,
>   A *is* 0, ..., Z *is* 25, 0 *is* 26, ..., 9 *is* 35
> $\leq$ *is* $\leq$
>   *endde*

The new sort "character" and the new operations "A", "B" etc. form an enrichment of Bool. The equations they obey are derived from those of Natleq, a theory of natural numbers with a "less than or equal" ordering, via the map which takes "character" to "nat", A to 0 etc. To find out whether an equation holds in the character theory we use this map to translate it into the number theory and check whether it holds there. Thus "$A \leq B$" holds because "$0 \leq 1$" holds for natural numbers. Note that Bool is a common subtheory of Natleq and the new theory of characters.

Here is another example, Rationals derived from integers. We first enrich the integers to get a theory, R, with a new sort, r, consisting of equivalence classes of pairs of integers. The binary operation "$//$", written as an infix,

---

* One of us (RMB) had heard a talk by Reichel in 1977 using his original notion but failed to appreciate the idea and later "re-invented" a slightly extended form of it.

takes a pair of integers to their equivalence class. We define operations of
addition, subtraction, etc. on these equivalence classes, and also the "injection", i, of the integers into R. Now R has the structure of the rationals
but it still bears marks of its construction, the operation $//$. So we derive
Rationals from R, "hiding" the $//$ operation. It is a nuisance to write out a
long description of the translation map with "0 *is* 0", "1 *is* 1" etc. so we
permit operations with the same name in each case to be omitted. This
example will involve "errors", the further discussion of which we defer
until after giving the Clear text.

> *const* Rat =
>> *let* R = Integers *enriched by*
>>> *data sorts* r
>>> *opns* $-//-$: int,int → r
>>> *err-opns* OVFL: r
>>> *eqns*
>>>> $(k*m)//(k*n) = m//n$ if $k \neq 0$ and $n \neq 0$
>>>> $(n//0)$ = OVFL *enden*
>>
>> *enriched by*
>>> *opns* i: int → r
>>> *eqns* i(n) = n//1 *enden*
>>
>> *enriched by*
>>> *opns* 0,1: r
>>>> $+, -, *, /$: r,r → r
>>> *eqns* 0 = i(0)
>>>> 1 = i(1)
>>>> $(m1//n1) + (m2//n2) =$
>>>>> $(m1*n2 + m2*n1)//(n1*n2)$
>>>> $(m1//n1) - (m2//n2) =$
>>>>> $(m1*n2 - m2*n1)//(n1*n2)$
>>>> $(m1//n1)*(m2//n2) = (m1*m2)*(n1*n2)$
>>>> $(m1//n1)/(m2//n2) = (m1*n2)//(n1*m2)$ *enden*
>>
>> *in*
>>> *derive sorts* rat
>>> *opns* 0,1: rat
>>>> $+, -, *, /$: rat,rat → rat
>>>> rational: int → rat
>>> *using* Integers
>>> *from* R
>>> *by* rat *is* r, rational *is* i   *endde*

The intuitive idea of errors is that the elements of sort s can be of two
subsorts: *ok* or *error*. The ok elements are the normal expected ones, and the

error elements are the exceptional ones, the error messages. Similarly, there are ok operators and error operators. The ok operators normally produce ok values, but may sometimes produce error values (e.g. $1//0 =$ OVFL, where "OVFL" is the error message for "overflow"); the error operators always produce error values (e.g. X IS-UNDEFINED-VARIABLE, where "IS-UNDEFINED-VARIABLE" is a post-fix error message producing function). It is required that all operations "preserve errors", in the sense that if any argument is an error, then so must the result be.

The above Clear text first defines, with an unnamed data theory, an error algebra having as its ok values of sort r equivalence classes of pairs of integers (e.g. $\{1//1, 2//2, 3//3, \ldots\}, \{2//1, 4//2, \ldots\}$) representing the usual rationals, and as its error values of sort r, the single equivalence class $\{$OVFL, $0//0$, $1//0, 2//0, \ldots\}$, using the convention that anything equivalent to an error is an error. We next form the theory R, which enriches this structure with some new operations, which are the usual field operations, and defines them, for ok-values, in terms of the previous values given by R. Because these definitions are given by "ok-eqns" (just called *eqns*), nothing is said about what is to happen if an error arises; in this sense the enrichment is "loose". For example, nothing is said about the value of $((1//0)//0) + 2$ (except that it is an error element). Finally, we use *derive* to hide the operation $//$ and change the operation "i" to "rational", thus arriving at a specification whose ok part of sort rat is the usual rationals, and whose error part of sort rat, is some algebra of error messages.

Clear gives you the choice of specifying what you mean (a) directly by a set of equations (abstract specification), or (b) by deriving it from some preexisting concepts by first constructing a model from these and then hiding or renaming some of the sorts and operators (constructive specification). The abstract method is more elegant but more prone to mistakes. The ordinary programmer would probably do better with constructive specification most of the time; an exception is when he wants to define an operation as the inverse of another operation.

2.3. Parameterized theories

We defined above the theory of boolean sequences. But what if we want sequences of natural numbers? Do we have to start all over again? We need a theory of sequences of anything. How about a theory of sorting which has an operation which sorts a sequence into ascending order? We would like to do that in general too, but it can only be done for elements which have a partial order defined on them. These are examples of *parameterized theories*, otherwise known as *theory procedures* since they take a theory as argument and deliver a new theory as result. As we have just seen the argument must satisfy certain conditions, for example the procedure which produces the theory of sorting will accept any theory which has a sort with a partial ordering over it. For instance given the natural numbers with the usual "less than or equal" operation it produces the theory of natural numbers, sequences of natural numbers and the operation for sorting these sequences. We express the constraint that the parameter must have a sort with a partial order by associating Poset, the theory of partial orders, with this parameter, writing:

$$\textit{procedure } \text{Sorting(P: Poset)} = \ldots$$

We call Poset the "requirement" for P ("requirement" replaces our previous term "metasort" in [4]). The procedure sorting will accept any theory T which is an "example" of Poset, in the sense that we can specify a map from the sorts of Posets to the sorts of T and from operations of Poset to operations of T such that if we translate via this map any equation holding in Poset then the translation holds in T. We write the map in brackets after the argument theory. As for derive, if an operation maps into another with the same name we may omit it. Thus

$$\text{Sorting(Natleq[element } \textit{is } \text{nat, } \leq \textit{is } \text{leq])}$$

We will work out this example in detail. We start with the notion of sequence. The sequence procedure has a quite trivial requirement, it just needs a sort and no operations. We first define this requirement theory, then sequences.

> *const* Triv = *theory sorts* element *endth*

> *procedure* Sequence(X: Triv) =
>   X *enriched by data sorts* sequence
>   *opns* empty: sequence
>   unit: element → sequence
>   −.− : sequence,sequence → sequence
>   *eqns* empty.s = s
>   s.empty = s
>   s.(t.u) = (s.t).u
>   *enden*

Note that we refer to "element"; this is more properly "element *of* X" since there might be another parameter "Y: Triv", but we may omit "*of* X" when no confusion is possible.

Now for Sorting we use the requirement Poset, then define the procedure Ascending which defines "ascending sequence".

procedure Ascending(SP: Sequence(Poset)) =
    SP *enriched by*
        opns $-\leq-$: sequence,sequence $\rightarrow$ bool
        eqns empty $\leq$ s = true
            unit(x) $\leq$ unit(y) = x $\leq$ y
            s $\leq$ t.u = s $\leq$ t and s $\leq$ u
            s.t $\leq$ u = s $\leq$ u and t $\leq$ u   *enden*
    enriched by
    opns ascending: sequence $\rightarrow$ bool
    eqns ascending(empty) = true
        ascending(unit(x)) = true
        ascending(s.t) = ascending(s) and s $\leq$ t and ascending(t)
    enden

We need to say that the ascending sequence is a permutation of the original one. How can we express this? A convenient way is to introduce the notion of "bag", that is, unordered sequence. A sequence is then a permutation of another if they yield the same bag. Bag and Perms define these concepts. We then use Ascending and Perms to define Sorting.

procedure Bag(X: Triv) =
    X *enriched by data sorts* bag
        opns empty: bag
            unit: element $\rightarrow$ bag
            $-$ union$-$: bag,bag $\rightarrow$ bag
        eqns empty union b = b
            b union c = c union b
            b union (c union d) = (b union c) union d
    enden

procedure Perms(ST: Sequence(Triv)) =
    ST + Bag(ST) *enriched by*
        opns bagof: sequence $\rightarrow$ bag
            is-perm: sequence,sequence $\rightarrow$ bool
        eqns bagof(empty) = empty
            bagof(unit(x)) = unit(x)
            bagof(s.t) = bagof(s) union bagof(t)
            is-perm(s,t) = (bagof(s) == bagof(t))
    enden

procedure Sorting(P: Poset) =
    Ascending(Sequence(P)) + Perms(Sequence(P)) *enriched by*
        opns sort-up: sequence $\rightarrow$ sequence
        eqns is-perm(s,sort-up(s)) = true
            ascending(sort-up(s)) = true *enden*

A facility which we have not mentioned so far is introducing a local name for a theory using *let* ... = ... *in* .... For example

> *proc* P(X: Poset) =
>   *let* F = Map(X,X) *in*
>   ...X...F...   (expression using F as well as X)

2.4. Shared subtheories

As we build up our Clear specification we define a number of constant theories (like Bool), and we introduce parameter theories (X in *proc* P(X:T) = ...) and local theories (Y in *let* Y = ... *in* ...). Now these theories are not independent. Bool may be used in defining T, and both X and Bool may be used in defining Y. If Bool is used to define T we may call it an "ancestor" of T. Clear keeps this ancestry relation as part of the environment so that when we combine two theories, Y + Z, the new theory has the *disjoint* union of their sorts and operators, *except* that common ancestor theories are not duplicated. This means that if two people working on different parts of the specification happen to choose the same name for an operator they are still regarded as distinct. Also each application of a procedure gives a fresh copy of the new sorts and operators which it introduces. For example Set(X) + Set(X) will have two sorts called Set and two union operators, but *let* S = Set(X) *in* S + S only has one sort and one operator.

It may be that in our desire to avoid global names and unintentional clashes we have gone a bit too far in making names different, one might like Set(X) to mean the same thing whenever it is written. Our semantics (using the notion of "pushout") is consistent but may cause undue "proliferation" of distinct names, an inconvenience when writing Clear specifications. This needs further exploration.

3. IMPLEMENTATION

Clear is a specification language, not a programming language; its purpose is communication rather than calculation. Nevertheless a computer implementation can help us to answer two questions:
(a) Have we written a valid specification?
(b) What are its consequences?
For the first of these, validation, we must show that: (1) the specification is syntactically correct; (2) it typechecks; (3) each time a Clear procedure is used its arguments fulfil their respective requirements.
Let us examine these in turn.

(1) For this we need a syntax checker. A general one written by David MacQueen has been adapted for Clear by Don Sannella.

(2) To typecheck the equations we need to determine the local environment of sorts and operators. This means implementing the signature part of the definitions of the Clear operations, "+", enrich and derive, also dealing with procedure application. Shared subtheories must be handled correctly. We then need a typechecker for expressions (again we have one provided by MacQueen but not yet adapted for Clear).

(3) To check that arguments of procedures satisfy the requirement theories we need to use the definitions of the Clear operations and of procedure applications, this time to determine what equations are in the environment at a particular point. We then need a theorem prover to show that each equation in the requirement, suitably instantiated, can be derived from the argument theory. For example if the requirement is for a partially ordered set and we supply the theory of natural numbers with arithmetic "less than or equal", we must show that this operation is reflexive, transitive and symmetric.

Turning to our second question, how do we discover the consequences of the specification? We may follow the Z language and allow the user to insert "theorems" at any point in addition to the specifying equations. To prove such a theorem follows from the specification involves just the same mechanisms as checking that a requirement is fulfilled.

Thus we have to implement the Clear operations on theories and provide a theorem prover. We have not attempted the latter, but Don Sannella and David Rydeheard as part of their Ph.D. work at Edinburgh have done a pilot implementation of the Clear operations, including procedure application, working from an abstract syntax. Their program is coded in the functional language Hope [6], and it follows closely the categorical semantics in [5]. The categorical definitions are implemented by the methods described in [3], an approach which we believe to be novel and interesting. However this implementation "from first principles", although very transparent, is far from efficient in time or space. It has recently been completed, compiled and run on some small examples; further testing is in progress. It has led to discovery of two "bugs" in the semantic definition. Part of the categorical definitions have been recoded more efficiently in POP-2 by Sannella, and he is designing a more practical implementation.

Coding up the mathematical definitions in a strongly typed functional language seems to provide a good basis for understanding and checking out the language definitions. We feel that we were right to do a formal semantics before attempting an implementation.

4. LIMITATIONS AND EXTENSIONS

The Clear language here described suffers from a number of limitations which make it more difficult to write certain specifications. In particular it lacks quantifiers, infinite data objects and higher order operators.

4.1. Quantifiers

We have an implicit universal quantifier around the equations, but no existential quantifier. So we cannot make a straightforward definition like

Prime(n) iff not *exists* i *exists* j. i $\neq$ 1 and j $\neq$ 1 and i*j = n

We can wriggle round this by using bounded quantifiers "*exists* x ε S" where S is a finite set. Thus since we need only check divisors up to n

Prime(n) = not *exists* i ε Upto(n). *exists* j ε Upto(n). 2 $\leq$ i and 2 $\leq$ j and i*j = n

where Upto(n) is (straightforwardly) defined to be {1, . . . , n}. This doesn't look much better, but in fact we can code up such bounded quantifiers in Clear. Consider

exists n ε S. Nice(n)

We can make an auxiliary definition of an operation

Exists-nice: set(nat) $\rightarrow$ bool

with

Exists-nice(empty-set) = false
Exists-nice({n}) = Nice(n)
Exists-nice(S1 union S2) = Exists-nice(S1) or Exists-nice(S2)

We can use this technique to code up the above definition of Prime with two auxiliaries; but it is rather clumsy.

Much better is to extend Clear to permit axioms using quantifiers. Now equational theories have a "best" model, the initial one, but predicate calculus theories do not. The solution is to use equations for introducing new data, with constructor operations, but to permit predicate calculus sentences with *for all* x and *exists* x when we introduce other operators. (We will call them axioms rather than equations.) Of course, we can still use equality in these predicate calculus axioms.

const Natprime =
    theory data sorts nat
        opns 0: nat
            succ: nat $\rightarrow$ nat   endth

enriched by opns − + − : nat,nat → nat
eqns 0 + n = n
　　　succ(m) + n = succ(m + n)
enriched by predicate − ≤ − : nat,nat
　　axioms m ≤ n iff *exists* k. (m + k = n)

Now the Clear semantics in [5] does not permit this. We need to extend the general scheme of semantics to deal with two kinds of theory, equational and predicate. We believe we know how to do this and it is not hard, but the technical details are out of place here.

4.2. Infinite values

The data sorts are introduced as initial algebras which may be thought of as consisting of equivalence classes of finite terms. Thus it is not possible to have a data type whose elements are infinite sequences. Even though such infinite objects do not occur as stored values in a computer they are very useful in describing computations, for example the infinite set of strings generated by a grammar, or the infinite sequences of values produced by a non-terminating program, say an airline reservation system.

One remedy is to pass from algebras to continuous algebras, for which some initiality results are known. The equations then involve infinite terms and a fixed point or recursive notation would have to be used for these.

Another remedy is to embed set theory, say presented in first order logic, in Clear. Data sorts would have to include (possibly infinite) sets, not just data defined by initial algebras. This would follow the lead of the Z language [1], which takes set theory as its basis and constructively defines all other data types in terms of sets. This follows the widely accepted approach for the foundations of mathematics. The question would then arise as to whether initial algebra definitions should be abolished or whether it would be convenient to retain them alongside the set constructions. How do you merge the good ideas in Clear with those in Z?

4.3. Scott domains

In programming language semantics, and more recently in tackling other specification problems, good use has been made of Scott domains. These can be defined as the solution of recursive domain equations. They permit infinite objects and partial functions and functionals to be described. These more sophisticated data types can also be introduced using initiality, but our thoughts in this direction are preliminary. We would like to explore the connection with Milner's work on LCF [13].

4.4. Higher order logic

Another related but distinct direction of development is higher order logic, dealing with total functions rather than partial functions. An equational system of higher order logic, based on Cartesian closed categories and total functions, is the subject of the forthcoming thesis at UCLA of K. Parsaye-Ghomi.

4.5. Intensional logics

Another direction of development for Clear is to incorporate intensional logics, algorithmic logic [23], dynamic logic [15]. These enable us to reason about imperative programs with implicit state. Another intensional logic is temporal logic [21] which has found favour recently as a means of reasoning about parallel programs. The possibility of putting these into the Clear framework is worth investigation; it would provide structure for large theories in intensional logics.

5. GENERALITY AND INSTITUTIONS

We have introduced operations for combining, enriching and deriving theories, together with a parameter mechanism. All this has been done for first order equational theories. But as we have suggested, analogous methods would work for "putting together" more sophisticated kinds of theory. What are the requirements on a notion of "theory" for it to be amenable to our "putting together" techniques? In [5] we provided a precise mathematical answer to this question. This is the notion of an *institution**. An institution is a kind of logical formalism with its semantics and including a means of changing the vocabulary. For example predicate calculus is an institution and it permits different vocabularies of functions and relation names. We give here a non-technical definition of institution; for a precise one couched in the elegant language of category theory see the paper cited above.

An institution has:

(1) A notion of *signature* (some vocabulary of names for sorts, operators, predicates or whatever) together with a notion of *translations* from one signature to another (mapping sorts of the first vocabulary to sorts of the other, operators to operators etc.).

(2) A notion of *combining* two signatures which share some common sub-signature (disjoint union of vocabularies but respecting the shared part).

---

* In [5] it is called a "language" (Section 2.9), but we now prefer the term" institution" as less overworked. Think of institutions such as the Bank of England or the Supreme Court.

(3) For each signature a set of *models*, together with a rule which given a translation from signature Σ to signature Σ' and a Σ'-model reduces it to a Σ-model.

(4) For each signature a set of *sentences*, together with a way of extending a translation from signature Σ to signature Σ' to a translation from Σ-sentences to Σ'-sentences.

(5) For each signature a binary relation "satisfies" between models of the signature and sentences of the signature. This relation must obey the "naturalness" condition: For any translation from Σ to Σ', a Σ'-model satisfies the translation of a Σ-sentence if and only if its reduction satisfies the Σ-sentence.

Consider, as an example, equational logic.

(a) A signature is a set of sorts with a set of operators, and translations map sorts to sorts and operators to operators in a compatible way.

(b) Combination of two signatures is just the disjoint union of the respective sort sets and operator sets respecting shared subsets.

(c) The models of a signature Σ are the algebras with sort and operator names in Σ.

(d) The sentences of Σ are the equations with sort and operator names in Σ.

(e) If f is a translation from Σ to Σ', then a Σ'-algebra is a map from operators in Σ' to functions over the carrier of the algebra. If we compose f with this map we get a Σ-algebra. This is the reduction of Σ'-models to Σ-models.

(f) Given such an f and a Σ-sentence "$t_1 = t_2$" we can get a Σ'-sentence by just replacing the operators in t_1 and t_2 by their translations under f.

(g) The satisfaction relation is rather obvious. We just evaluate the terms in the equation "$t_1 = t_2$" using the operations of the algebra, doing this for all possible values of the variables. If t_1 always has the same value as t_2 then the algebra satisfies the equation. It is easy to see that this satisfaction relation has the naturalness property required.

Thus equational logic is an institution. So are predicate calculus and the various other systems in the previous section. It also turns out that given an institution with suitable initial models the corresponding data theory is itself an institution [5].

(a) Data enrichment for institutions: duplicity

How do we handle data enrichment in such a general setting? Given a signature the set of its models must have some extra structure, so that we can talk about initial models, and a translation from one theory to another must define the *free* extension of a model of the source theory.

At first sight this imposes considerable limitations on the kind of institution we may deal with, for example, predicate calculus does not enjoy these free extensions (or even initial models). Recently, however, we have seen how to get around this, by a device which we like to call "duplicity". The idea is that although arbitrary translations in the institution may not give rise to free extensions there may be a well-defined subclass of translations between theories which do. For example if we take a predicate calculus theory and just add new sorts, operators and *equations* (no quantified sentences) then we do get a free extension of any model. So the "duplicity" idea is to have an institution together with a "sub-institution" with limited kinds of translation which permit free extensions.* In data enrichments we restrict ourselves to these simpler translations. Thus we might use just equations to introduce new data types but allow ourselves quantifiers when we define new operators over them. A finite graph may be defined equationally, but the operator "paths-from_ to _" might be specified using quantifiers.

Such duplicity may seem obvious, but in fact lack of initial algebras has tended to inhibit people from developing richer specification languages in the algebraic style.

6. SYNTACTIC SUGAR

Clear was designed in an attempt to understand what mathematical operations on theories are needed to build up large theories from small pieces. In order to make the underlying operations on theories transparent we kept the syntax as simple as possible making only minor concessions to readability. The user of a specification language would like a little more "syntactic sugar". A pleasanter syntax would make use of the fact that many definitions of theories take standard forms; we could thus avoid the use of words like *theory*, *enrich* and *derive* as far as possible and thus keep the declarations and equations uncluttered. Proposals in this direction have been made by Don Sannella at Edinburgh, and we are engaged at SRI in the design of a more readable specification language "Ordinary" which has its semantics defined by translation into Clear.

In order to make the example which follows a little more readable we will introduce a little syntactic sugar in this paper. Note that we will use predicate calculus in enrichments which are not data enrichments (the notation is as usual *exists, all, and, or, not, iff, if . . . then* and for convenience Q *if* P as a synonym for *if* P *then* Q). This extension was justified informally by "duplicity" in our previous discussion of institutions. The syntactic changes are as follows.

---

* Technically we have an institution with a category of theories and a subcategory in which each theory morphism gives rise to a free functor between the category of models of its source and those of its target. (We have not yet written this up.)

(1) Write *spec* for *const* and for *proc*.

(2) Omit = after *const* P and after *proc* P(. . .).

(3) Omit *in* after *let* . . . = . . .

(4) Write *end* for *endth* and for *enden*.

(5) Omit X *enriched by* where X is the sum of the formal parameters and locals.

(6) Write *axioms* for *eqns* when an enrichment is not a data enrichment.

(7) In an equation or axiom omit the *for all* $x_1, \ldots, x_n$, relying on the reader to recognise the variables.

(8) Write . . . *where*. . . = . . .*for*. . . *if* . . . = . . . to introduce local definitions. Thus a = f(a) *where* a = b + 1 means a = f(a) *if* a = b + 1.

With these rules the following transformation takes place

proc P(X:T) =
    let Y = . . . *in*
    let Z = . . . *in*
    X + Y + Z *enriched by*
    sorts . . .
    opns . . .
    eqns . . .
enden

spec P(X:T)
    let Y = . . .
    let Z = . . .
    sorts . . .
    opns . . .
    axioms . . .
end

We also introduce one simple new semantic construct "renaming"; this is very useful although its effects can be obtained using derive. Thus

$$T \; renaming \; x1 \; is \; x, \; y1 \; is \; y$$

means T with sort or operator names x and y replaced by x1 and y1 (its semantics is very similar to that of enrich: composition of a based theory with a name-changing signature morphism).

7. AN EXAMPLE: LIST PROCESSING WITH GARBAGE COLLECTION

We now present a somewhat more substantial example, list processing with garbage collection.

We assume the existence of a theory Set analogous to Bag already given, adding just the equation S union S = S. This must provide the usual operations such as membership. It has requirement Ident, a theory like Triv but with an equality. We also assume a theory Map with requirement Ident, where a map is a finite function, with operations

f[x] — applying the map f to argument x
insert(f,x,y) — takes f and produces a new map with the addition of (x,y)
domain(f) — the domain Set of a map, i.e. all first members of (x,y)-pairs
f restricted-to S — the restriction of map f to the set S of arguments.

We further assume a theory Relation. A relation R over a finite set S is S together with a set of pairs of S elements. We define a sort rel with

domain(R) — the set S
R[x,y] — true iff (x,y) is one of the pairs
empty(S) — the empty relation over S
insert(R,x,y) — takes R and produces a relation with the addition of (x,y)

Note that if S is a set of elements of sort t then the requirement of Relation is a theory of sets of t.* We define the state of a list processing machine as a finite function (map) taking a cell to a pair of values, its car and cdr, where a value is either a cell or an atom. This requires a theory Sum, giving the disjoint union of two sorts with injection functions, and a theory Prod, giving the Cartesian product of two sorts with a pairing function.

We can now define the operation of garbage collection which takes a root cell and a state and produces a "cleaned" state by removing all cells not reachable from the root. In order to define this notion of "reachable" we need a theory of "Reachability"; this is quite general and not restricted to list processing.

We can also define list operations. The operation "cons" takes a pair of values and a state and produces a new cell together with a new state in which the new cell has the given values as its car and cdr. To define cons we need a general theory "Choice" to provide an operation "new" which given a set produces some element not in the set. We also define car, cdr, newcar and newcdr; the latter update the car and cdr parts, respectively, of a given cell with a given value.

All this is done for some arbitrary notion of atom. Finally we take atoms to be character sequences and combine garbage collection with the list operations to produce a theory of list processing.

>   *spec* Sum(X: Triv, Y: Triv)
>   *data sorts* sum
>   *opns* inl: X → sum
>   inr: Y → sum
>   *end*

>   *spec* Prod(X: Triv, Y: Triv)
>   *data sorts* prod
>   *opns* ⟨−,−⟩: X, Y → prod
>   *end*

---

* If this theory were defined internally in Relation using Set it would give a different copy from any use of Set outside; this is an irritating feature of our semantics which we referred to above as "proliferation".

spec Choice(S: Set(Ident))
    opns new: set → element
    axioms not (new(S) member S)
    end

spec Reachability(R: Relation(Set(Ident)))
    opns −.− : rel, rel → rel
          −power− : rel, nat → rel
          repeat: rel → rel
          reachables: element, rel → set
    axioms
        (R.R1)[x,z] iff exists y (R[x,y] and R1[y,z])
        (R power 0)[x,y] = (x==y) and x member domain(R)
        R power (n + 1) = (R power n).R
        (repeat R)[x,y] iff exists n ((R power n)[x,y])
        y member reachables(x,R) iff (repeat(R))[x,y]
    end

spec State(Atom: Ident)
    let Cell = *derive sorts* cell
                      opns − == − : cell,cell → bool
                using Bool *from* Nat *by* cell *is* nat
                endde
                enriched by opns nil: cell *end*
    let Value = Sum(Atom, Cell) *renaming* value *is* sum
    Map(Cell, Prod(Value,Value))
                  renaming state *is* map,
                        cell-set *is* domain-set,
                        empty-state *is* nilmap

spec Garbage-collection(S: State(Ident))
    let R = Reachability(Relation(S[element *is* cell,
                              set *is* cell-set]))
                  renaming cellrel *is* rel
    opns cellsof: value → cell-set
         cellrelof: state → cellrel
         cleaned-state: cell, state → state
    axioms
        cellsof(inl(a)) = empty-set
        cellsof(inr(c)) = {c}
        cellrelof(s)[c,c1] = c1 member cellsof(v1) or
                        c1 member cellsof(v2)
                      where ⟨v1, v2⟩ = s[c]

cleaned-state(rootcell,s) = s restricted-to
                            reachables(cellrelof(s), rootcell)
end

spec List-operations(S: State(Ident))
    let Ch = Choice(S[element *is* cell, set *is* cell-set])
    opns cons: value,value,state → Prod(State[element *is* cell],
                                    State[element *is* state])
        car,cdr: cell,state → value
        newcar,newcdr: value,cell,state → state
    axioms
        cons(v1,v2,s) = ⟨c, insert(s,c,⟨v1, v2⟩)⟩
                    where c = new(domain(s) union {nil})
        car(c, insert(s, c, ⟨v1,v2⟩) = v1
        cdr(c, insert(s, c, ⟨v1,v2⟩) = v2
        newcar(v,c,s) = insert(s, c, ⟨v, v2⟩)
                    where ⟨v1, v2⟩ = s[c]
        newcdr(v,c,s) = insert(s, c, ⟨v1, v⟩)
                    where ⟨v1, v2⟩ = s[c]
end

spec List-processing
    let Atom = Sequence(Character)
    let St = State(Atom[element *is* sequence])
    Garbage-collection(St) + List-operations(St)

8. PROGRAM DEVELOPMENT

We have shown how to write specifications in Clear but so far we have said nothing about program development. First we should emphasize that even without any formal tools for program development the precise specification of the concepts involved is a valuable aid to writing correct programs. But what can we say about systematic development of programs?

One would like the development to be as well-structured as the Clear specification, that is one should be able to develop implementations of the individual pieces of the Clear specification and then combine these implementations (perhaps breaking the modularity structure in places for the sake of efficiency). This suggests some "calculus of program development", but we are still groping for a suitable mathematical formulation, possibly one based on the notion of 2-category [10].

Another approach is to note that Clear has an executable sub-language. First consider data. A data sort whose constructor operations are subject to no equations is immediately implementable, for example stack with empty and push; call this an *anarchic* data definition. Next consider functions defined over such data. We can implement them if each equation has a simple left-hand side of the form $f(x, \ldots, z)$ where $x, \ldots, z$ are variables, or more generously $f(s, \ldots, t)$ where $s, \ldots, t$ are terms using only anarchic constructor operations. (The implementation does not guarantee termination.) Call these definitions *explicit,* as opposed to implicit ones like $f(g(x)) = x$. Anarchic data and explicit function definitions form the executable sublanguage.

Now we can take a Clear specification and rewrite it a piece at a time, *preserving its denotation,* until we arrive at a version in the executable sublanguage. This can be done by introducing *derive* expressions. Note that we do not restrict Clear itself to this sublanguage because non-anarchic data and implicit function definitions may give much simpler specifications, easier to get right.

Thus we could do program development in Clear if we are content with a functional programming language. Using, say, dynamic logic as the institution we might be able to have an imperative target language.

There are still problems, notably connected with many-one representations and quotienting, but we think that this approach may be fruitful.

For other interesting work in this area see [7], [8] and [16].

9. CONCLUSION

Our research on the Clear project has concentrated on a specific issue: modularity in specifications. We have devoted little attention to the other important issues of good notation for the detailed presentation and of a good library of primitive concepts. Rather we have striven to make these issues orthogonal to the modularity issue and we have managed to express this orthogonality in mathematical form. We have also shown how the data/procedure distinction can be handled in a general way using the idea of free constructions and "data theories". Quite apart from the particular language, Clear, which we have defined, we hope that our approach to orthogonality in semantics may be fruitful. We hope that the discussion here may motivate some people to read our semantics paper [5].

Open areas for future investigation include:

(a) implementation of Clear;

(b) a more model-theoretic semantics for Clear with procedure denotations being functors instead of theory morphisms (Jim Thatcher has argued forcefully for this);

(c) various mutations, both semantic and syntactic, to make Clear more useable;

(d) a theory of the modular development of programs from Clear specifications.

ACKNOWLEDGEMENTS

Our work on Clear stemmed from work of the ADJ group (Goguen, Thatcher, Wagner and Wright), and we have continued to benefit from the insights of the other members of this group. Our students David Rydeheard, Don Sannella and Joe Tardo have done a lot of hard work on implementations; they have provided valuable discussions, as have other colleagues at Edinburgh and Los Angeles. Don Sannella has done a number of Clear examples and has helped with the ones herein. David MacQueen's work on Hope provided a valuable tool. We much appreciate Eleanor Kerse's typing. RMB would like to thank IBM for the Visiting Professorship at the University of Liège, and the Computer Science Department there, especially Professor Danny Ribbens, for their friendly and stimulating reception. The work has been funded by the Science Research Council and the National Science Foundation.

REFERENCES

1. J. R. Abrial, S. A. Schuman, B. Meyer (1979). Specification language Z. Massachusetts Computer Associates Inc., Boston.
2. D. Bjorner (1980). "Formal Description of Programming Concepts—A Software Engineering Viewpoint." Proceedings of Mathematical Foundations of Computer Science, Lecture Notes in Computer Science, Vol. 88, 1–21. Springer-Verlag, Berlin.
3. R. M. Burstall (1980). "Electronic Category Theory." Proceedings of Mathematical Foundations of Computer Science, Lecture Notes in Computer Science, Vol. 88, 22–39. Springer-Verlag, Berlin.
4. R. M. Burstall and J. A. Goguen (1977). "Putting Theories Together to Make Specifications." Proceedings of Fifth International Joint Conference on Artificial Intelligence, 1045–1058. Carnegie-Mellon University, Pittsburgh.
5. R. M. Burstall and J. A. Goguen (1980). "The Semantics of CLEAR, a Specification Language." Proceedings of Advanced Course on Abstract Software Specifications, Lecture Notes in Computer Science, Vol. 86. Springer-Verlag, Berlin.
6. R. M. Burstall, D. B. MacQueen and D. T. Sannella (1980). "HOPE: An Experimental Applicative Language." Proceedings of 1980 LISP Conference, 136–143. Stanford University Computer Science Department, Palo Alto.
7. H. D. Ehrich (1978). "Extensions and Implementations of Abstract Data Type Specifications." Proceedings of Mathematical Foundations of Computer Science, Lecture Notes in Computer Science, Vol. 64, 155–163. Springer-Verlag, Berlin.

8. H. Ehrig, H.-J. Kreowski, B. Mahr and P. Padawitz (1980). "Compound Algebraic Implementations: An Approach to Stepwise Refinement of Software Systems." Proceedings of Mathematical Foundations of Computer Science, Lecture Notes in Computer Science, Vol. 88, 231–245. Springer-Verlag, Berlin.

9. J. A. Goguen (1971). "Mathematical Representation of Hierarchically Organized Systems," 112–128. Global Systems Dynamics, S. Karger, Basle.

10. J. A. Goguen and R. M. Burstall (1980). "CAT, a System for the Structured Elaboration of Correct Programs from Structured Specifications." Computer Science Department, SRI International, Menlo Park.

11. J. A. Goguen and J. Tardo (1979). An introduction to OBJ: a language for writing and testing algebraic specifications. Proceedings of Conference on Specifications of Reliable Software 170–189. IEEE Computer Society.

12. J. A. Goguen, J. W. Thatcher and E. G. Wagner (1978). An initial algebra approach to the specification, correctness and implementation of abstract data types. "Current Trends in Programming Methodology," Vol. 4, 80–149. Data Structuring, Prentice-Hall, Englewood Cliffs, New Jersey.

13. M. J. Gordon, A. J. R. Milner and C. P. Wadsworth (1979). "Lecture Notes in Computer Science," Vol. 78, *Edinburgh LCF.* Springer-Verlag, Berlin.

14. J. Guttag and J. J. Horning (1980). "Formal Specification as a Design Tool," 251–261. Proceedings of the 7th Annual ACM Symposium on Principles of Programming Languages, ACM, Las Vegas, Nevada.

15. D. Harel (1979). "Lecture Notes in Computer Science. Vol. 68: First-order Dynamic Logic." Springer-Verlag, Berlin.

16. U. Hupbach (1980). "Abstract Implementation of Abstract Data Types," Vol. 88, 291–304. Mathematical Foundations of Computer Science, Lecture Notes in Computer Science. Springer-Verlag, Berlin.

17. U. Hupbach, H. Kaphengst and H. Reichel (1980). Initiale algebraische Spezifikation von Datentypen, parameterisierten Datentypen und Algorithmen. VEB Robotron, Zentrum fur Forschung und Technik, Dresden, WIB.

18. H. Kaphengst and H. Reichel (1971). Algebraische algorithmentheorie. VEB Robotron, Zentrum fur Forschung und Technik, Dresden, WIB.

19. H. A. Klaeren (1980). "A Simple Class of Algorithmic Specifications for Abstract Software Modules," Vol. 88, 362–374. Proceedings of Mathematical Foundations of Computer Science, Lecture Notes in Computer Science. Springer-Verlag, Berlin.

20. K. Levitt, L. Robinson and B. Silverberg (1979). HDM Handbook, 1, 2, 3. SRI International.

21. A. Pnueli (1979). "The Temporal Semantics of Concurrent Programs," Vol. 70, 1–20. Proceedings of Conference on Semantics of Concurrent Computation, Lecture Notes in Computer Science. Springer-Verlag, Berlin.

22. H. Reichel (1980). "Initially-Restricting Algebraic Theories," Vol. 88, 504–514. Proceedings of Mathematical Foundations of Computer Science, Lecture Notes in Computer Science. Springer-Verlag, Berlin.

23. A. Salwicki (1970). Formalized algorithmic languages. *Bull. Acad. Pol. Sci. Ser. Math.* **18,** 227–232.

5. Verification of concurrent programs: the temporal framework

Z. MANNA and A. PNUELI

ABSTRACT

This is the first in a series of reports describing the application of Temporal Logic to the specification and verification of concurrent programs.

We first introduce Temporal Logic as a tool for reasoning about sequences of states. Models of concurrent programs based both on transition graphs and on linear-text representations are presented and the notions of concurrent and fair executions are defined.

The general temporal language is then specialized to reason about those execution states and execution sequences that are fair computations of a concurrent program. Subsequently, the language is used to describe properties of concurrent programs.

The set of interesting properties is classified into *Invariance* (Safety), *Eventuality* (Liveness) and *Precedence* (Until) properties. Among the properties studied are: Partial Correctness, Global Invariance, Clean Behavior, Mutual Exclusion, Deadlock Absence, Termination, Total Correctness, Intermittent Assertions, Accessibility, Starvation Freedom, Responsiveness, Safe Liveness, Absence of Unsolicited Response, Fair Responsiveness and Precedence.

In the following reports of this series, we use the temporal formalism to develop proof methodologies for proving the properties discussed here.

1. INTRODUCTION

Temporal Logic is a special branch of logic that deals with the development of situations in time. Whereas ordinary logic is adequate for describing a *static* situation, Temporal Logic enables us to discuss how a situation *changes* due to the passage of time. An execution of a program is precisely a chain of situations, called execution states, that undergo a series of transformations

215

determined by the program's instructions. This suggests that Temporal Logic is the appropriate tool for reasoning about the execution of programs. The uniqueness of this approach is that it enables us to formalize the entire *execution* of a program and not just the *function* or *relation* it computes.

The temporal logic approach offers special advantages for the formalization and analysis of the behavior of *concurrent programs*. Concurrent programs have long been a difficult subject to formalize and have often defied generalization of methods that worked perfectly for sequential programs.

One inherent difficulty in analysing a concurrent program is that when combining two processes to be run in parallel, we cannot infer the *input-output relations* computed by the conbined program from just the input-output relation computed by each of the individual component processes. The obvious reason for this is that, running in parallel, the processes may interfere with one another, altering the behavior each would have when run alone. Consequently, in order for any approach to stand a chance of success, it must deal with more than the input-output relation computed by a program. It should be concerned with *execution sequences* in one form or another, as well as be able to discuss mid-execution events.

Another inherent difficulty is the *discontinuity* associated with the simulation of concurrency by *multiprogramming*. A very convenient and widely used model of real concurrency is to regard the participating events as composed of many atomic basic steps. Then instead of requiring that these basic steps occur concurrently, we consider sequences in which these steps are *interleaved* in all possible ways. The problem with modelling concurrency by multiprogramming (interleaving) is that without further restrictions a certain process can be discriminated against by having its execution continuously delayed. Disallowing this discrimination introduces a discontinuity into the set of interleaved execution sequences.

Consequently, any approach which is strongly based on the concept of continuity, such as the denotational approach or equivalent relational ones, is bound to face severe difficulties when extended to deal with concurrency.

Temporal Logic avoids both these difficulties by (*a*) being geared from the start to analyse and formalize properties in terms of execution sequences, and (*b*) not being based on limits and assumptions of continuity. In fact, it can very easily and naturally express such concepts as "eventually" which describes an event arbitrarily ahead in the future, but still a finite duration away.

In this report we introduce the framework and language of Temporal Logic and demonstrate its appropriateness for describing properties of programs.

We start by an exposition of *modal logic* whose domain of interpretation is a set of states and (general) accessibility relations between these states. We then specialize to *temporal logic* which requires that the states form a *linear discrete sequence.* Linear discrete sequences can be used to describe a dynamic process which goes through changes at discrete instants. Consequently, temporal logic is suitable for reasoning about such dynamic processes and their behavior in time.

Next, we present a *model of concurrent programs*. The basic model is based on several concurrent processes, each of which is given in the form of a transition graph or a linear-text program. Executions of concurrent programs are defined to be an interleaving of execution steps, each taken from one of the processes. We discuss the conditions under which an interleaved execution faithfully represents real concurrency. One of these conditions calls for the interleaving to be *fair* in not neglecting any of the processes for too long.

We then show how the language of temporal logic can be further specialized to reason about *execution sequences* of programs. In this way, properties of programs which are expressible as properties of their executions are readily formalizable.

The rest of the report overviews in a systematic manner the different properties of interest. They are classified into:

(a) *Invariance properties*, stating that some condition holds continuously throughout the computation.

(b) *Eventuality properties*, stating that under some initial conditions, a certain event (such as the program's termination) must eventually be realized.

(c) *Precedence properties*, stating that a certain event always precedes another.

Several typical and useful properties are discussed in each class, together with sample programs illustrating these properties.

2. THE GENERAL CONCEPTS OF TEMPORAL LOGIC

In the development of logic as a formalization tool, we can observe an increasing ability to express change and variability. *Propositional Calculus* was developed to express constant or absolute truth, stating basic facts about the universe of discourse. The propositional framework mainly deals with the question of how the truth of a composite sentence depends on the truth of its constituents. In *Predicate Calculus* we deal with variable or relative truth by distinguishing the statement (the predicate) from its arguments. It is understood that the statement may be true or false according to the particular individuals it is applied to. Thus we may regard predicates as parameterized propositions. The *Modal Calculus* adds another dimension of variability to the description by predicates. If we contemplate a major transition in which the complete structure of basic premises and meaning of functions and predicates is changed (and not only individuals), then the Modal Calculus provides a special notation for this major change. For instance, any chain of reasoning which is valid on earth may become invalid on Mars because some of the basic concepts naturally used on earth may assume completely different meanings (or become meaningless) on Mars. Conceptually, this calls for a partition of the universe of discourse into worlds of similar structure but different contents. Variability within a world is handled by changing the arguments of predicates, while changes between worlds are expressed by the special modal formalism.

Consider for example the statement: "It rains today". Obviously, the truth of such a statement depends on at least two parameters: the date and the location at which it is stated. Given a specific date t_0 and location l_0, the specific statement: "It rains at l_0 on t_0" has propositional character, i.e. it is fully specified and must either be true or false. We may also consider the fully variable predicate $rain(l, t)$: "It rains at l on t" which gives equal priority to both parameters. The modal approach distinguishes two levels of variability. In this example, we may choose time to be the major varying factor, and the universe to consist of worlds which are days. Within each day we consider the predicate $rain(l)$ which, given the date, depends only on the location. Alternately, one can choose the location to be the major parameter and regard the raining history of each location as a distinct world.

As is seen from this example the transition from Predicate Logic to Modal Logic is not as sharp as the transition from Propositional Logic to Predicate Logic. For one thing it is not absolutely essential. We could manage quite reasonably with our two parameter predicate. Secondly, the decision as to which parameter is chosen to be the major one may seem arbitrary. It is strongly influenced by our intuitive view of the situation.

In spite of these reservations there are some obvious advantages to the introduction and use of modal formalisms. It allows us to explicitly make one parameter more significant than all the others, and makes the dependence on that parameter implicit. Nowadays, when increasing attention is being paid to the clear correspondence between syntax and natural reasoning (as is repeatedly stressed by the discipline of structured programming), it seems only appropriate to introduce extra structure into the description of varying situations. Thus a clear distinction is made between variation within a world, which we express using predicates and quantifiers, and variation from one world to another, which we express using the modal operators.

Another way to view the generalization offered by Modal Logic is to claim that Predicate Calculus is appropriate for describing *static situations*. It gives statements about basic objects and their interrelation. The additional dimension provided by the Modal Logic is that of *dynamic change* from one situation into the other. Characteristic to changes effected by time transitions is the fact that the same basic objects and entities exist in each of the static situations but that their attributes and interrelations may change. Thus Modal Logic faithfully and conveniently portrays for us a *dynamic situation* consisting of a set of static situations and rules of change between them.

2.1. The modal framework

The general modal framework [5] considers therefore a *universe* which consists of many similar *states* (or *worlds*) and a basic *accessibility relation* between the states, $R(s, s')$, which specifies the possibility of getting from one state s into another state s'.

Consider again the example of rainy days. There, each state in the universe is a day. A possible accessibility relation might hold between two days s and s' if s' is in the future of s.

The main notational idea is to avoid any explicit mention of either the state parameter (date in our example) or of the accessibility relation. Instead we introduce two special operators which describe properties of states which are accessible from a given state in a universe.

The two *modal operators* introduced are $\Box$ (called the *necessity operator*) and $\Diamond$ (called the *possibility operator*). Their meaning is given by the following rules of interpretation in which we denote by $|w|_s$ the truth value of the formula w in a state s:

$$|\Box w|_s = \forall s'[R(s, s') \supset |w|_{s'}]$$
$$|\Diamond w|_s = \exists s'[R(s, s') \wedge |w|_{s'}].$$

Thus, $\Box w$ is true at a state s if the formula w is true at all states R-accessible from s. Similarly, $\Diamond w$ is true at a state s if w is true in at least one state R-accessible from s.

A *modal formula* is a formula constructed from proposition symbols, predicate symbols (including equality), function symbols, individual constants and individual variables, the classical operators and quantifiers, and the modal operators. A formula without any modal operators is called a *static formula*. A fully modal (*dynamic*) formula is conveniently viewed as consisting of static subformulas to which modal and classical operators are applied. The truth value of a modal formula at some state of a given universe is found by a repeated use of the rules above for the modal operators and evaluation of any static subformula on the state itself. It is assumed that every state contains a full interpretation of all the classical symbols in the formula, so that the truth of any static formula is fully determined.

For example, the formula

$$rain(l) \supset \Diamond \sim rain(l)$$

is interpreted in our model of rainy days as stating: for a given day and a given location l, if it rains on that day at l then there exists another day in the future on which it will not rain at l; thus any rain will eventually stop. Similarly,

$$rain(l) \supset \Box rain(l)$$

claims that if it rains on that day it will rain everafter. Note that any modal formula is always considered with respect to some fixed reference state, which may be chosen arbitrarily. In our example, it has the meaning of "today".

Consider the general formula

$$\Box \sim w \equiv \sim \Diamond w.$$

As we can see from the definitions this claims that all R-accessible states satisfy $\sim w$ if and only if there does not exist an R-accessible state satisfying w. This formula is true in any state for any universe with an arbitrary R.

Giving a more precise definition, a *universe* U of a modal formula w consists of a set of *states* (or *worlds*) S, a binary relation R on S, called the *accessibility relation*, and a *domain* D. Each state s provides a first-order interpretation over the domain for all the proposition symbols, predicate symbols, function symbols, individual constants, and (free) individual variables in w. A *model* (U, s_0) is a universe U with one of the states of U, $s_0 \in S$, designated as the initial or reference state. In short,

$$\text{universe of w} = \begin{cases} \text{set of states} - S \\ \text{accessibility relation between states} - R \\ \text{domain} - D \end{cases}$$

where

$$\text{state} = \text{assignment to symbols of w over D}$$

We define the truth value of a modal formula w at a state s (denoted by $|w|_s$) in a given universe U inductively:

(1) If w is static, i.e. contains no modal operators, then the truth value of $|w|_s$ is found by interpreting w in s.

(2) $|\Box w|_s$ is $\forall s'[R(s, s') \supset |w|_{s'}]$.

(3) $|\Diamond w|_s$ is $\exists s'[R(s, s') \wedge |w|_{s'}]$.

(4) $|w_1 \vee w_2|_s$ is true iff either $|w_1|_s$ is true or $|w_2|_s$ is true.

(5) $|\sim w|_s$ is true iff $|w|_s$ is false.

(6) $|\exists x w|_s$ is true iff there exists a universe U' differing from U by at most the interpretation given to x in each state of U, such that $|w|_s$ is true in U'.

The rules for the other operators and the universal quantifier are derivable from the ones above

Example. Consider the interpretation of the formula w

$$\forall x \square \exists y.p(x, y)$$

for a universe U with a set of states S, accessibility relation R and domain D. The meaning of $|w|_s$, for $s \in S$, is

$$(\forall x \in D)(\forall s' \in S)[R(s, s') \supset (\exists y \in D)|p(x, y)|_{s'}].$$

Thus, this formula will be true at state s in a universe U if for all assignments of values to x, and for each state s' accessible from s, there is a value assignment to y, possibly dependent on the x assignment and the choice of s', which will make p(x, y) true in s'. ∎

Note that by our notation

- $|\Diamond(\square w)|_s$ means that $|\square w|_{s'}$ is true at some state s', R-accessible from s. That is,

$$\Diamond\square w$$

stands for: we can get to a point where w is true everafter; i.e. there is a state s', R-accessible from s, such that s' itself and all of its R-descendants satisfy w.

- $|\square(\Diamond w)|_s$ means that $|\Diamond w|_{s'}$ is true for all states s', R-accessible from s. That is,

$$\square\Diamond w$$

stands for: wherever we go w is still realizable; i.e. for every state s' accessible from s it is possible to find an R-descendant of s' which satisfies w.

- $|\square(w \supset \square w)|_s$ means that $|w \supset \square w|_{s'}$ is true for all states s', R-accessible from s. That is,

$$\square(w \supset \square w)$$

stands for: if w ever becomes true in some s' a descendant of s, it remains true for all descendants of s'.

If a formula w is true in a state s_0 in a universe U we say that (U, s_0) is a *satisfying model* for that formula, or that the formula is *satisfied* in (U, s_0).

A formula w which is true in all states of every universe is called *valid*; that is, for every universe U of w and for every state s in U, $|w|_s$ is true. For example, the formula

$$\square\sim w \equiv \sim\Diamond w$$

is a valid formula. This formula establishes the connection between "necessity" and "possibility". Another valid formula is

$$\Box(w_1 \supset w_2) \supset (\Box w_1 \supset \Box w_2),$$

i.e., if in all accessible states $w_1 \supset w_2$ holds and if w_1 is true in all accessible states, then w_2 must also be true in all of those states.

Both formulas are valid for any accessibility relation. If we agree to place further general restrictions on the relation R, we obtain additional valid formulas which are true for any model with a relation satisfying these restrictions. According to the different restrictions we may impose on R we obtain different modal systems. In our discussion we stipulate that R *is always reflexive and transitive*; i.e. we consider a formula to be valid if it is true in all states of every universe with reflexive and transitive accessibility relation.

For example, the formula

$$\Box w \supset w$$

is valid since it is true for any reflexive model. It claims for a state s that if all states accessible from s satisfy w, then w is satisfied by s itself. This is obvious since s is accessible from itself (by reflexivity).

The formula

$$\Diamond \Diamond w \supset \Diamond w,$$

which stands for $(\Diamond(\Diamond w)) \supset (\Diamond w)$, is valid since it is true for all transitive models. It claims for a state s_0: if there exists an s_2 accessible from s_1 which is accessible from s_0 such that s_2 satisfies w, then there exists an s_3 accessible from s_0 which satisfies w. This always holds in a transitive model since by transitivity, s_2 is also accessible from s_0 and we may take $s_3 = s_2$.

2.2. The temporal framework

The framework of temporal logic is a derivation of the modal framework in which we impose further restrictions on the models of interpretation [16, 17]. The interpretation given by the temporal logic to the basic accessibility relation is that of the passage of time. A world s' is accessible from a world s if through development in time s can change into s'. We concentrate on histories of development which are linear and discrete. Thus, the models of temporal logic consist of ω-sequences, i.e. sequences of the form $\sigma = s_0, s_1, \ldots$. In such a sequence, s_j is accessible from s_i iff $i \leq j$. Due to the discreteness of the sequences we can refer not only to states that lie in the future of a given state, but also to the (unique) immediate future state or next state.

This leads to the introduction of an additional operator, the *next instant* operator denoted by $\bigcirc$.

Relating these concepts to the general modal framework, a universe consists again of a collection of states (worlds). On these states we define an *immediate accessibility relation* ρ which is required to be a function. That means that every world s has exactly one other world s' such that $\rho(s, s')$. This corresponds to our intuition that in a discrete time model each instant has exactly one immediate successor. The transitive reflexive closure of ρ, $R = \rho^*$, is the accessibility relation discussed under the general modal framework and is indeed both reflexive and transitive. Intuitively $R(s, s')$ holds when s' is either identical to s or lies in the future of s.

By the restrictions imposed on R, the resulting model (U, s_0) can be represented as an infinite sequence of states,

$$\sigma = s_0, s_1, s_2, \ldots,$$

where $\rho(s_i, s_{i+1})$ is true for $i \geq 0$. This intuitively corresponds to the temporal developments of a process observed at a sequence of discrete points in time.

We will now give a more complete definition of the language we are going to use. Note that this language is designed specially for the application we have in mind, namely reasoning about programs, and is not necessarily the most general language possible.

(a) Symbols

The language uses a set of basic symbols consisting of individual variables and constants, and proposition, function and predicate symbols. The set is partitioned into two subsets: global and local symbols. The *global symbols* have a uniform interpretation over the complete universe and do not change their values or meanings from one state to another. The *local symbols*, on the other hand, may assume different meanings and values in different states of the universe. For our purpose, the only local symbols that interest us are local individual variables and local propositions. We will have global symbols of all types.

Our symbols are further partitioned into different *sorts*. Each sort corresponds to a different domain, and the interpretation will associate a domain with every sort. Corresponding to a sort we may have individual constants that are interpreted over the associated domain, individual variables that assume values from that domain, function symbols that represent functions over the domain, and predicate symbols that represent predicates over the domain. The symbols used for individual constants, functions and predicates will be typical to the first-order theory of the domain we wish to formalize.

For example, in dealing with the theory of natural numbers we use the conventional symbols:

$$\{0, 1, \ldots, +, -, \times, \div, \ldots, >, \geq, \ldots\}.$$

Note that some functions and predicates may have a non-homogenous signature, i.e. they may have different sorts associated with different argument positions. A typical example is the if-then-else function which accepts one boolean argument and two arguments of possibly another sort.

(b) Operators and quantifiers

We use the regular set of boolean connectives: $\wedge$, $\vee$, $\supset$, $\equiv$ and $\sim$ together with the equality operator $=$ and the first-order quantifiers $\forall$ and $\exists$. This set is referred to as the *classical operators*. For *modal operators* we use the operators:

$$\square, \diamond, \bigcirc \text{ and } U$$

which are called respectively the *always*, *sometimes*, *next* and *until* operators. The first three operators are unary while the U operator is binary.

The quantifiers $\forall$ and $\exists$ are to be applied only to global individual variables.

(c) Terms

Terms are constructed from individual constants and individual variables to which we apply functions. The application must conform with the arity and sort signature restrictions associated with each symbol. An additional rule is that if t is a term so is $\bigcirc$t—referred to as the *next* (value of) t. Note that we use the *next* operator $\bigcirc$ in two different ways—as a temporal operator applied to formulas and as a temporal operator applied to terms.

(d) Formulas (sentences)

Formulas are constructed from atomic formulas to which we apply the boolean connectives, the modal operators and quantification over global individual variables. *Atomic formulas* consist of propositions and predicates (including the "$=$" operator) applied to terms of the appropriate sorts.

A formula is said to be *classic* (*static*) if it involves no modal operators.

We will sometimes regard propositions and (closed) formulas as integer-valued functions yielding 1 for true and 0 for false. These functions can then be combined arithmetically in order to provide a compact representation for equivalent but long propositional formulas. For example, for propositions $p_1, \ldots, p_n$, the statement

$$p_1 + \ldots + p_n = 1 \quad \text{or} \quad \sum_{i=1}^{n} p_i = 1$$

states that exactly one of the p_i's is true. This is of course equivalent to the formula

$$\bigvee_{1 \leq i \leq n} p_i \wedge \bigwedge_{1 \leq i < j \leq n} \sim (p_i \wedge p_j).$$

2.3. Models (environments)

A model (I, α, σ) for our language consists of a (global) interpretation I, a (global) assignment α and a sequence of states σ.

The *interpretation* I specifies a domain corresponding to each sort, and assigns concrete elements, functions and predicates to the (global) individual constants, function and predicate symbols.

The *assignment* α assigns a value over the appropriate domain to each of the global free individual variables and propositions.

The *sequence* $\sigma = s_0, s_1, \ldots$ is an infinite sequence of states. Each state s_i assigns values to the local free individual variables and propositions.

For a sequence

$$\sigma = s_0, s_1, \ldots$$

we denote by

$$\sigma^{(i)} = s_i, s_{i+1}, \ldots$$

the i-truncated suffix of σ.

Given a temporal formula w, we present below an inductive definition of the truth value of w in a model (I, α, σ). The value of any subformula or term τ under (I, α, σ) is denoted by $\tau|_\sigma^\alpha$, I being implicitly assumed.

Consider first the evaluation of terms:

- For a local individual variable or local proposition y:

$$y|_\sigma^\alpha = ys_0,$$

i.e. the value assigned to y in s_0, the first state of σ.

- For a global individual variable or global proposition u:

$$u|_\sigma^\alpha = \alpha[u],$$

i.e. the value assigned to u by α.

- For an individual constant the evaluation is given by I:

$$c|_\sigma^\alpha = I[c].$$

- For a function $f(x_1, \ldots, x_k)$:

$$f(t_1, \ldots, t_k)|_\sigma^\alpha = I[f](t_1|_\sigma^\alpha, \ldots, t_k|_\sigma^\alpha),$$

i.e. the value is given by the application of the interpreted function $I[f]$ to the values of $t_1, \ldots, t_k$ evaluated in the environment (I, α, σ).
- For a term t:

$$\bigcirc t|_\sigma^\alpha = t|_{\sigma^{(1)}}^\alpha,$$

i.e. the value of $\bigcirc t$ in $\sigma = s_0, s_1, \ldots$ is given by the value of t in the shifted sequence $\sigma^{(1)} = s_1, s_2, \ldots$.

Consider now the evaluation of sentences:
- For a predicate $p(x_1, \ldots x_k)$ (including equality):

$$p(t_1, \ldots, t_k)|_\sigma^\alpha = I[p](t_1|_\sigma^\alpha, \ldots, t_k|_\sigma^\alpha).$$

Here again, we evaluate the arguments in the environment and then test $I[p]$ on them.
- For a disjunction:

$$(w_1 \lor w_2)|_\sigma^\alpha = \text{true} \quad \text{iff} \quad w_1|_\sigma^\alpha = \text{true or } w_2|_\sigma^\alpha = \text{true}.$$

- For a negation:

$$(\sim w)|_\sigma^\alpha = \text{true} \quad \text{iff} \quad w|_\sigma^\alpha = \text{false}.$$

- For a next-time application:

$$\bigcirc w|_\sigma^\alpha = w|_{\sigma^{(1)}}^\alpha.$$

Thus $\bigcirc w$ means: w will be true in the next instant—read "next w".
- For an all-times application:

$$\square w|_\sigma^\alpha = \text{true} \quad \text{iff} \quad \text{for every } k \geq 0, \; w|_{\sigma^{(k)}}^\alpha = \text{true},$$

i.e. w is true for all suffix sequences of σ. Thus $\square w$ means: w is true for all future instants (including the present)—read "always w" or "henceforth w".
- For a some-time application:

$$\diamondsuit w|_\sigma^\alpha = \text{true} \quad \text{iff} \quad \text{there exists a } k \geq 0 \text{ such that } w|_{\sigma^{(k)}}^\alpha = \text{true},$$

i.e. w is true on at least one suffix of σ. Thus $\diamondsuit w$ means: w will be true for some future instant (possibly the present)—read "sometimes w" or "eventually w".
- For an until application:

$$w_1 U w_2|_\sigma^\alpha = \text{true} \quad \text{iff} \quad \text{for some } k \geq 0, \; w_2|_{\sigma^{(k)}}^\alpha = \text{true and}$$
$$\text{for all } i, \; 0 \leq i < k, \; w_1|_{\sigma^{(i)}}^\alpha = \text{true}.$$

Thus $w_1 U w_2$ means: there is a future instant in which w_2 holds, and such that until that instant w_1 continuously holds—read "w_1 until w_2" [4, 6].
● For a universal quantification:

$$(\forall u.w)|_\sigma^\alpha = \text{true iff for every } d \in D, \; w|_\sigma^{\alpha'} = \text{true},$$

where $\alpha' = \alpha \circ [u \leftarrow d]$ is the assignment obtained from α by assigning d to u. D is the domain over which u ranges.
● For an existential quantification:

$$(\exists u.w)|_\sigma^\alpha = \text{true iff for some } d \in D, \; w|_\sigma^{\alpha'} = \text{true},$$

where $\alpha' = \alpha \circ [u \leftarrow d]$.
Following are some examples of temporal expressions and their intuitive interpretations:

$u \supset \Diamond v$ — If u is presently true, v will eventually become true.
$\Box(u \supset \Diamond v)$ — Whenever u becomes true it will eventually be followed by v.
$\Diamond \Box w$ — At some future instant w will become permanently true.
$\Diamond(w \wedge \bigcirc \sim w)$ — There will be a future instant such that w is true at that instant and false at the next.
$\Box \Diamond w$ — Every future instant is followed by a later one in which w is true, thus w is true infinitely often.
$\Box(u \supset \Box v)$ — If u ever becomes true, then v is true at that instant and ever after.
$\Diamond v \supset ((\sim v)Uu)$ — If v ever happens, its first occurrence is preceded by (or coincides with) u.

If w is true under the model (I, α, σ) we say that (I, α, σ) *satisfies* w or that (I, α, σ) is a *satisfying model* for w. We denote this by

$$(I, \alpha, \sigma) \models w.$$

A formula w is *satisfiable* if there exists a satisfying model for it.
A formula w is *valid* if it is true in every model, denoted by

$$\models w.$$

Sometimes we are interested in a restricted class of models C. A formula w which is true for each model in C is said to be C-*valid*, denoted by

$$C \models w.$$

2.4. A repertoire of valid temporal statements

Following is a list of valid temporal statements which we justify by semantic considerations. There are two reasons for presenting them here. First we would like to illustrate the type of temporal reasoning we will later use. Second, we will refer in later proofs to the statements presented here as established valid statements to be used freely in other proofs. When, in a later part of this work, we present a formal deductive system for temporal reasoning, we will take some of the valid statements listed here as axioms and deduce the others as theorems.

1. $\models \square \sim w \equiv \sim \diamond w$
2. $\models \diamond \sim w \equiv \sim \square w$
3. $\models \bigcirc \sim w \equiv \sim \bigcirc w$

These statements point out the duality between the operators.

Statement 1 says that w is false in all states (instants) of a sequence iff there is no state in which w is true.

Statement 2 says that there is a state in which w is false iff it is not the case that w is true in all states.

Statement 3 says that w is false in the next state iff it is not the case that w is true in the next state. This statement restricts each state to have no more than a single successor.

4. $\models w \supset \diamond w$
5. $\models \square w \supset w$
6. $\models \bigcirc w \supset \diamond w$
7. $\models \square w \supset \bigcirc w$
7'. $\models \square w \supset \diamond w$
8. $\models \square w \supset \bigcirc \square w$
9. $\models w_1 U w_2 \supset \diamond w_2$
10. $\models \diamond \square w \supset \square \diamond w.$

The statements 4 to 10 indicate implication relations between the operators.

Statement 4 says that if w is true now, then it will be true sometime in the future. This is an immediate consequence of the fact that the present is considered to be a part of the future.

Statement 5, a dual of 4, says that if w is true in all future instants it is also presently true.

Statement 6 says that if w is true at the next instant it will sometime be true. This is because the next instant is also a part of the future.

Statement 7, a dual of 6, says that if w is true in all future instants it is also true for the next instant.

Statement 7' says that if w is always true then it is sometimes true.

Statement 8 says that if w is true in all future instants it is also true for all future instants of the next instant, i.e. all future instants excluding the present.

Statement 9 says that if w_1 is true until w_2 will happen then w_2 will eventually happen.

Statement 10 says that if w is permanently true beyond a certain instant then it is true infinitely often.

11. $\models \Box w \equiv \Box\Box w$
12. $\models \Diamond w \equiv \Diamond\Diamond w.$

The statements 11 and 12 show that both $\Box$ and $\Diamond$ are idempotent. Intuitively speaking both imply that the future is equivalent to the future of the future.

13. $\models \Box \bigcirc w \equiv \bigcirc \Box w$
14. $\models \Diamond \bigcirc w \equiv \bigcirc \Diamond w$
15. $\models ((\bigcirc w_1) U (\bigcirc w_2)) \equiv \bigcirc(w_1 U w_2).$

Statements 13 to 15 indicate the commutativity of the next operator $\bigcirc$ with each of the others. It amounts to a shift of our reference point from the present to the immediately next instant.

Statement 13 says that w holds for the instant next to every future instant iff w holds for all future instants, barring the present.

Statement 14 says that w is realized in an instant next to some future instant iff it is realized sometimes in the future, excluding the present.

Statement 15 says that $\bigcirc w_1$ holds until an instance of $\bigcirc w_2$ iff w_1 holds until w_2 starting from the next instant.

16. $\models \Box(w_1 \wedge w_2) \equiv (\Box w_1 \wedge \Box w_2)$
17. $\models \Diamond(w_1 \vee w_2) \equiv (\Diamond w_1 \vee \Diamond w_2)$
18. $\models \bigcirc(w_1 \wedge w_2) \equiv (\bigcirc w_1 \wedge \bigcirc w_2)$
19. $\models \bigcirc(w_1 \vee w_2) \equiv (\bigcirc w_1 \vee \bigcirc w_2)$
20. $\models \bigcirc(w_1 \supset w_2) \equiv (\bigcirc w_1 \supset \bigcirc w_2)$
21. $\models ((w_1 \wedge w_2) U w_3 \equiv ((w_1 U w_3) \wedge (w_2 U w_3))$
22. $\models (w_1 U(w_2 \vee w_3)) \equiv ((w_1 U w_2) \vee (w_1 U w_3)).$

Statements 16 to 22 indicate distributivity relations between the temporal operators and the boolean connectives.

The $\Box$ operator has a universal character—stating w for all future instants, and the $\Diamond$ operator has an existential character—stating w for some future instant. Consequently $\Box$ distributes with $\wedge$ (16) stating that both w_1 and w_2 hold in every future instant iff w_1 holds for all future instants and so does w_2. The $\Diamond$ operator distributes with $\vee$ (17) stating that there will be an instant in which either w_1 or w_2 hold iff there either will be an instant in which w_1 holds or there will be an instant in which w_2 holds.

The $\bigcirc$ operator has both universal and existential character because it refers to a unique instant—the next one. Therefore it distributes with both $\vee$ and $\wedge$, as is shown by statements 18 and 19.

Since the $\bigcirc$ operator has been shown to distribute with the basic boolean connectives $\sim$, $\wedge$, $\vee$, it will also distribute over any other boolean connective such as $\supset$. Statement 20 says that if in the next instant w_1 implies w_2 and w_1 is known to hold at the next instant then w_2 does also.

The *until* operator has a different character with respect to its two arguments. It is universal with respect to its first argument which appears in the semantic definition under a $\forall i(0 \leq i < k)$ quantification. It is existential with respect to its second argument which appears in the semantic definition under a $\exists k(k \geq 0)$ quantification.

Statement 21 says that w_1 and w_2 both hold until an instance of w_3 iff w_1 holds until an instance of w_3 and w_2 holds until an instance of w_3. To justify the implication from right to left, we are guaranteed of having a t_1 such that w_3 is true at t_1 and w_1 holds until then, and a t_2 such that w_3 is true at t_2 and w_2 holds until then. By considering the earliest of these two instants $t = \min(t_1, t_2)$ we know that w_3 is true at t and both w_1 and w_2 hold until then.

Statement 22 says that w_1 holds until an instance of either w_2 or w_3 iff either w_1 holds until an instance of w_2 or w_1 holds until an instance of w_3. This is seen by observing that we can make the same selection between the two disjuncts on both sides of the equivalence.

23. $\models (\Box w_1 \vee \Box w_2) \supset \Box(w_1 \vee w_2)$
24. $\models \Diamond(w_1 \wedge w_2) \supset (\Diamond w_1 \wedge \Diamond w_2)$
25. $\models ((w_1 U w_3) \vee (w_2 U w_3)) \supset (w_1 \vee w_2) U w_3$
26. $\models (w_1 U(w_2 \wedge w_3)) \supset ((w_1 U w_2) \wedge (w_1 U w_3))$.

Statements 23 to 26 indicate implications that hold when interchanging the order between temporal operators and the boolean connectives. They are not equivalences and only the direction of the given implication is true.

Statement 23 says that if either w_1 is true for all future instants or w_2 is true for all future instants then in every future instant either w_1 or w_2 holds.

Statement 24 says that if there exists an instant in which both w_1 and w_2 are true then there exists an instant in which w_1 is true and there exists an instant in which w_2 is true.

Statement 25 says that if either w_1 holds until w_3 or w_2 holds until w_3 then there is an instance of w_3 such that until then either w_1 or w_2 holds.

Statement 26 says that if w_1 holds until an instant t in which both w_2 and w_3 are true then both w_1 holds until w_2 at t and w_1 holds until w_3 at t.

27. $\models \Box(w_1 \supset w_2) \supset (\Box w_1 \supset \Box w_2)$
28. $\models \Box(w_1 \supset w_2) \supset (\Diamond w_1 \supset \Diamond w_2)$
29. $\models \Box(w_1 \supset w_2) \supset (\bigcirc w_1 \supset \bigcirc w_2)$
30. $\models \Box(w_1 \supset w_2) \supset ((w_1 U w_3) \supset (w_2 U w_3))$
31. $\models \Box(w_1 \supset w_2) \supset ((w_0 U w_1) \supset (w_0 U w_2))$

Statements 27 to 31 indicate the monotonicity of each of the temporal operators; that is, if its application to a formula w_1 is true and w_1 universally implies w_2 (for all instants) then its application to w_2 is also true.

This property is stated respectively for $\square$ in 27, $\Diamond$ in 28, $\bigcirc$ in 29 and the two positions of U in 30 and 31.

32. $|= (\square w_1 \wedge \bigcirc w_2) \supset \bigcirc(w_1 \wedge w_2)$
33. $|= (\square w_1 \wedge \Diamond w_2) \supset \Diamond(w_1 \wedge w_2)$
34. $|= (\square w_1 \wedge (w_2 U w_3)) \supset (w_1 \wedge w_2)U(w_1 \wedge w_3)$.

Statements 32 to 34 are *frame rules*. They say that if w_1 is known to hold for all states then w_1 may be added as a conjunct under any other temporal operator. This is respectively stated for $\bigcirc$ in 32, for $\Diamond$ in 33 and for both argument positions of U in 34.

35. $|= \square(w \supset \bigcirc w) \supset (w \supset \square w)$
36. $|= (w \wedge \Diamond \sim w) \supset \Diamond(w \wedge \bigcirc \sim w)$.

Statements 35 and 36 are *induction rules*.

Statement 35 (corresponding to computational induction) says that if the fact that w holds at any instant implies that it also holds at the next instant, and w holds in the present, then w holds at all future instants.

Statement 36 (corresponding to the least number principle) is the dual of 35. It says that if w is true now and is false sometime in the future, then there exists some instant such that w is true at that instant and false at the next.

37. $|= \square w \equiv (w \wedge \bigcirc \square w)$
38. $|= \Diamond w \equiv (w \vee \bigcirc \Diamond w)$
39. $|= w_1 U w_2 \equiv w_2 \vee (w_1 \wedge \bigcirc(w_1 U w_2))$

Statements 37 to 39 explain the $\square$, $\Diamond$ and U operators respectively by distributing their effect into what is implied for the present and what is implied for the next instant.

Statement 37 says that w is true for all future instants iff w is true for the present and for all instants lying in the future of the next instant.

Statement 38 says that w is true in some future instance iff it is either true now or true at an instant not earlier than the next.

Statement 39 says that "w_1 until w_2" is presently true iff either w_2 is true now or w_1 holds now and "w_1 until w_2" is true for the next instant.

40. $|= (\sim w U w) \equiv \Diamond w$
41. $|= (\square w_1 \wedge \Diamond w_2) \supset (w_1 U w_2)$
42. $|= ((w_1 \supset w_2)U w_3) \supset ((w_1 U w_3) \supset (w_2 U w_3))$
43. $|= ((w_1 U w_2) \wedge (\sim w_2 U w_3)) \supset (w_1 U w_3)$
44. $|= (w_1 U(w_2 \wedge w_3)) \supset ((w_1 U w_2)U w_3)$
45. $|= ((w_1 U w_2)U w_3) \supset ((w_1 \vee w_2)U w_3)$
45′. $|= (\Diamond w_1 \wedge \Diamond w_2) \supset ((\sim w_1 U w_2) \vee (\sim w_2 U w_1))$.

This list of statements illustrates some properties of the until operator.

Statement 40 says that w is guaranteed to happen iff there is an instant in which w is true and until this instant w is false. This states of course that w happens iff there is an earliest occurrence of w.

Statement 41 says that if w_2 is guaranteed to happen and w_1 is constantly true, then w_1 will be true until a guaranteed occurrence of w_2.

Statement 42 says that if w_1 implies w_2 until w_3 happens and w_1 is true until an instance of w_3 (not necessarily the same instance) then w_2 will hold until an instance of w_3 (which can be taken as the earlier of the two).

Statement 43 says that if w_1 holds until w_2 and w_2 is false until w_3 then w_1 is true until w_3. To justify this let (a) $w_1 U w_2$ and (b) $\sim w_2 U w_3$ be the two clauses given as premises. By (b) we know that w_3 will happen say at t_3 and w_2 will be false until then. By (a) w_2 must happen, say at t_2 and w_1 be true until then. By (b) $t_2 \geq t_3$ so that w_1 must certainly be true until t_3, an instance of w_3.

Statement 44 can be justified as follows. The premise guarantees an instant t_2 such that w_2 and w_3 are both true at t_2 and w_1 is true until then. Clearly, taking any $0 \leq t_1 < t_2$ we know that w_2 will be true at t_2 and w_1 is true for every t, $t_1 \leq t < t_2$, thus $w_1 U w_2$ at t_1. Since $w_1 U w_2$ is true for every t_1, $0 \leq t_1 < t_2$ and w_3 is true at t_2, $w_1 U w_2$ is true until w_3.

Statement 45 says that if $w_1 U w_2$ is continuously true until an instance of w_3 then so is $w_1 \lor w_2$.

Statement 45' says that if both w_1 and w_2 are guaranteed to happen then one of them will happen first; that is, either w_2 happens first and w_1 is false until then, or w_1 happens first and w_2 is false until then.

46. $\models \Diamond \exists xw \equiv \exists x \Diamond w$
47. $\models \Box \forall xw \equiv \forall x \Box w$
48. $\models \bigcirc \exists xw \equiv \exists x \bigcirc w$
49. $\models \bigcirc \forall xw \equiv \forall x \bigcirc w$
50. $\models ((\forall xw_1) U w_2) \equiv \forall x(w_1 U w_2)$ provided x is not free in w_2
51. $\models (w_1 U(\exists xw_2)) \equiv \exists x(w_1 U w_2)$ provided x is not free in w_1

Statements 46 to 51 indicate the commutativity relations between the temporal operators and the quantifiers. They follow from our restriction that the quantifiers $\forall$ and $\exists$ are to be applied only to global individual variables. Statements 46 and 47 are known as Barcan's formulas.

Statement 46 demonstrates once more the existential character of the operator $\Diamond$. It says that in some instant there exists an x satisfying w(x) iff there exists an x such that in some instant w(x) is satisfied.

Statement 47 demonstrates the universal character of the $\Box$ operator. It says that w is true in all instants for all values of x iff it is true for all values of x for every instant.

Statements 48 and 49 demonstrate the dual character of the $\bigcirc$ operator, which is both universal and existential.

Statements 50 and 51 demonstrate that the until operator has a universal character with respect to its first argument and an existential character with respect to its second argument.

The preceeding statements were all of the form

$$|= w$$

and they stated formulas which are true in every model. The next list of statements contains *inferences* of the form

$$|= w_1 \Rightarrow |= w_2.$$

They state that if w_1 has been shown to be a valid statement then so will be w_2. The inference statements enable us to deduce the validity of one formula from the other. For every valid formula $|= w_1 \supset w_2$ there is a corresponding inference $|= w_1 \Rightarrow |= w_2$, and this is a standard way of justifying an inference. However, there are inferences $|= w_1 \Rightarrow |= w_2$ such that $w_1 \supset w_2$ is not a valid statement (see, for example, the following inference 52).

52. $|= w \Rightarrow |= \Box w$ $\Box$—generalization
53. $|= w \Rightarrow |= \Diamond w$ $\Diamond$—generalization
54. $|= w \Rightarrow |= \bigcirc w$ $\bigcirc$—generalization

Inference 52 states that if w is valid then so is $\Box w$. The fact that w is valid means that it is true for any sequence and therefore for all suffixes $\sigma^{(i)}$ of a given sequence. Thus $\Box w$ is true for every sequence σ and is therefore a valid statement.

Inference 53 may be deduced by inferring first $|= \Box w$ and then using the valid statement $|= \Box w \supset \Diamond w$ (number 7' in our list), to infer $|= \Diamond w$.

Inference 54 may be deduced similarly by using statement 7, $|= \Box w \supset \bigcirc w$.

55. $|= w_1 \supset w_2 \Rightarrow |= \Box w_1 \supset \Box w_2$ $\Box\Box$—introduction
56. $|= w_1 \supset w_2 \Rightarrow |= \Diamond w_1 \supset \Diamond w_2$ $\Diamond\Diamond$—introduction
57. $|= w_1 \supset w_2 \Rightarrow |= \bigcirc w_1 \supset \bigcirc w_2$ $\bigcirc\bigcirc$—introduction

These inferences are all obtained by infering first $|= \Box(w_1 \supset w_2)$ by Inference 52 and then using statements 27 to 29, respectively.

58. $\left. \begin{array}{l} |= w_1 \supset \Box w_2 \\ |= w_2 \supset \Box w_3 \end{array} \right\} \Rightarrow |= w_1 \supset \Box w_3$ $\Box$—concatenation

59. $\left. \begin{array}{l} |= w_1 \supset \Diamond w_2 \\ |= w_2 \supset \Diamond w_3 \end{array} \right\} \Rightarrow |= w_1 \supset \Diamond w_3$ $\Diamond$—concatenation

Inference 58 is obtained by first deriving $|= \Box w_2 \supset \Box\Box w_3$ by Inference 55, observing that $\Box\Box w_3 \equiv \Box w_3$, and then using propositional reasoning. Inference 59 is obtained similarly by applying Inference 56.

$$60. \quad \left. \begin{array}{l} |= w_1 \supset w_2 \\ |= w_2 \supset \square w_3 \\ |= w_3 \supset w_4 \end{array} \right\} \Rightarrow \quad |= w_1 \supset \square w_4 \qquad \square\text{---consequence}$$

$$61. \quad \left. \begin{array}{l} |= w_1 \supset w_2 \\ |= w_2 \supset \Diamond w_3 \\ |= w_3 \supset w_4 \end{array} \right\} \Rightarrow \quad |= w_1 \supset \Diamond w_4 \qquad \Diamond\text{---consequence}$$

$$62. \quad \left. \begin{array}{l} |= w_1 \supset w_2 \\ |= w_2 \supset \bigcirc w_3 \\ |= w_3 \supset w_4 \end{array} \right\} \Rightarrow \quad |= w_1 \supset \bigcirc w_4 \qquad \bigcirc\text{---consequence}$$

Inference 60 is obtained by deriving first $|= \square w_3 \supset \square w_4$ by $\square\square$—introduction (55) and then applying propositional reasoning. Similarly, inferences 61 and 62 are obtained by deriving $|= \Diamond w_3 \supset \Diamond w_4$ and $|= \bigcirc w_3 \supset \bigcirc w_4$ by 56 and 57, respectively.

3. CONCURRENT PROGRAMS AND THEIR EXECUTION

In the following we introduce the model of concurrent programs that we will study here (for simpler models see [7] and [8]).

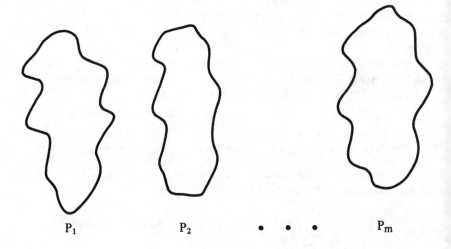

In our model a concurrent program $P_1 \| \ldots \| P_m$ consists of m, $m \geq 1$, processes $P_1, \ldots, P_m$ which are running in parallel. Each process P_i, $i = 1$, ..., m is an independent transition graph with nodes (locations) labeled by

$l_0^i, l_1^i, \ldots, l_e^i$. The sets of labels $L_i = \{l_0^i, \ldots, l_e^i\}$ of the different processes are taken to be disjoint. The edges (or transitions) in each process are labeled by instructions of the form:

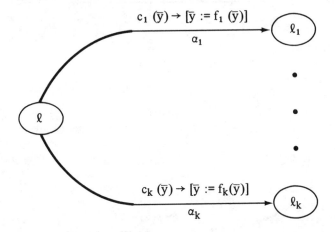

where $c_\alpha(\bar{y})$ is a condition called the *enabling condition* of the transition α, and f_α is the *transformation* associated with the transition α. If $c_\alpha(\bar{\eta})$ is true we say that the transition α is *enabled* for $\bar{y} = \bar{\eta}$.

For a given node l with k outgoing transitions

we define $E_l(\bar{y}) = c_1(\bar{y}) \vee \ldots \vee c_k(\bar{y})$ to be the *full-exit condition* at node l. We do not require that the individual conditions are exhaustive, i.e. that $E_l(\bar{y}) = $ true for every $\bar{y}$; thus, deadlocks are allowed in our semantics. Nor do we require the conditions to be exclusive; thus, each individual process can be nondeterministic. A location whose individual conditions are exclusive is called a *deterministic location*. If $E_l(\bar{\eta})$ is true, i.e. at least one of the α_i, $i = 1, \ldots, k$, transitions originating from l is enabled, we say that the location l is *enabled for* $\bar{y} = \bar{\eta}$. If a process P_j is currently at $l \in L_j$ which is enabled, we say that the *process is enabled*.

The set of program variables $\bar{y} = (y_1, \ldots, y_n)$ is accessible and shared by all the processes. This model of concurrent programs is therefore called the *shared-variables model*. In this model, communication and synchronization between processes are managed via the shared variables. A full specification of a concurrent program also includes a specification of the initial values of the program variables $y_1, \ldots, y_n$.

We will often represent a process in a linear-text form instead of a graph.

In such a case the nodes are the places (labels) just before each statement, and the transitions are the statements themselves. The linear-text form restricts us to having at most two transitions out of each node.

We list below the types of statements that we allow in the linear-text form and their representation in the graph model:

l: $\bar{y} := f(\bar{y})$
l':

is represented as

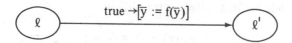

l: if $p(\bar{y})$ then go to m
l':

is represented as

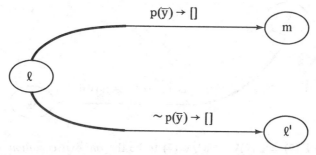

l: if $p(\bar{y})$ then $\bar{y} := f(\bar{y})$
l':

is represented as

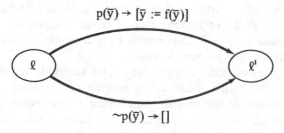

l: loop until $p(\bar{y})$
l':

This statement loops until the condition $p(\bar{y})$ becomes true. It is represented as

l: loop while $p(\bar{y})$
l':

This statement is the complement of the above statement: it loops until condition $\sim p$ is true. It is represented as

l: compute $u_1, \ldots, u_p$ using $v_1, \ldots, v_s$
l':

This statement is representative of a segment of terminating computation in whose details we are not interested. The only facts we assume about this segment are:

(1) The segment may modify only the program variables $u_1, \ldots, u_p, p \geq 0$, and may reference only the program variables $v_1, \ldots, v_s, s \geq 0$.

(2) The segment must eventually terminate.

The statement is represented as

We will often use compute segments of the form

l: compute
l':

for the case $p = s = 0$ to refer to a segment of terminating computation that does not modify or access any program variables.

l: execute $u_1, \ldots, u_p$ using $v_1, \ldots, v_s$
l':

This statement represents an arbitrary program segment that may modify only the program variables $u_1, \ldots, u_p, p \geq 0$, and may reference only $v_1, \ldots, v_s, s \geq 0$. Here we do not require that the segment must eventually terminate. Consequently its representation is given by:

$$\text{true} \rightarrow [(u_1, \ldots, u_p) := f(v_1, \ldots, v_s)]$$

ℓ $\longrightarrow$ ℓ'

true → []   true → []

l_e: halt

is represented as:

i.e. a node with no exits.

Note that for all the statements considered so far, except for the halt statement, the full-exit condition is always identically true. Also all the instructions (and their corresponding locations), except for the execute $u_1, \ldots, u_p$ instruction, are deterministic, i.e., they have exclusive transitions.

Example. Consider the following concurrent program for computing the binomial coefficient $\binom{n}{k}$ for integers n and k, such that $0 \leq k \leq n$:

Program BC (Binomial Coefficient):

$$y_1 = n, \quad y_2 = 0, \quad y_3 = 1$$

l_0: if $y_1 = (n - k)$ then go to l_e m_0: if $y_2 = k$ then go to m_e

l_1: $y_3 := y_3 \cdot y_1$ m_1: $y_2 := y_2 + 1$

l_2: $y_1 := y_1 - 1$ m_2: loop until $y_1 + y_2 \leq n$

l_3: go to l_0 m_3: $y_3 := y_3/y_2$

l_e: halt m_4: go to m_0

                                                              m_e: halt

— Process P_1 —   — Process P_2 —

The computation follows the formula

$$\binom{n}{k} = \frac{n \cdot (n - 1) \cdot \, \cdots \, \cdot (n - k + 1)}{1 \cdot 2 \cdot \, \cdots \, \cdot k}$$

The values of y_1, i.e. n, n − 1, ..., n − k + 1, (and n − k), are used to compute the numerator in P_1, and the values of y_2, i.e. (initially 0), 1, 2, ..., k, are used to compute the denominator. The process P_1 multiplies $n \cdot (n - 1) \cdot \, \cdots \, \cdot (n - k + 1)$ into y_3 while P_2 divides y_3 by $1 \cdot 2 \cdot \, \cdots \, \cdot k$.

The instruction

$$m_2: \text{loop until } y_1 + y_2 \leq n$$

synchronizes P_2's operation with P_1 to ensure that y_3 is divided by i only after it has been multiplied by n − i + 1 to guarantee even divisibility. We rely here on the mathematical theorem that the product of i consecutive positive integers: $k \cdot (k + 1) \cdot \, \cdots \, \cdot (k + i - 1)$ is always divisible by i!. Consider the intermediate expression at m_2:

$$y_3 = \frac{n \cdot (n - 1) \cdot \, \cdots \, \cdot (n - j + 1)}{1 \cdot 2 \cdot \, \cdots \, \cdot (i - 1)},$$

where $1 \leq i \leq j \leq n$, $y_1 = n - j$ and $y_2 = i$. The numerator consists of a multiplication of i consecutive positive integers and it is therefore divisible by i. If $j = i$, we have to wait until y_1 is decremented by the instruction in l_2 from $n - i + 1$ to $n - i$ before we can be absolutely sure that $(n - i + 1)$ has been multiplied into y_3. Thus, Process P_2 waits at m_2 until $y_1 + y_2$ drops to a value smaller than or equal to n. ∎

In order to keep track of the progress of the execution in each process we may envisage a vector of *location variables* $\bar{\pi} = \{\pi_1, \ldots, \pi_m\}$ where each π_i ranges over the label set L_i of process P_i.

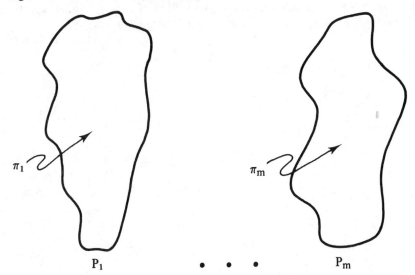

$$P_1 \quad \bullet \quad \bullet \quad \bullet \quad P_m$$

The location variable π_i points to the location in P_i which is next to be executed.

Let us consider now the notion of execution in our model. A major simplifying assumption is that the program is executed by *multiprogramming* or *interleaving*. Under this assumption, the execution proceeds as a sequence of discrete steps. In each step one enabled process is selected and its enabled transition is executed. We personify this selection by conceiving a *scheduler* who performs the selection.

At any step of the computation the scheduler selects an enabled process and lets that process execute one instruction (transition). For the sake of completeness we also allow the scheduler to arbitrarily insert an *idling step* in which no process is scheduled, no instruction is performed, and the values of all program and location variables remain the same. In the case that no enabled processes are available, an idling step is the only choice that the scheduler has thereafter. In such a case we say that the program is *deadlocked*.

A special case of this situation is when the program has *terminated*, i.e. all the processes have terminated.

Since by the assumption of interleaving, each transition is fully executed with no interference from the other processes, we call the instructions labelling the transitions *indivisible* or *atomic*.

3.1. Multiprogramming versus concurrency

At first glance the simplification of replacing real concurrency by interleaving may seem counterintuitive to our notion of a truly parallel execution. Consider for example the following concurrent program A:

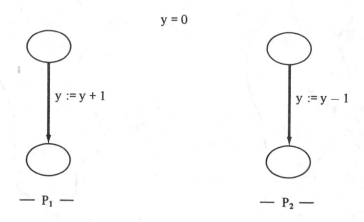

A *multiprogramming execution* of this program can yield only $y = 0$ as the result on termination, because either we first add 1 to y (in P_1) and then subtract 1 (in P_2), or we first subtract 1 from y (in P_2) and then add 1 (in P_1). However, a truly *concurrent execution* of the above can also yield $y = 1$ and $y = -1$ as possible results, depending on the exact timing of the concurrent execution events. For example, consider two processors sharing the variable y, each executing one of the processes. Suppose that both processors start computing the right-hand side of their respective expressions at about the same time. Naturally, they both retrieve the value 0 as the current value of y. When the computations are done one processor obtains the value 1 to be stored into y, while the other wants to store -1 into y. If P_1 stores its value later than P_2 we would have $y = 1$ as the result; if P_1 is earlier we obtain -1 as the final result. Thus our multiprogramming execution model does not reflect the real concurrent execution in this example.

The problem is that the instructions $y := y + 1$ and $y := y - 1$, which were considered to be "atomic" in the mutliprogramming execution, contained too many events, namely: fetching the value of a shared variable, computing an expression, and storing a value into a shared variable. In real concurrent execution these events may be interleaved with similar events of the other process, causing interference. A close examination reveals that the critical events are the fetching and storing into shared variables. Let us define a variable which is modifiable only by P_1 to be *private to* P_1, while all the other variables are called *shared in* P_1.

An occurrence of a variable on the left-hand side of an assignment is called a *modification reference,* and any other occurrence of a variable is called an *accessing reference.*

An occurrence of a variable in a statement is defined to be a critical reference if it is either a modification of a variable which is accessible by other processes or an access of a variable which is modifiable by other processes [12].

Under the following assumption multiprogramming execution reflects real concurrency:

The Rule of Single (Critical) Reference: every instruction may have at most one critical reference.

Reviewing the above example we see that the instruction $y := y + 1$ violates the single access rule. We can transform this program into an equivalent program A' (with respect to true concurrent executions) that will satisfy this rule:

$$y = 0$$

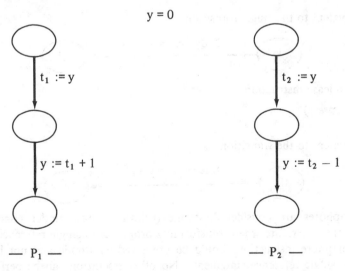

$$t_1 := y \qquad\qquad\qquad t_2 := y$$

$$y := t_1 + 1 \qquad\qquad y := t_2 - 1$$

$$— P_1 — \qquad\qquad\qquad — P_2 —$$

Here, t_1 and t_2 are private variables of P_1 and P_2, respectively. It is obvious that if executed by multiprogramming, the program A' can now yield any of $\{0, -1, +1\}$ as possible results, depending on the scheduling.

We may summarize this discussion on the relations between concurrency and multiprogramming by the following facts:

(a) A program that obeys the single reference rule can yield the same set of results when executed concurrently or by multiprogramming.

(b) For every program there exists an equivalent (concurrent) program that obeys the single reference rule.

Thus, using multiprogramming, it is possible to represent all the possible situations arising under concurrency. Since it greatly simplifies the analysis, we adopt the multiprogramming approach in our treatment of parallel programs.

One necessary exception to the single reference rule is *semaphores*—a standard synchronization device in concurrent programs [2].

3.2. Semaphores

Semaphores are special atomic instructions denoted by *request*(y) (also known as P(y)), and *release*(y) (also known as V(y)), operating on the semaphore variable y.

The request instruction

l: *request*(y)
l':

is equivalent to the single transition

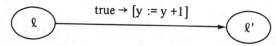

The release instruction

l: *release*(y)
l':

is equivalent to the transition

$$\ell \xrightarrow{\text{true} \to [y := y + 1]} \ell'$$

Semaphores are considered atomic (primitive) even under concurrent executions. Therefore when transforming programs to single reference form the semaphore instruction should be preserved as atomic and not broken up into single reference statements. No other operation can be performed on semaphore variables.

Usually the semaphore variable y is initialized to 1 (or occasionally to some other positive value). A process reaching a *request*(y) instruction will proceed beyond it only if y > 0 and then it will decrement y by 1, setting it to 0. Thus a location containing a *request*(y) instruction can be used as a checkpoint synchronizing the process with other processes containing *request*(y) and *release*(y) instructions operating on the same y.

Consider a concurrent program of form

$$y = 1$$

$$
\begin{array}{ccc}
\vdots & \vdots & \vdots \\
l^1\!: request(\text{y}) & l^2\!: request(\text{y}) & l^k\!: request(\text{y}) \\
\vdots & \vdots & \vdots \\
m^1\!: release(\text{y}) & m^2\!: release(\text{y}) & m^k\!: release(\text{y}) \\
\vdots & \vdots & \vdots \\
- \text{P}_1 - & - \text{P}_2 - & \quad\bullet\ \bullet\ \bullet \qquad - \text{P}_k -
\end{array}
$$

Assume, for example, that P_1 arrived first at l^1 when y was 1. It then went beyond l^1 and set y to 0. As long as P_1 is between l^1 and m^1, y will remain 0 and any process, say P_2, which will attempt to go beyond its request statement l^2 will be held there since the enabling condition y > 0 is false. It must wait there for y to turn positive, which can only be caused by P_1 performing the *release*(y) operation at m^1. Even if P_1 and P_2 reached l^1 and l^2 simultaneously, the atomicity of the request instruction (which is required for exactly this reason) ensures that only one process can gain access to its region lying between l and m. This region is called a *critical section*, and our use of semaphores in this example ensured mutual exclusion of access to the critical sections; that is, at most one of the processes may execute its critical section at any instant. Semaphores may also be used for a variety of other signalling and synchronization tasks.

Mutual exclusion of critical sections is necessary whenever two or more processes need to access a shared variable or device (such as disk) and wish to be protected from interference or attempts of the other processes to access the same resource while doing so.

Example. Consider once more program BC (Binomial Coefficient). In order to recast it in a single reference form we notice that the variable y_3 is the critically shared variable. Hence, we have to break the instruction

$$l_1\!: \text{y}_3 := \text{y}_3 \cdot \text{y}_1$$

into the sequence

$$l_1\!: t_1 := \text{y}_3 \cdot \text{y}_1$$
$$l_1'\!: \text{y}_3 := t_1$$

Note that y_1 is private in P_1, hence its access at l_1 is non-critical. Similarly we have to break the instruction

$$m_3: y_3 := y_3/y_2$$

into

$$m_3: t_2 := y_3/y_2$$
$$m_3': y_3 := t_2.$$

Note that both the assignments $y_2 := y_2 + 1$, $y_1 := y_1 - 1$ and the test $y_1 + y_2 \leq n$ already satisfy the single reference rule.

The problem now is that of interference between the two new processes. Consider for example an execution which includes the sequence:

$$l_1, m_3, l_1', m_3'.$$

Following this execution we find that while l_1' stores a certain value into y_3, it is immediately overwritten by the value stored into it by m_3'. Thus the value of the computation performed in l_1 is completely lost and the result is of course invalid. To prevent such a mishap we must protect each of the sequences (l_1, l_1') and (m_3, m_3') from interference by the other. The protection is done by using a semaphore variable y_4; the modified program appears below:

Program BC' (modified Binomial Coefficient):

$$y_1 = n, \ y_2 = 0, \ y_3 = 1, \ y_4 = 1$$

l_0: if $y_1 = (n - k)$ then go to l_e m_0: if $y_2 = k$ then go to m_e

l_1: request(y_4) m_1: $y_2 := y_2 + 1$

$\boxed{\begin{array}{l} l_2: t_1 := y_3 \cdot y_1 \\ l_3: y_3 := t_1 \\ l_4: release(y_4) \end{array}}$ $\begin{array}{l} m_2: \text{loop until } y_1 + y_2 \leq n \\ m_3: request(y_4) \end{array}$

l_5: $y_1 := y_1 - 1$ $\boxed{\begin{array}{l} m_4: t_2 := y_3/y_2 \\ m_5: y_3 := t_2 \\ m_6: release(y_4) \end{array}}$

l_6: go to l_0

l_e: halt m_7: go to m_0

                                     m_e: halt

The mutually protected critical sections are (l_2, l_3, l_4) and (m_4, m_5, m_6) respectively. Their exclusion ensures that each computed value of y_3 is assigned to y_3 without any interference. Under multiprogramming executions, BC' is equivalent to BC and is in single reference form. ∎

Example. Consider the following program CP modelling a producer-consumer situation:

Program CP (Consumer Producer):

$$b = \Lambda, \; s = 1, \; cf = 0, \; ce = N$$

l_0: compute y_1	m_0: *request*(cf)
l_1: *request*(ce)	m_1: *request*(s)
l_2: *request*(s)	m_2: $y_2 :=$ head(b)
l_3: $t_1 := b \circ y_1$	m_3: $t_2 :=$ tail(b)
l_4: $b := t_1$	m_4: $b := t_2$
l_5: *release*(s)	m_5: *release*(s)
l_6: *release*(cf)	m_6: *release*(ce)
l_7: go to l_0	m_7: compute using y_2
	m_8: go to m_0
— P_1: Producer —	— P_2: Consumer —

The producer P_1 computes a value into y_1 without using any other program variables; the computation details are irrelevant. It then adds y_1 to the end of the buffer b. The consumer P_2 removes the first element of the buffer into y_2 and then uses this value for its own purposes (at m_7). It is assumed that the maximal capacity of the buffer b is $N > 0$. The "compute using y_2" instruction references y_2 but does not modify any of the program variables.

In order to ensure the correct synchronization between the processes we use three semaphore variables:

(a) The variable s ensures that the accesses to the buffer are protected and provides exclusion between the sections (l_3, l_4, l_5) and (m_2, m_3, m_4, m_5).

(b) The variable ce, standing for "count of empties" counts the number of free available slots in the buffer b. It protects the buffer b from overflowing. The producer cannot deposit a value in the buffer if ce = 0, and when it does deposit it decrements ce by 1. Since we start with ce = N, the producer cannot deposit more than N items before the consumer has removed any of them. The consumer, on the other hand, increments ce by 1 whenever it removes an item and creates a new vacancy.

(c) The variable cf ("count of fulls") counts how many items the buffer currently holds. It is initialized to 0, incremented by the producer whenever a new item is deposited and decremented by the consumer whenever an item is removed. It ensures that the consumer does not attempt to remove an item from an empty buffer. ∎

3.3. Fairness

Another problem with modelling concurrency by multiprogramming is fairness. Consider first a program with no semaphore instructions, and where the full-exit condition $E_l(\bar{y})$ at each nonterminal location l (i.e. $l \neq l_e$) is identically true, i.e. $E_l(\bar{y}) = $ true for every $\bar{y}$. Note that the latter is true for every linear-text program without semaphores. Under these restrictions every process that has not yet terminated is enabled, i.e. it always has an enabled transition, and if selected by the scheduler can always execute this transition. Running under a true concurrent execution, every process will go on executing until it reaches the termination label l_e.

In order to model the same property under multiprogramming execution we require the scheduler to be *fair*. By that we mean that no process which is ready to run (i.e., enabled) will be neglected forever. Stated more precisely, we exclude infinite executions in which a certain process which has not terminated is never scheduled from a certain point on. Note that all finite terminating sequences are necessarily fair. This will also prevent the scheduler from going on a spree of idling steps when at least one process is enabled.

Coming back to the more general situation, we have to consider the possibility that a non-terminated process is not continuously enabled. Furthermore, its being enabled may depend on the action of the other processes, since in general the full-exit condition $E_l(\bar{y})$ may depend on the shared variables $\bar{y}$.

Our requirement of fairness for this more general case will be formulated as:

We disallow infinite sequences in which a certain process is enabled infinitely often and is scheduled only a finite number of times.

Consider the simplest case of two processes synchronized by a semaphore:

$$y = 1$$

l_0: *request*(y)	m_0: *request*(y)
l_1: *release*(y)	m_1: *release*(y)
l_2: go to l_0	m_2: go to m_0
$-P_1-$	$-P_2-$

Obviously the infinite execution sequence (where we only mention the label arrived at as a result of the current transition)

$$l_1, l_2, l_0, m_1, m_2, m_0, l_1, l_2, l_0, m_1, m_2, m_0, \ldots$$

is fair. On the other hand the sequence:

$$l_1, l_2, l_0, l_1, l_2, l_0, \ldots$$

while constantly $\pi_2 = m_0$ is unfair. This is so because whenever $\pi_1 = l_0$ or $\pi_1 = l_2$, P_2 is enabled. Thus in this sequence even though P_2 is not continuously enabled (it is not enabled when $\pi_1 = l_1$) it is enabled infinitely often. Since P_2 is never scheduled while being enabled infinitely often this sequence is unfair.

In practice any particular scheduler which is fair satisfies a stronger requirement: it is fair within a finite bound, i.e. no enabled process may be neglected for more than k instants of being enabled. Here k is a constant, characteristic of the scheduler.

Generalizing the semaphore instruction *request*(y) which waits for y to turn positive and then decrements it, we have the "wait until p(ȳ)" and "wait while p(ȳ)" instructions. They are modeled as follows:

l: wait until p(ȳ)
l':

is represented by

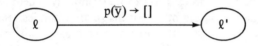

and

l: wait while p(ȳ)
l':

is represented by

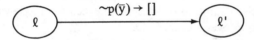

The wait instructions are similar to the request instruction in that the full-exit condition is not identically true. Thus for the "wait until p(ȳ)" instruction, the full-exit condition $E_l(ȳ)$ is equal to p(ȳ). Consequently fairness considerations ensure that if p(ȳ) turns true infinitely often while a process is waiting at *l* it will eventually be scheduled (exactly when p(ȳ) is true) and proceed to *l'*.

Let us compare the "wait until p(ȳ)" instruction with the "loop until p(ȳ)" instruction whose graph representation is

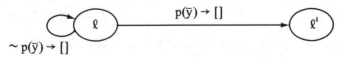

Note that the full-exit condition for this instruction is E_l = true. Thus even if p(ȳ) turns true infinitely often we are not assured of ultimately reaching *l'*. This is so because the only requirement implied by fair scheduling is that if E_l is infinitely often true the process waiting at *l* must eventually be scheduled at an instant in which E_l is true. However this instant may always happen to be one in which p(ȳ) = false and the instruction executed is a transition back to *l*.

The only condition which will guarantee for a loop instruction the eventual exit to l' is that $p(\bar{y})$ becomes permanently true beyond a certain stage in the computation.

There are practical implications to the distinction between the wait and loop instructions. If we wish to implement an actual fair multiprogramming scheduler, it is easier to be fair to the loop instruction than to the wait instruction. Since for the loop instruction, E_l is identically true, in order to be fair to a process which is at l, the scheduler has just to make sure it does not neglect it and eventually comes around to scheduling it. In order to be fair to a wait instruction, whose full-exit condition is $p(\bar{y})$, we have to monitor the instants in which $p(\bar{y})$ is true. Then when it is observed that $p(\bar{y})$ is true many times the relevant process has to be eventually scheduled.

On the other hand, the use of a wait instruction implies greater efficiency since the scheduler may place the process executing a wait instruction on a suspension list, from which it will be removed only when $p(\bar{y})$ is true and the scheduler decides to schedule that process.

3.4. Execution sequences

Having discussed the notions of multiprogramming and fairness we can give a more precise definition of acceptable execution sequences for a given concurrent program over a domain D.

An execution state of a concurrent program is of the form:

$$s = \langle \bar{\lambda}; \bar{\eta} \rangle$$

where $\bar{\lambda} = \langle \lambda_1, \ldots, \lambda_m \rangle$ is the vector of current values held by the location variables $\bar{\pi}$ and $\bar{\eta} = \langle \eta_1, \ldots, \eta_n \rangle \in D^n$ is the vector of data values assumed by the program variables $\bar{y}$ in the state s. Obviously each $\lambda_i \in L_i$ points to the next instruction to be executed.

An execution sequence of the program $P = P_1 \| \ldots \| P_m$ is an infinite sequence of states:

$$\sigma = s_0, s_1, s_2 \ldots$$

An execution sequence σ is *legal* if each $s_{k+1} = \langle \bar{\lambda}'; \bar{\eta}' \rangle$ is related to $s_k = \langle \bar{\lambda}; \bar{\eta} \rangle$ by one of the following rules:

(a) *Idling step:* $s_{k+1} = s_k$ (i.e. $\bar{\lambda}' = \bar{\lambda}, \bar{\eta}' = \bar{\eta}$).

(b) *An i-step:* for some $1 \le i \le m$ we have the following: The process P_i contains a transition such that $c(\bar{\eta}) = $ true (i.e. the transition is enabled) and $\bar{\eta}' = f(\bar{\eta})$. For all j, $j \neq i$, we have $\lambda'_j = \lambda_j$.

Note that in the presence of self loops, i.e.

such as in loop instructions, we cannot always uniquely decide whether an idling step or an i-step led from state s_k to state s_{k+1}.

An execution sequence σ is *fair* if it is legal, and furthermore satisfies the following requirement:

If a process P_i is enabled infinitely often, the sequence must contain an infinite number of i-steps.

Note that in checking for fairness we are allowed to take a given step both as an i-step and as a j-step if both interpretations are possible. Thus the following degenerate program

$$l_0: \text{go to } l_0 \qquad\qquad m_0: \text{go to } m_0$$

possesses the execution sequence

$$\langle (l_0, m_0);() \rangle, \quad \langle (l_0, m_0);() \rangle, \dots$$

which is legal and fair. Each step here may be interpreted as an idling step, a 1-step or a 2-step. Because of this multiple interpretation the sequence is indeed fair.

Consider the sequence corresponding to a terminating computation, i.e. all processes have terminated. Since in a terminating state ($\pi_i = l^i_e$) the process P_i is never enabled, the fairness criterion does not require further scheduling of P_i, and the only possible steps from that point on are idling steps. Thus our representation of a terminating computation as an infinite sequence in which from a certain point on all states are identical is consistent with fairness. This state, to which the sequence has "converged", is the terminal state.

4. THE TEMPORAL DESCRIPTION OF PROGRAM PROPERTIES

As we have seen, the behavior of a concurrent program is characterized by the set of its fair execution sequences. We have also developed the formalism of temporal logic whose formulas are interpreted over sequences. We now combine the two and utilize temporal logic to state properties of the execution sequences of a given program, thus describing properties of the dynamic behavior of the program [9, 10, 14, 15].

In order to apply the general temporal formalism to execution sequences, it is convenient to introduce additional structure and special notation into the temporal language. For the concept of a state we will take an "execution state" which consists of the vector of current locations in the program and the current values of all program variables at a certain stage in the execution. The accessibility relation between execution states will represent "derivability" by the program's execution. We will use predicates and propositions to describe properties of a single state, and modalities to describe properties of the execution leading from one state to another.

Consider a typical concurrent program

$$P = P_1 || \ldots || P_m$$

with input variables $\bar{x} = (x_1, \ldots, x_k)$ and shared program variables $\bar{y} = (y_1, \ldots, y_n)$ over a domain D. (For simplicity, we do not consider many-sorted domains.)

An *execution state* for this program has the general structure $s = \langle \bar{\lambda}; \bar{\eta} \rangle$ with $\bar{\lambda} = (\lambda_1, \ldots, \lambda_m)$ where each $\lambda_i \in L_i$ and $\bar{\eta} = (\eta_1, \ldots, \eta_n) \in D^n$. In such an execution state

(a) λ_i is the label of the node in the transition graph of process P_i where execution is next to resume. (It is the label of the next instruction to be executed in the linear-text representation.)

(b) $\bar{\eta}$ are the current values of the variables $\bar{y}$ in the state s.

An *execution sequence* is any sequence of execution states of the program P:

$$\sigma = s_0, s_1, \ldots.$$

Corresponding to the structure of execution states and sequences we will consider temporal formulas with the following individual variables:

(a) *Local program variables:* $y_1, \ldots, y_n$.
These represent the current values of the program variables which of course may vary from one execution state to the other.

(b) *Local location variables:* $\pi_1, \ldots, \pi_m$.
These represent the location of each process in a given state. Each π_i will range over the set L_i.

(c) *Global variables:* $x_1, \ldots, x_k, u_1, u_2, \ldots$.
These are the input variables $x_1, \ldots, x_k$, and auxiliary variables $u_1, u_2, \ldots$ which stay constant over the complete execution, i.e. they do not vary from state to state. The auxiliary variables are used to express relations between local values in different states. For example:

$$\forall u[(y = u) \supset \Diamond(y = u + 1)]$$

express the statement that there will be a future instant in which the value of the variable y will be greater by 1 than its current value.

For a label $l \in L_j$, we abbreviate the atomic formula $(\pi_j = l)$ to at$l$, i.e.

$$\text{at}l \text{ is true iff } \pi_j = l,$$

which may therefore be considered a local proposition. Thus, for a given state $s = \langle \bar{\lambda}; \bar{\eta} \rangle$ and location $l \in L_j$, at$l$ is true at s if the process P_j is currently at l, i.e. $\lambda_j = l$.

More generally, for a set of labels $L \subseteq L_j$ the local proposition atL is defined to be true if P_j is anywhere within L, i.e.

$$\text{atL is true iff } \pi_j \in L.$$

If L consists of all the labels l_i within a segment, i.e. $L = \{l_a, l_{a+1}, \ldots, l_b\}$ for some $0 \leq a < b$, we will also write atL as at$l_{a..b}$. Thus,

$$\text{atL} = \text{at}l_{a..b} = \text{at}\{l_a, l_{a+1}, \ldots, l_b\} = \bigvee_{i=a}^{b} \text{at}l_i.$$

For a given program P let $\varphi(\bar{x})$ be a restriction (precondition) on the input values $\bar{x}$; the program variables $\bar{y}$ are initialized to $f_0(\bar{x})$. Usually φ characterizes the inputs we expect the program to operate on.

(1) An execution sequence is said to be a (P, φ)-*initialized computation* if it is a sequence σ such that:

(a) It is a fair execution sequence of P, and

(b) It is properly φ-initiated; that is, if $s_0 = \langle \bar{\lambda}; \bar{\eta} \rangle$ is the first state of σ we require that $\lambda = (l_0^1, \ldots, l_0^m)$, the set of initial locations in each of the processes, and that $\eta = f_0(\bar{x})$ for some input values $\bar{x}$ such that $\varphi(\bar{x})$ holds.

(2) An execution sequence is said to be a (P, φ)-*computation* (*admissible computation*) if it is a suffix of a (P, φ)-initialized computation.

(3) We define the set $F(P, \varphi)$ to be the set of all (P, φ)-computations. Obviously for every $\sigma \in F(P, \varphi)$ and every $i \geq 0$ also $\sigma^{(i)} \in F(P, \varphi)$. We thus say that $F(P, \varphi)$ has the suffix closure property.

(4) A formula w is $F(P, \varphi)$-*valid* if it is true for every sequence in $F(P, \varphi)$. Such a formula is obviously an established valid property of (the φ computations of) P. We will be interested in these formulas that express valid program properties.

In this section we study the expression of program properties as temporal formulas; in the next sections we will also consider how to reason about (P, φ)-valid formulas and prove them.

Since most of our reasoning will be done in the context of a fixed program P and a fixed precondition φ, we introduce a special notation for $F(P, \varphi)$ validity. We denote

$$|\equiv w \Rightarrow F(P, \varphi) |= w.$$

The statement $|\equiv w$ thus means that w is true for every suffix of a fair execution of P which is initiated at $\bar{l}_0 = (l_0^1, \ldots, l_0^m)$ with $\varphi(\bar{x})$ holding and $\bar{y} = f_0(\bar{x})$.

Facts of the form $\models w$ will serve as the basic statements in our specification and description of program properties. Consequently we will be very much interested in proof rules for deriving such statements.

For example the following is an important valid derivation

$$\models w \Rightarrow \models w$$

It states that if w is true for every possible sequence it is true in particular for every (P, φ)- computation.

This enables us to transport all the generally known valid temporal statements ($\models$-valid) into reasoning about a particular program ($\models$-valid). Thus the following are $\models$ valid formulas:

$$\models \Box \sim w \equiv \sim \Diamond w$$
$$\models \Box(w_1 \supset w_2) \supset (\Box w_1 \supset \Box w_2)$$
$$\models \Box(w \supset \bigcirc w) \supset (w \supset \Box w)$$

etc.

Another valid inference is

$$\models w \Rightarrow \models \Box w$$

This rule states that if w is true for all the (P, φ)-computations then $\Box w$ is also true for them. This rule is a direct consequence of the suffix closure property of $F(P, \varphi)$. One can prove similarly that all the inference rules (numbers 52 to 62) proven in the earlier repertoire still hold after replacing $\models$ by $\models$.

We will now review the expression of program properties by temporal formulas. The properties will be classified according to the form of the temporal formulas expressing them.

4.1. Invariance (safety) properties

Consider first the class of program properties that hold continuously throughout the execution. They are expressible by formulas of the form:

$$\models \Box w.$$

Such a formula states that $\Box w$ holds for every admissible computation, i.e. w is an invariant of every computation. By the generalization rule this could have been written as $\models w$, but we prefer the above form since it emphasizes that we are discussing invariance properties.

Note that the initial condition associated with the admissible computation is:

$$at\bar{l}_0 \wedge \bar{y} = f_0(\bar{x}) \wedge \varphi(\bar{x})$$

which characterizes the initial state for input $\bar{x}$ satisfying the precondition $\varphi(\bar{x})$.

Here, $\bar{l}_0 = (l_0^1, \ldots, l_0^m)$ is the set of initial locations in each of the processes. To emphasize the precondition $\varphi(\bar{x})$ we sometimes express $|\equiv \Box w$ as

$$|\equiv \varphi(\bar{x}) \supset \Box w.$$

A formula in this form therefore expresses an *invariance property*. The properties in this class are also known as *safety properties*, based on the premise that they ensure that "nothing bad will ever happen" [8].

We give below a sample of important properties falling under this category.

(a) Partial correctness

This property is meaningful only for programs in which each process contains a terminal location l_e. We call such programs *terminating programs*, in contrast with *continuous programs* that are supposed to run forever and therefore do not contain terminal locations.

Let $\varphi(\bar{x})$ be the precondition that restricts the set of inputs for which the program is supposed to be correct, and $\psi(\bar{x}, \bar{y})$ the statement of its correctness, i.e. the relation that should hold between the input values $\bar{x}$ and the output values $\bar{y}$. Then in order to state partial correctness with respect to a specification (φ, ψ) we can write:

$$|\equiv \varphi(\bar{x}) \supset \Box(\text{at}\bar{l}_e \supset \psi(\bar{x}, \bar{y})),$$

where $\bar{l}_e = (l_e^1, \ldots, l_e^m)$ is the set of terminal locations in each of the processes. This formula claims that if the initial state satisfies the restricting precondition then in any state accessible from the initial state: if that state happens to be an exit state, i.e. $\bar{\lambda} = \bar{l}_e$, then the relation $\psi(\bar{x}, \bar{y})$ holds between the input values $\bar{x}$ and the current values of $\bar{y}$. Thus this formula states that all convergent φ-initialized computations terminate in a state satisfying ψ, but it does not guarantee termination itself. Note the use of the global variables $\bar{x}$ which remain constant throughout the computation.

Example. Let us consider as a concrete example, a single program for computing x! over the nonnegative integer.

Program F (Factorial Program):

$$y_1 = x, \ y_2 = 1$$
$$l_0: \text{if } y_1 = 0 \text{ then go to } l_e$$
$$l_1: (y_1, y_2) := (y_1 - 1, y_1 \cdot y_2)$$
$$l_2: \text{go to } l_0$$
$$l_e: \text{halt.}$$

The statement of its partial correctness is

$$|\equiv (x \geq 0) \supset \Box(\text{at}l_e \supset y_2 = x!),$$

where the initial condition associated with the admissible computation is actually

$$at l_0 \land y_1 = x \land y_2 = 1 \land x \geq 0.$$

We are justified in regarding partial correctness as an invariance property since it is actually a part of a "network of invariants" normally used in the Invariant-Assertion Method; namely, for Program F above:

$$
\begin{aligned}
\models (x \geq 0) \supset \Box\{ \quad & [at l_0 \supset (y_1 \geq 0) \land (y_2 \cdot y_1! = x!)] \\
\land \; & [at l_1 \supset (y_1 > 0) \land (y_2 \cdot y_1! = x!)] \\
\land \; & [at l_2 \supset (y_1 \geq 0) \land (y_2 \cdot y_1! = x!)] \\
\land \; & [at l_e \supset (y_1 = 0) \land (y_2 = x!)]\}.
\end{aligned}
$$

And in fact, in order to prove the partial correctness property, we usually prove the invariance of this larger formula, from which partial correctness follows. ∎

Example. As another example consider a program TN counting the number of nodes in a binary tree X.

Program TN (Counting the nodes of a tree).

$$S = (X), \; C = 0$$

l_0: if $S = (\;)$ then go to l_e
l_1: $(T, S) := (hd(S), tl(S))$
l_2: if $T = \Lambda$ then go to l_0
l_3: $C := C + 1$
l_4: $S := lt(T) \cdot rt(T) \cdot S$
l_5: go to l_0
l_e: halt.

The program operates on a tree variable T and a variable S which is a stack of trees. The input variable X is a tree. The ouput is the value of the counter C. Each node in a tree may have zero, one or two descendants.

The possible operations on trees are the functions $lt(T)$ and $rt(T)$ which yield the left and right subtrees of a tree T respectively. If the tree does not possess one of these subtrees the functions return the value Λ.

The stack S is initialized to contain the tree X. Taking the head and tail of a stack (functions hd and tl respectively) yields the top element and rest of the stack respectively. The operation in l_1 pops the top of the stack into the variable T. The operation at l_4 stacks both the right subtree and the left subtree of T onto the top of the stack.

At any iteration of the program the stack S contains the list of subtrees of X whose nodes have not yet been counted. The iteration removes one such subtree from the stack. If it is the empty subtree, $T = \Lambda$, we proceed to examine the next subtree on the stack. If it is not the empty subtree we add one to the counter C and add to the stack the left and right subtrees of T. When the stack is empty, S = (), the program halts.

Denoting by |T| the number of nodes in a tree T we can express the statement of partial correctness of the program TN by:

$$\models \Box[\text{at}l_e \supset C = |X|].$$

The actual initial condition associated with the admissible computation is

$$\text{at}l_0 \wedge S = (X) \wedge C = 0. \quad \blacksquare$$

Example. As a more complex example consider again the program BC' for the concurrent computation of a binomial coefficient.

The statement of partial correctness to be proved there is:

$$\models (0 \leq k \leq n) \supset \Box[(\text{at}l_e \wedge \text{at}m_e) \supset y_3 = \binom{n}{k}].$$

That is, every properly initialized execution of the program BC' that terminates satisfies at its termination point $y_3 = \binom{n}{k}$. The actual initial condition associated with the admissible computation is

$$\text{at}l_0 \wedge \text{at}m_0 \wedge y_1 = n \wedge y_2 = 0 \wedge y_3 = 1 \wedge y_4 = 1 \wedge 0 \leq k \leq n. \quad \blacksquare$$

(b) Clean behavior

For every location in a program we can formulate a *cleanness* condition that states that the instruction at this location will execute successfully and will generate no fault. Thus if the statement contains a division, the cleanness condition will include the clause specifying that the divisor is nonzero or not too small (to avoid arithmetic overflow). If the statement contains an array reference, the cleanness condition will state that the subscript expressions are within the declared range. Denoting the cleanness condition at location l by α_l, the statement of clean behavior is:

$$\models \varphi(\bar{x}) \supset \Box \bigwedge_l (\text{at}l \supset \alpha_l).$$

The conjunction is taken over all "potentially dangerous" locations in the program.

Example. The factorial program F above should produce only natural number values during its computation. A cleanness condition at l_1, which is clearly a critical point, is (under the precondition $x \geq 0$)

$$\models (x \geq 0) \supset \Box[\text{at}l_1 \supset (y_1 > 0)]$$

guaranteeing that the subtraction performed at l_1 always yields a natural number. Note that we have not indicated that y_1 is an integer; such type considerations will be ignored in our discussions. $\quad \blacksquare$

Example. If a program contains the instruction

$$l: \text{ if } y_1 > y_2 \text{ then } y_1 := (S[i] \div y_2),$$

where $\div$ is the integer-division operator and the range of the array subscript i is between 1 and m. Then the cleanness condition at l can be expressed as follows:

$$\models \Box \{[atl \wedge (y_1 > y_2)] \supset [(1 \leq i \leq m) \wedge (y_2 \neq 0)]\}. \quad \blacksquare$$

Example. A clean behavior statement for the tree node counting program TN is given by:

$$\models \Box[(atl_1 \supset S \neq (\ ) \wedge (atl_4 \supset T \neq \Lambda)].$$

This ensures that no attempt is made to pop an empty stack or to decompose an empty tree. ■

Example. In the binomial coefficient program BC' an appropriate and crucial cleanness statement is given by:

$$\models (0 \leq k \leq n) \supset \Box\{atm_4 \supset [(y_2 \neq 0) \wedge (y_3 \bmod y_2 = 0)]\}.$$

That is, whenever we reach the location m_4 in an admissible computation of BC', y_3 is evenly divisible by y_2. ■

(c) Global invariants

Very frequently, invariant properties are not related to any particular location. In general, some properties may be invariant independent of the location. In these cases we speak of *global invariants*, i.e. invariants unattached to any particular location. The expression of global invariance is even more straightforward. Thus, we write

$$\models \varphi(\bar{x}) \supset \Box \beta,$$

to state that property β holds at all times during an admissible execution.

Example. In the factorial program F above, to claim that y_1 is always a natural number, we may write:

$$\models (x \geq 0) \supset \Box(y_1 \geq 0).$$

Another valid global invariant for this program is:

$$\models (x \geq 0) \supset \Box(y_2 \cdot y_1! = x!),$$

which states that $y_2 \cdot y_1! = x!$ at all steps of the execution. ■

Example. For the binomial coefficient program BC′, an appropriate global assertion would be:

$$|\equiv (0 \leq k \leq n) \supset \Box[(n - k \leq y_1 \leq n) \wedge (0 \leq y_2 \leq k)].$$

We can use the same notation to refer to a local invariant, a statement that is true whenever we are at a certain location l. In this case we write

$$|\equiv \Box(atl \supset \beta). \qquad \blacksquare$$

Example. In the TN program for counting the nodes in a tree, we can express a fact which is true whenever we visit the location l_0; namely,

$$|\equiv \Box[atl_0 \supset (\sum_{t \in S} |t| + C = |X|)],$$

i.e. the sum of the number of nodes in all the subtrees currently in the stack plus the current value of the counter C is invariant at l_0 and equals the number of the nodes in the tree X. $\blacksquare$

Invariants can also be used in the context of a program whose output is not necessarily apparent at the end of the execution; for example, a sequential program whose output is printed on an external file during the computation.

Example. Consider the following program PR for printing the infinite sequence of successive prime numbers

$$2, \quad 3, \quad 5, \quad 7, \quad 11, \quad 13, \quad 17, \quad \ldots.$$

Program PR (Printing the prime numbers):

$$y_1 = 2$$

l_0: print(y_1)
l_1: $y_1 := y_1 + 1$
l_2: $y_2 := 2$
l_3: if $(y_2)^2 > y_1$ then go to l_0
l_4: if $(y_1 \bmod y_2) = 0$ then go to l_1
l_5: $y_2 := y_2 + 1$
l_6: go to l_3

A part of the correctness statement for such a program is:

$$|\equiv \Box(atl_0 \supset prime(y_1));$$

it indicates that only primes are printed. $\blacksquare$

Next we will examine some properties which are meaningful only for concurrent programs.

(d) Mutual exclusion

The notions of critical sections and mutual exclusion were introduced earlier, but let us briefly review them.

Consider two processes P_1 and P_2 being executed in parallel. Assume that each process contains a section $C_i \subseteq L_i$, for i = 1, 2, which includes some task critical to the cooperation of the two processes. For example, it might access a shared device (such as a disk) or a shared variable. If the nature of the task is such that it must never be done by both of them simultaneously, we call these sections *critical sections*. The property stating that the processes will never simultaneously execute their respective critical sections is called *mutual exclusion* with respect to this pair of critical sections.

The property of mutual exclusion for C_1 and C_2 can be described by:

$$\models \varphi(\bar{x}) \supset \Box \sim (\text{atC}_1 \wedge \text{atC}_2).$$

This states that it is never the case that the joint execution of the processes reaches C_1 and C_2 simultaneously. Hence, mutual exclusion is implied.

Example. Consider again the consumer-producer program CP. The sections

$$C_1 = \{l_3, l_4, l_5\} \text{ in } P_1$$

and

$$C_2 = \{m_2, m_3, m_4, m_5\} \text{ in } P_2$$

are obviously critical sections since they make several accesses to the shared variable b. In order to obtain the correct result it must be ensured that no other accesses (or modifications) to b are made during the computation involving b.

The mutual exclusion property in this case can be expressed by:

$$\models \Box \sim (\text{atC}_1 \wedge \text{atC}_2),$$

where the initial condition associated with the admissible computation is:

$$\text{at}l_0 \wedge \text{at}m_0 \wedge b = \Lambda \wedge s = 1 \wedge cf = 0 \wedge ce = N.$$

The formula states that we can never simultaneously be in both critical sections C_1 and C_2. Note that actually it suffices to prove

$$\models \Box \sim (\text{at}l_3 \wedge \text{at}m_2).$$

This is so because there exists an execution in which $\text{at}l_3 \wedge \text{at}m_2$ in some state if and only if there exists an execution in which $\text{atC}_1 \wedge \text{atC}_2$ in some state. ∎

Example. Similarly a statement of mutual exclusion for the program BC′ computing the binomial coefficient is given by:

$$|\equiv (0 \le k \le n) \supset \Box \sim (\text{at}l_{2..4} \land \text{atm}_{4..6}).$$

Here, following our convention, $\text{at}l_{2..4}$ denotes $\pi_1 \in \{l_2, l_3, l_4\}$ and $\text{atm}_{4..6}$ denotes $\pi_2 \in \{m_4, m_5, m_6\}$.

(e) Deadlock freedom

A concurrent program consisting of m processes is said to be *deadlocked* if no process is enabled. This leaves the idling step as the only possible choice of the scheduler. The rest of the computation will therefore consist of an endless repetition of the current deadlocked state. Clearly in a deadlock situation each process P_j must be blocked at a location $l \in L_j$ whose full-exit condition is false for the current value $\bar{\eta}$ of $\bar{y}$. Therefore the only potential deadlock locations are those l for which E_l is not identically true. We refer to such locations as *waiting locations*. The terminal location l_e is also considered to be a waiting location. However, the special case in which all processes are at their respective l_e locations is not considered to be a deadlock but rather a termination.

Let us therefore consider a tuple $\bar{l} = (l^1, \ldots, l^m)$ of waiting locations, $l^j \in L_j$, not all of which are terminal locations. Let $E_1, \ldots, E_m$ be their associated full-exit conditions. To prevent a deadlock at l we require:

$$|\equiv \varphi(\bar{x}) \supset \Box (\bigwedge_{j=1}^{m} \text{at}l^j \supset \bigvee_{j=1}^{m} E_j(\bar{y})).$$

This indicates that whenever all the processes are each at $l^j, j = 1, \ldots, m$, at least one of them is enabled. The corresponding process can then proceed and deadlock is averted.

In order to eliminate the possibility of a deadlock in the full program, we must impose a similar requirement for every possible n-tuple of waiting locations, excluding $\bar{l}_e = (l_e^1, \ldots, l_e^m)$.

Example. In the consumer producer program CP, the complete deadlock freedom condition will be expressed as

$$|\equiv \Box \{ \quad [(\text{at}l_1 \land \text{atm}_0) \supset (ce > 0 \lor cf > 0)]$$
$$\land [(\text{at}l_1 \land \text{atm}_1) \supset (ce > 0 \lor s > 0)]$$
$$\land [(\text{at}l_2 \land \text{atm}_0) \supset (s > 0 \lor cf > 0)]$$
$$\land [(\text{at}l_2 \land \text{atm}_1) \supset (s > 0)]\}. \quad \blacksquare$$

Example. Similarly for the binomial coefficient program BC' statement of the impossibility of deadlock is given by:

$$|\equiv (0 \le k \le n) \supset \Box \{ \quad [(\text{at}l_1 \land \text{atm}_3) \supset (y_4 > 0)]$$
$$\land [(\text{at}l_1 \land \text{atm}_e) \supset (y_4 > 0)]$$
$$\land [(\text{at}l_e \land \text{atm}_3) \supset (y_4 > 0)]\}.$$

This statement ensures that if execution is at (l_1, m_3) then $y_4 > 0$ and one of the processes is able to proceed, and if one of the processes is ever at its terminal location, the other process is not deadlocked at its *request* instruction. ■

4.2. Eventuality (liveness) properties

A second category of properties are those expressible by formulas of the form:

$$|\equiv w_1 \supset \Diamond w_2$$

This formula states that for every admissible computation, if w_1 is initially true then w_2 must eventually be realized. In comparison with invariance properties that only describe the preservation of a desired property from one step to the next, an eventuality property guarantees that some event will finally be accomplished. It is therefore more appropriate for the statement of goals which need many steps for their attainment.

Note that because of the suffix closure of the set of admissible computations this formula is equivalent to:

$$|\equiv \Box(w_1 \supset \Diamond w_2)$$

which states that whenever w_1 arises during the computation it will eventually be followed by the realization of w_2.

A property expressible by such a formula is called an *eventuality* (*liveness*) *property* [12, 13]. Following are some samples of eventuality properties.

(a) Total correctness

This property, like partial correctness, is relevant only for programs with terminal locations.

A program is said to be *totally correct* w.r.t. a specification (φ, ψ), if for every input values $\bar{x}$ satisfying $\varphi(\bar{x})$, termination is guaranteed, and the output values $\bar{y}$ upon termination satisfy $\psi(\bar{x}, \bar{y})$. Once more, let $\bar{l}_e$ denote the exit points of the program. Total correctness w.r.t. (φ, ψ) is expressible by:

$$|\equiv \varphi(\bar{x}) \supset \Diamond(\text{at}\bar{l}_e \wedge \psi(\bar{x}, \bar{y})).$$

This says that if we have an admissible execution sequence beginning in a state which is at locations $\bar{l}_0$ and has values $\bar{y} = f_0(\bar{x})$ where $\varphi(\bar{x})$ is true, then later in that execution sequence we are guaranteed to have a state which is at $\bar{l}_e$ and satisfies $\psi(\bar{x}, \bar{y})$.

Example. The statement of total correctness for the factorial program F is:

$$|\equiv (x \geq 0) \supset \Diamond(\text{at}l_e \wedge y_2 = x!).$$

Example. The expression of total correctness for the tree node counting program TN is given by:

$$\models (S = (X)) \supset \Diamond(atl_e \wedge C = |X|).$$

Example. The statement of total correctness for the binomial coefficient program BC' is given by:

$$\models (0 \leq k \leq n) \supset \Diamond[atl_e \wedge atm_e \wedge y_3 = \binom{n}{k}].$$

(b) Intermittent assertions

Eventuality formulas enable us to express a causality relation between any two events, not only between program initialization and termination but also between events arising during the execution. This becomes especially important when discussing continuous (cyclic) programs, i.e. programs that are not supposed to terminate but are to operate continuously. The general form of such an eventuality is:

$$\models (atl \wedge \phi) \supset \Diamond(atl' \wedge \phi')$$

and it claims that whenever (in an admissible computation) ϕ arises at l we are guaranteed of eventually reaching l' with ϕ' true. This is the exact formalization of the basic Intermittent-Assertion statement [1, 11]:

"If sometime ϕ at l then sometime ϕ' at l'".

Example. Consider the program TN for counting the number of nodes in a tree. An important intermittent assertion that serves as a basis for the proof of its correctness is:

$$\models [atl_0 \wedge S = u \cdot s \wedge C = c] \supset \Diamond[atl_0 \wedge S = s \wedge C = c + |u|].$$

Here, u, s and c are used in the role of global variables, while S and C are local program variables. This statement says that being at l_0 with a nonempty stack ensures a later arrival to l_0. In a subsequent arrival (not necessarily the next one), the top element of the stack will be removed and the value of C will have been incremented by the number of nodes in the top element. ∎

Example. Consider again the program PR for printing successive prime numbers. Under the invariance properties we expressed the claim that nothing but primes is printed

(1) $$\models \Box(atl_0 \supset prime(y_1)).$$

Now we can state that the proper sequence of primes is produced. The property that every prime number is printed can be expressed by

(2) $$\models [atl_0 \wedge y_1 = 2 \wedge prime(u)] \supset \Diamond(atl_0 \wedge y_1 = u).$$

In conjunction with the invariance property (1), this statement guarantees that all printed results are primes and that a subsequence of the printed results is the desired sequence of primes

$$2, \quad 3, \quad 5, \quad 7, \quad 11, \quad 13, \quad 17, \quad \ldots,$$

but they do not guarantee that some primes are not printed more than once or out of sequence. For example, the sequence of integers

$$3, \quad 2, \quad 5, \quad 3, \quad 7, \quad 5, \quad 11, \quad 7, \quad 13, \quad 11, \quad \ldots$$
$$\quad\uparrow \qquad\quad \uparrow \qquad\quad \uparrow \qquad\quad\quad \uparrow \qquad\quad\quad \uparrow$$

satisfies the statements above.

We thus have to add an additional statement that will guarantee that the printed sequence is exactly the desired one. We have to be careful in devising a solution: note that the statement

$$[atl_0 \wedge y_1 = u] \supset \square(atl_0 \supset y_1 > u)$$

does not resolve the problem! Why?

The property that the primes are printed in order can be expressed by

$$(3) \qquad\qquad |\equiv [atl_1 \wedge y_1 = u] \supset \square(atl_0 \supset y_1 > u).$$

This ensures monotonicity for any future visit to l_0. ∎

The following properties are of interest mainly for concurrent programs having more than one process.

(c) Accessibility

Consider again a process that has a critical section C. In the previous discussion we have shown how to state exclusion (or protection) for that section. A related and complementary property is *accessibility*. That is, if a process wishes to enter its critical section it will eventually get there and will not be indefinitely held up by the protection mechanism. Obviously a fool-proof protection mechanism is worthless if it does not eventually admit the process into its critical section.

Let l_1 be a location just before the critical section. The fact that the process is at l_1 indicates an intention to enter the critical section. Let C be the set of locations in the critical section. The property of accessibility can then be expressed by

$$|\equiv atl_1 \supset \Diamond atC;$$

namely, whenever the program is at l_1, it will eventually get to C.

A correct construction of critical sections should ensure these two complementary properties: protection (exclusiveness) and accessibility.

Example. For the consumer-producer program CP, we wish to express the property that whenever the producer is at l_1 it will eventually get to l_3 and be able to deposit y_1 in the buffer. A symmetric statement expresses accessibility for the consumer: whenever the consumer is at m_0 it will eventually get to m_2. The conjunction of these two properties, expressing the accessibility property of the program is, given by:

$$|\equiv [\text{at}l_1 \supset \Diamond \text{at}l_3] \wedge [\text{at}m_0 \supset \Diamond \text{at}m_2]. \qquad \blacksquare$$

(d) Liveness

A more general class of eventuality properties arises when we consider the notion that the computation of any particular process must eventually progress. Here we do not necessarily restrict ourselves to locations containing semaphore instructions.

Consider an arbitrary non-terminal location l in some process P_i, i.e. $l \neq l_e$ for that process. If the computation of this process is to proceed we cannot remain blocked at l due to a failure of the scheduler to schedule process P_i. Assuming that our program contains self loops only for waiting purposes, such as in the loop instruction, progress in P_i is observable by seeing P_i moving from a state where at$l$ to a state where $\sim$at$l$. Consequently, the property of liveness for a general location l, $l \neq l_e$, can be expressed by:

$$|\equiv \text{at}l \supset \Diamond(\sim \text{at}l),$$

i.e. if we arrive at this location we will eventually move out. In fact we can simplify this formula to

$$|\equiv \Diamond(\sim \text{at}l)$$

which is equivalent to

$$|\equiv \sim \Box \text{at}l,$$

meaning that we cannot get blocked at the location l.

The property of liveness is also known as absence of livelock or freedom from individual starvation. A *livelock* (or *individual starvation*) is defined as a situation in which some processes which are not in a terminal location cannot proceed even though the full program may still progress by having some other processes execute. Note that this is a stronger requirement than the absence of deadlock. As long as at least one of the processes can proceed the program is not deadlocked.

(e) Responsiveness

A very important class of programs that are usually modeled as concurrent programs are operating systems and real-time programs such as airline reservation systems and other online data-base systems. These programs can conveniently be considered as continuous (cyclic) programs which are to run forever. A halt in these programs usually indicates an error condition. Consequently these programs are not run for their end results but for the effects produced during their endless operation. Thus the notions of total and partial correctness are meaningless and have to be replaced by statements about the programs' continuous behavior.

One desired property of such programs is *responsiveness*.

Example. Consider a continuous program (*granter*) G modelling an operating system. Assume that it serves a number of customer programs (*requesters*) $R_1, \ldots, R_t$ by scheduling a shared resource between them. The resource here can be a shared disk, main memory, etc. Let the customer programs communicate with the operating system concerning the resource via a set of boolean variables $\{r_i, g_i\}$, for $i = 1, \ldots, t$. r_i is set to true by the customer program R_i to signal a request for the resource. g_i is set to true by G signalling to R_i that it has been granted (allocated) the resource. After using the resource, the customer R_i releases the resource back to the system G by setting r_i to false, which is then acknowledged by the system G by setting g_i to false.

To summarize:

$$R_i \text{ signals a request} \Rightarrow r_i := \text{true}$$
$$G \text{ allocates a resource} \Rightarrow g_i := \text{true}$$
$$R_i \text{ releases the resource} \Rightarrow r_i := \text{false}$$
$$G \text{ acknowledges the release} \Rightarrow g_i := \text{false}.$$

The statement that the operating system fairly responds to the customer requests—responsiveness—is given by:

$$a_i: \quad r_i \supset \Diamond g_i,$$

i.e. whenever r_i becomes true, eventually g_i will turn true. Note that this statement does not stipulate that r_i becomes true when G is at a particular location. Consequently it can express events such as interrupts or unsolicited signals which may occur at any arbitrary moment.

Similarly we have to ensure that the system acknowledges the release of the resource by turning g_i to false:

$$b_i: \quad \sim r_i \supset \Diamond(\sim g_i).$$

Furthermore, the system cannot hope to operate successfully if it does not enjoy the cooperation of the customer programs. For example, the system cannot promise R_2 an eventual grant of the resource if R_1 who currently has hold of it does not ever release it. Consequently we will expect the R_i's to satisfy some proper behavior requirements, namely for each i:

$$c_i: \quad g_i \supset \Diamond(\sim r_i).$$

This statement ensures that when the resource is granted to R_i, it will eventually be released.

To these statements we will usually add some more invariance statements ensuring the correct continuous behavior of G. One such statement is

$$d: \quad \Box(\sum_{i=1}^{t} g_i \leq 1)$$

meaning that at any particular time the system grants the resource to at most one customer. This is a type of a mutual exclusion.

Denote the correct behavior statement of G by

$$\psi = \bigwedge_{i=1}^{t} a_i \; \wedge \; \bigwedge_{i=1}^{t} b_i \; \wedge \; d$$

and the correct behavior expected from the R_i's by

$$\varphi = \bigwedge_{i=1}^{t} c_i$$

The problem of proving the correct behavior of G can be approached in two different ways:

(1) Consider a concurrent program P that consists of G alone. The r_i's and g_i's are then considered as input/output variables, where the r_i's are supposed to be set by the external agents $R_1, \ldots, R_t$.

For this program we would prove:

$$\models \Box\varphi \supset \Box\psi$$

That is, provided the external communication φ continuously behaves properly we can promise the correct behavior ψ of G.

(2) As another alternative consider the concurrent program P that consists of G run together with $R_1, \ldots, R_t$, i.e.

$$P = G\|R_1\| \ldots \|R_t.$$

For each R_i here we substitute a simplified model that guarantees to maintain c_i. Such a model can be presented as:

$$r_i = \text{false}$$

l_0: execute
l_1: $r_i := \text{true}$
l_2: wait until g_i
l_3: compute {use resource}
l_4: $r_i := \text{false}$
l_5: wait until $\sim g_i$
l_6: go to l_0

— Customer Program R_i —

If we believe that our model for R_l faithfully represents the real R_l as far as communication with G is concerned, we can proceed to prove

$$\models \Box(\varphi \wedge \psi)$$

as ensuring the correct behavior of P.

Thus the two modelling alternatives available to us are: considering G alone communicating with the external world via the r_l, g_l variables, or considering a combined system of G together with $R_1, \ldots, R_t$. In the first case the proper behaviour of the external world has to be promised through a continuous maintainance of φ. In the second case the proper behavior of the R_i's is proven at the same time as the proper behavior of G.

The same analysis can of course be conducted for other situations where a program communicates with external devices and is expected to respond properly to incoming signals. ∎

The application of the temporal formalism to the problems of responsiveness points out its power. Invariances and eventualities are long-known properties and many special formal systems and methodologies have been proposed and successfully implemented for their analysis and proofs. The temporal logic contribution to this problem is a uniform treatment and an explicit direct expressibility. In contrast, the discussion of responsiveness is relatively recent; no prior formalism addressed itself to the description and proof of these properties.

4.3. Precedence (until) properties

The third class of properties to be considered are those properties which are expressible using the until operator.

In their simplest form they will be expressed by statements of the type:

$$\models w_1 \, U \, w_2.$$

This statement says that in all admissible computations of P there will be a future instance in which w_2 holds and such that w_1 will hold until that instance. Our until operator is exclusive in the sense the w_1 does not necessarily hold in that instance. Recall that the formal meaning of the until operator was given by

$$w_1 \, U \, w_2|_\sigma^\alpha = \text{true} \quad \textit{iff} \quad \text{for some } k \geq 0, \, w_2|_{\sigma(k)}^\alpha = \text{true and}$$
$$\text{for all } i, \, 0 \leq i < k, \, w_1|_{\sigma(i)}^\alpha = \text{true.}$$

Note that we require $i < k$ and not $i \leq k$.

The until operator is also very useful in expressing precedence relations between events. We define the derived *precede operator* P by:

$$w_1 \, P \, w_2 \quad \text{is} \quad \sim((\sim w_1) U \, w_2).$$

The statement $w_1 P w_2$, reading w_1 *precedes* w_2, says that if w_2 ever happens it will not happen until w_1 happens first. This is equivalent to stating that the first instance of w_1 (observed from the present) comes before the first instance of w_2. The formal meaning of the precede operator can be given by

$$w_1 P w_2|_\sigma^\alpha = \text{true} \;\; \textit{iff} \;\; \text{for every } k \geq 0, \text{ if } w_2|_\sigma^{\alpha(k)} = \text{true}$$
$$\text{then for some } i, 0 \leq i < k, w_1|_\sigma^{\alpha(i)} = \text{true}.$$

The precede operator is also exclusive, since we have $i < k$ and not $i \leq k$.

Notice that while $w_1 U w_2$ implies that w_2 will indeed happen, this is not guaranteed by $w_1 P w_2$. In fact, if w_2 never happens then $w_1 P w_2$ holds for every w_1.

Several obvious properties of the precede operator may be derived from corresponding properties of the U operator and the definition of P. Among them are:

1. $\models wPw \equiv \square \sim w$
2. $\models w_1 P w_2 \wedge w_2 P w_3 \supset w_1 P w_3$
3. $\models w_1 P w_2 \equiv \sim w_2 \wedge [w_1 \vee \bigcirc(w_1 P w_2)]$
4. $\models \square \sim w_2 \supset w_1 P w_2$
5. $\models w_1 P w_2 \vee w_2 P w_1 \vee \diamondsuit(w_1 \wedge w_2)$

Statement 1 says that every w always precedes itself iff w is always false, since no event can come before the first occurrence of itself.

Statement 2 indicates the transitivity of the precedence relation. It says that if w_1 precedes w_2 which precedes w_3 then w_1 precedes w_3.

Statement 3 gives an inductive characteristic of the P operator. It says that w_1 precedes w_2 iff w_2 is not true now and either w_1 is true now or w_1 precedes w_2 when observed from the next instant.

Statement 4 says that if w_2 never happens then obviously w_1 precedes w_2, for every w_1.

Statement 5 characterizes the linearity of time. It says that for every two events w_1 and w_2, either w_1 precedes w_2 or w_2 precedes w_1 or both occur at the same time.

We will consider formulas involving the P operator as belonging to the class of until properties. We discuss below several subclasses of properties involving the U and P operators.

(a) Safe liveness

Following Lamport [8] we may interpret invariance properties as an assurance that nothing bad will happen, and liveness properties as a promise that something good will eventually happen. Consistent with this, we may want to ascertain that nothing bad happens until something good happens. This is exactly expressible by

$$\models w_1 U w_2,$$

where w_1 is a safety property that we wish to maintain (e.g. clean behavior and global assertions), while w_2 is a liveness property that we want ultimately to achieve (e.g. termination and correctness). We strongly suggest that a full specification of a program should always be expressed as an until expression $|\equiv w_1 U w_2$, i.e. achieve w_2 while maintaining w_1.

In some cases the "until" statement is just a conveniently expressed combination of safety and liveness properties since:

$$|\equiv (\Box w_1 \land \Diamond w_2) \supset w_1 U w_2.$$

However the more interesting case is when w_1 holds up to but not including the instant in which w_2 happens. Then it is no longer true that $\Box w_1$ is a program-valid statement.

The until operator can also be used to express "first-time" properties. Recall that a formula of form

$$|\equiv (\text{at}l \land \phi) \supset \Diamond(\text{at}l' \land \phi')$$

expresses the some-time property: if the program is at l and ϕ is true, then sometime (eventually) the program must reach l' with ϕ' being true. Similarly, a formula of form

$$|\equiv (\text{at}l \land \phi) \supset [(\sim\text{at}l')U(\text{at}l' \land \phi')]$$

expresses the first-time property: If the program is at l and ϕ is true, then sometime the program must reach l', and on the first visit, ϕ' will be true.

Example. The safety and liveness properties for the binomial coefficient program BC' can be stated as:

$$|\equiv (0 \leq k \leq n) \supset$$
$$\{[(\text{at}m_4 \supset (y_2 \neq 0) \land (y_3 \bmod y_2 = 0)) \land$$
$$(n - k \leq y_1 \leq n) \land (0 \leq y_2 \leq k)]$$
$$U$$
$$[\text{at}l_e \land \text{at}m_e \land y_3 = \binom{n}{k})]\}.$$

That is, achieve termination and correct result while maintaining a clean behavior and global invariances.

(b) Absence of unsolicited response

Let $w_1 \supset \Diamond w_2$ be a statement of responsiveness which guarantees that to every situation in which w_1 is true the program responds by making w_2 true. We often wish to complement this statement by requiring that on the other hand, w_2 will never happen unless preceded by w_1, i.e. the program does not respond unless explicitly requested. This of course is expressible as:

$$|\equiv w_1 P w_2,$$

meaning that there is always a w_1 preceding any w_2.

There is however a problem associated with the interpretation of the formal statement above as expressing our intuitive requirement. Assume a situation in which w_1 occurs at t_1 and w_2 indeed follows at t_2, $t_2 > t_1$, and neither w_1 nor w_2 is true between t_1 and t_2. If we try to test the statement: "w_1 precedes w_2" at any t_3, $t_1 < t_3 < t_2$, it will turn out to be false, since the first event following t_3 is w_2 rather than w_1. Thus we have to be careful to restrict our statement to only such reference points from which the precedence relation can be safely observed.

Thus a more careful description of the no-request-no-response statement is:

$$|\equiv (at l_0 \supset w_1 P w_2) \wedge [(w_2 \wedge \bigcirc \sim w_2) \supset \bigcirc(w_1 P w_2)].$$

This selects as good reference points from which the precedence of w_1 to w_2 may be observed, either the starting point of the computation, or an instant in which w_2 is true and is changing to false in the next instant.

In most practical cases we have additional information about the behavior of w_1 and w_2 that helps us formulate the requirements in simpler terms.

Example. Let us reconsider the example of the operating system model: an allocator (granter) G that allocates a resource between customers (requesters) $R_1, \ldots, R_t$. Customer R_1 signals its requests by setting r_1 to true. The allocator G eventually responds by setting g_1 to true. The customer eventually releases the resource by setting r_1 to false which the allocator acknowledges by setting g_1 to false.

This simple communication protocol between a particular customer R_1 and the allocator can be specified by the following four invariants:

(1) $|\equiv (r_1 \wedge \sim g_1) \supset \bigcirc r_1.$

This says that if r_1 is true and g_1 is false, meaning that R_1 is requesting the resource but has not yet been granted its request, R_1 should persist in its request by leaving r_1 on for the next instant.

(2) $|\equiv (r_1 \wedge g_1) \supset \bigcirc g_1.$

This states that if the resource has been granted to R_1, then the allocator is not allowed to withdraw its grant until the resource is released by R_1, by setting r_1 to false.

(3) $|\equiv (\sim r_1 \wedge g_1) \supset \bigcirc \sim r_1.$

This states that if the allocator has not yet acknowledged the release of the resource by R_1, then R_1 may not issue a new request.

(4) $|\equiv (\sim r_1 \wedge \sim g_1) \supset \bigcirc \sim g_1.$

This states that if the resource is not currently allocated to R_1 nor is R_1 requesting it, the allocator should not grant the resource to a process which is not requesting it. This is exactly our requirement of no unsolicited responses for this case.

These four demands with the additional responsiveness requirement

(5) $\models r_i \supset \Diamond g_i$

(6) $\models g_i \supset \Diamond \sim r_i$

(7) $\models \sim r_i \supset \Diamond \sim g_i$

ensure the correct and proper behavior of the system.

The four statements 1–4 above characterize the behavior of the program by immediate transition rules. Since it is not always obvious what are the global consequences of such local constraints, we would prefer to specify them in a more global style. Such specifications can be given by:

(a) $\models r_i \supset [r_i U(g_i \wedge r_i)]$

(b) $\models g_i \supset [g_i U(\sim r_i \wedge g_i)]$

(c) $\models \sim r_i \supset [\sim r_i U(\sim g_i \wedge \sim r_i)]$

(d) $\models \sim g_i \supset (r_i P g_i)$

which replace 1–7.

Statement (a) says that if r_i is true it will remain true until g_i is granted. Statement (b) says that if the resource is granted it will remain granted until released. Statement (c) says that if the resource has been released it will not be requested again until the release has been acknowledged. Statement (d) says that if g_i is not currently allocated, its next allocation must be preceded by a request. ∎

(c) Fair responsiveness

In many situations we have the precedence of two events ψ_1 and ψ_2, i.e. ψ_1 precedes ψ_2 only when two earlier events ϕ_1 and ϕ_2 occurred in the same order, i.e. ϕ_1 precedes ϕ_2. We will refer to such situations as *conditional precedence*. It is expressible by the statement:

$$\models (\phi_1 P \phi_2) \supset (\psi_1 P \psi_2).$$

This says that if ϕ_1 precedes ϕ_2 then ψ_1 will precede ψ_2.

Coupled with the implications

$$\models \phi_1 \supset \Diamond \psi_1 \quad \text{and} \quad \models \phi_2 \supset \Diamond \psi_2$$

which ensure responsiveness, the conditional precedence sharpens our committment to *fair responsiveness*. That is, if we interpret $\models \phi_1 \supset \Diamond \psi_1$ and $\models \phi_2 \supset \Diamond \psi_2$ as describing a response ψ_i to a request ϕ_i, then responsiveness says that every request will eventually be honored by a response. The fair responsiveness establishes a first-come-first-serve discipline by ensuring that if ϕ_1 preceded ϕ_2 then the response to ϕ_1, namely ψ_1, will precede the response to ϕ_2, i.e. ψ_2.

Example. Let us consider again the problem of the granter (allocator) and his serviced customers (requesters). We may impose a fairness requirement on his responsiveness obligations by insisting on a first-come-first-serve policy. This would be expressed by:

$$|\equiv (r_iPr_j) \supset (g_iPg_j).$$

This means that if customer R_i placed his request before customer R_j he will be serviced prior to customer R_j. However, we again must be careful to state this only in "quiescent" reference points. For example, if g_j is currently true, while both $r_i = r_j =$ false, a situation which may occur just at the end of a granting period to R_j, we certainly cannot promise that g_i will precede g_j.

A reasonable set of reference points is such instants in which g_j is currently false. Thus the conditional precedence statement restricted to these observation points is:

$$|\equiv (\sim g_j) \supset [(r_iPr_j) \supset (g_iPg_j)] \qquad \blacksquare$$

Example. Consider a pair of processes where the critical sections $C_1 = \{l_2, l_3\}$ and $C_2 = \{m_2, m_3\}$ are mutually protected by semaphores:

$$y = 1$$

l_0: execute	m_0: execute
l_1: *request*(y)	m_1: *request*(y)
l_2: compute	m_2: compute
l_3: *release*(y)	m_3: *release*(y)
l_4: go to l_0	m_4: go to m_0
— P_1 —	— P_2 —

We discussed previously the statement of accessibility for such a program; namely, that if P_1 is waiting at l_1 it will be eventually admitted into C_1. This ensures only the absence of infinite overtaking, i.e. the possibility of P_1 waiting at l_1 forever while P_2 enters it own critical section infinitely often. Yet, can we prevent overtaking altogether; i.e. can we prevent P_2 from overtaking P_1 and entering C_2 even though P_1 reached l_1 before P_2 reached m_1?

We may impose fair responsiveness on this situation by requiring that the first process to reach its request instruction will be the first to be admitted into its critical section. We may attempt to state this property by:

$$|\equiv [(atl_1 \; P \; atm_1) \supset (atC_1 \; P \; atC_2)] \wedge$$
$$[(atm_1 \; P \; atl_1) \supset (atC_2 \; P \; atC_1)].$$

This states that if P_1 gets to l_1 before P_2 gets to m_1 then P_1 will gain access to C_1 before P_2 gets to C_2, and similarly for the dual case in which P_2 gets to m_1 before P_1 gets to l_1.

However we again face the question of appropriate reference points. The statement would certainly not be true if P_2 is currently at C_2. In the above example we may be aided by the location variables in order to select appropriate reference points. One correct specification of fairness of the semaphores in this case is:

$$| \equiv [(\text{at}l_1 \wedge \text{at}\{m_4, m_0\}) \supset (\text{at}l_2 \; P \; \text{at}m_2)] \wedge$$
$$[(\text{at}m_1 \wedge \text{at}\{l_4, l_0\}) \supset (\text{at}m_2 \; P \; \text{at}l_2)].$$

This says that if we are at an instant in which P_1 is already at l_1 while P_2 is both out of C_2 and has not yet arrived at m_1 then P_1 will be admitted to its critical section first, and similarly for the dual case.   ∎

One should not be confused by the double appearance of the notion of fairness, once when discussing fair scheduling and fair execution sequences, and here when discussing fairness as a program property. The concepts are very similar, but previously we assumed fairness as a restriction on execution sequences, since we were interested only in fair execution sequences. Here we consider (and later prove) fairness as a property of the program that gives rise to those sequences. A badly designed program could fail to achieve fairness in responding even when each of the executions we examine is fair as a computation, i.e. the scheduler may be doing its best but the program failed to ensure correct (and timely) response to each request.

Consequently, when we prove that a program has the fair responsiveness property for every admissible computation, we assume that the computation is scheduled fairly and prove that it responds fairly.

ACKNOWLEDGEMENT

We thankfully acknowledge the help extended to us by Yoni Malachi, Ben Moszkowski, Richard Schwartz, Pierre Wolper, Frank Yellin and Rivi Zarhi in reading the earlier drafts of the manuscript. Special thanks are due to Connie Stanley for typing the infinitely often ($\square \diamondsuit$) changing versions of the manuscript.

REFERENCES

1. R. M. Burstall (1974). "Program Proving as Hand Simulation with a Little Induction," 308–312. Proc. IFIP Congress, Amsterdam.
2. E. W. Dijkstra (1968). Cooperating processes *In* "Programming Languages and Systems" (F. Genvys, ed.), 43–112. Academic Press, New York.
3. E. W. Dijkstra (1968). A constructive approach to the problem of program correctness. *BIT* **8**, 179–186.
4. D. Gabbay, A. Pnueli, S. Shelah and J. Stavi (1980). "The Temporal Analysis of Fairness," 163–173. Proc. 7th POPL, Las Vegas, NV.

5. G. E. Hughes and M. J. Cresswell (1968). "An Introduction to Modal Logic." Methuen & Co., London.
6. H. W. Kamp (1968). "Tense Logic and the Theory of Linear Order," Ph.D. Thesis, University of California, Los Angeles.
7. R. M. Keller (1976). Formal verification of parallel programs. *CACM* **19**, 371–384.
8. L. Lamport (1977). Proving the correctness of multiprocess programs. *IEEE Transactions on Software Engin.* SE-3, 125–143.
9. Z. Manna (1980). "Logics of Programs," 41–51. Proc. IFIP Congress, Tokyo and Melbourne.
10. Z. Manna and A. Pnueli (1979). "The Modal Logic of Programs," Proc. 6th International Colloquium on Automata, Languages and Programming, Graz, Austria. Lecture Notes in Computer Science, Springer Verlag, Berlin **71**, 385–409.
11. Z. Manna and R. Waldinger (1978). "Is 'Sometime' Sometimes Better Than 'Always'?: Intermittent Assertions in Proving Program Correctness," *CACM* **21**, 159–172.
12. S. Owicki and D. Gries (1976). "Verifying Properties of Parallel Programs: An Axiomatic Approach," *CACM* **19**, 279–284.
13. S. Owicki and L. Lamport (1980). "Proving Liveness Properties of Concurrent Programs," unpublished report.
14. A. Pnueli (1977). "The Temporal Logic of Program," 46–57. Proc. 18th FOCS, Providence, RI.
15. A. Pnueli (1979). "The Temporal Semantics of Concurrent Programs," Proc. Symposium on Semantics of Concurrent Computations, Evian, France. Lecture Notes in Computer Science, Springer Verlag, Berlin **70**, 1–20.
16. A. Prior (1967). "Past, Present and Future". Oxford University Press, Oxford.
17. N. Rescher and A. Urquart (1971). "Temporal Logic." Springer Verlag, Berlin.

Subject index

275